E.H. Alh

Krishna: Myths, Rites, and Attitudes

KRISHNA:
Myths, Rites, and Attitudes

Edited by Milton Singer

with a Foreword by Daniel H. H. Ingalls

THE UNIVERSITY OF CHICAGO PRESS
Chicago and London

THE UNIVERSITY OF CHICAGO PRESS, CHICAGO 60637
THE UNIVERSITY OF CHICAGO PRESS, LTD., LONDON

Published 1966. Phoenix edition published 1968
Printed in the United States of America

82 81 80 79 78 7 6 5 4 3

International Standard Book Number: 0–226–76101–0
Library of Congress Catalog Card Number: 65–20585

FOREWORD

In the pages that follow, six American and three Indian scholars, each trained in a different specialty, have joined in the study of Krishna. Since the study of Krishna is a field almost as large as India itself, our scholars have set some limits to their treatment. It is to the legends of Krishna as divine child and divine lover that they have turned their attention, and the question they ask is how those legends are related to the societies of India, past and present. What needs have the legends filled? What thoughts, what actions, what attitudes, have they prompted?

Since a foreword should be lighter fare than the work it introduces, I shall begin with the most elementary question of all. Who was Krishna? It is a foolish question if one expects a religious answer, for the worshiper will reply that Krishna was what he is, that Krishna is everything. But if one expects a historical answer, the question is not foolish; it is merely difficult to answer. It has been usual to speak historically of three Krishnas, although each melts into the others, it seems to me, more readily than most historians will admit. There is Krishna the chief of the Yādavas, who served as Arjuna's charioteer in the Bhārata epic. There is Krishna the god incarnate, the instructor of Arjuna and through him of all mankind, who appears, not in the old epic, but in that larger religious work, the *Mahābhārata,* into which it was expanded. Then there is Krishna of Gokula, the god brought up among cowherds, the mischievous child, the endearing lover, the eternal paradox of flesh and spirit.

E. Washburn Hopkins and R. G. Bhandarkar long ago did their best to distinguish these three Krishnas by reference to the chronology of the texts in which they appear. Using dates of which the sequence is reliable, although the absolute figures may be wrong by more than a century, they placed the first Krishna before 300 B.C., the second Krishna sometime thereafter, and the third Krishna after A.D. 200.

One must add two reservations. The dates refer, not to different persons, as one might refer to King George I, II, or III, but to different characters of a hero or god who was always thought to be one and the same. Furthermore, the characters are cumulative, not discrete. The god Krishna of the late *Mahābhārata* possesses all the paradoxical qualities of the earlier hero; he remains the trigger of action, the prime mover beyond normal distinctions of good and evil, but a new dimension of divinity has been added. In similar fashion, the divine herdsman preserves both the ambiguity and the divinity of the earlier characters; what have been added are the scenery of Gokula and a new emphasis on love of children and on the love between man and woman.

The Krishna with which the present book is concerned is the Krishna of the third and therefore of the most complete and also the most complex character. The legends and myths of this Krishna fill many volumes. There has been in India, beginning with the *Harivaṃśa* and the *Viṣṇu Purāṇa,* a steady stream of Krishna poetry that has lasted from roughly A.D. 200 to the present time. One work in the stream stands out by reason of its literary excellence, the organization that it brings to its vast material, and the effect that it has had on later writers. That work is the *Bhāgavata Purāṇa,* written by an anonymous author, probably a Tamilian, probably in the ninth or tenth century. Among the papers of the present volume, two deal entirely with the *Bhāgavata,* and the others refer to it time and again. The poetry of Sūrdās in the sixteenth century, the works of Caitanya's followers in Bengal from the sixteenth century onward, and even the present-day *bhajans* of Madras and the folk festivals of Barabhum and Kishan Garhi are inexplicable without reference to the *Bhāgavata.*

I shall not encroach on the papers of Thomas J. Hopkins and J. A. B. van Buitenen by discussing the *Bhāgavata* in detail. I shall point out, though, one of its qualities that I have felt more deeply than its other qualities and that, I think, cannot have been without effect in winning the *Bhāgavata* the position that it has attained. For all its traditional lore and traditional piety, and despite its frequent archaisms, the *Bhāgavata* remains, especially in its tenth book, the most enchanting poem ever written. One might call its tenth book "The *Geste* of

Krishna," intending, in Sanskrit style, a double meaning by the title. For the tenth book not only relates the *gesta,* the deeds, of the divine child and the divine lover, but impresses one throughout that those deeds were not just what they appeared, but rather were hints or symbols or epiphanies of some truth that lies beyond. The peasant woman Yaśodā ties her child to a stone mortar to keep him from stealing, but the string always falls an inch short. She looks into his laughing face, and in his mouth she thinks for half a minute that she sees the universe. The book is a jest as well as a *geste,* a jest that is serious only in that its subject is the ultimate truths, for it is told with a kindliness that I have observed in no other sermon. The poet handles this ambiguous history with consummate skill. In his pages the world appears as a magic land where every object, if only it is rightly seen, is a key to truth and to eternity. What else is poetry than just that? And how, if one had once read the *Bhāgavata,* could one write of Krishna without holding it in mind?

It is strange that Western scholars have paid so little attention in recent years to the Krishna legend. If I am not mistaken, the present work is the first Western effort in the field—I trust the three Indian contributors will allow the appellation—since Walter Ruben's collation of the Krishna legends some twenty years ago. I say it is strange, because the subject of Krishna was of deep interest and concern to those Westerners who rediscovered India in the eighteenth and nineteenth centuries. It will not be without use to inquire why they were concerned and why that concern has since lagged.

Western visitors to India of one or two centuries past were interested in Krishnaism on two counts. First, they found the poetry of Krishna, the legends of Krishna, and the worship of Krishna to be widespread in the everyday life of the Indians whom they met. Secondly, after an initial shock of strangeness, many Westerners became aware of elements in Krishnaism that seemed surprisingly familiar. The early missionaries had tried to equate the word *"Kṛṣṇa,"* pronounced "krishto" in some parts of India, with the word *Christos.* After scientific philology had put an end to that attempt, there still remained some extraordinary similarities between the worship of Krishna and Christianity: in cult there was the worship of God as a child; in legend there was the slaughter of the innocents; and in religious attitude there were the faith in the grace of God and the insistence upon complete devotion.

As always, it was the *Bhāgavata* that carried the message. Just how it first carried its message to Western Indianists makes a curious tale. Sometime in the mid-eighteenth century, a Malabari interpreter named Méridar Poullé wrote out, for some interested gentlemen at the factory of Pondichéry, a French translation of a Tamil summary of the Sanskrit *Bhāgavata*. Somehow a copy of Poullé's translation, in manuscript, found its way to Europe and to the library of that notable internationalist Voltaire, who read and discussed the work with great interest before it was finally published, anonymously, in Paris in 1788. It so happens that the Harvard College Library has a copy of the work; I am therefore able to say at first hand that the pure stream of the *Bhāgavata* in passing through three linguistic sieves was sadly altered. But Poullé's work led, at least indirectly, to a masterpiece of scholarship fifty years later. In 1840, Eugène Burnouf published the first volume of his great edition and translation of the original *Bhāgavata*. With Burnouf's *Bhāgavata* and the works of H. H. Wilson, which began appearing at about this time, the West had attained a fairly broad view of Krishnaism.

H. H. Wilson studied both the past and the present. His *Viṣṇu Purāṇa* was a translation of an ancient text; *A Sketch of the Religious Sects of the Hindoos* brought matters down to his own times. The same combination of interests was to be characteristic of those few scholars who continued in later years to work on the Krishna tradition, notably Sir George Grierson, R. G. Bhandarkar, and, in our own times, S. K. De. They were few because their ranks were thinned from two sides. The professional Sanskritists of the West, from 1840 on, turned ever more backward to a period that was older, older than the third Krishna, older even than the first. They were interested above all in the common roots of the Indo-Iranian and Germanic languages, and for that purpose their best evidence came from the earliest of all Indian texts, the Veda. On the other hand, the anthropologists and district magistrates, faced with what William James called the "blooming welter" of current phenomena—a British magistrate, understanding the term in his own slang, might well have accepted it—had no time for the study of ancient texts. Hence arose that great divorce that continues to impoverish Indian studies. Those who see the present reality find no time for the study that most of all might make their observations understandable, while those who hold the ancient knowledge have grown too proud—or should one say afraid?—to confront their knowledge with life.

Here lies the great merit of the present volume, a merit added to the particular merits of its papers, so that the whole in a sense exceeds the sum of its parts. For in bringing these papers together Professor Singer has reversed the tendency of recent times and has laid a stimulus on Indologists to return to the wider view, the less astigmatic vision, of the great explorers.

Although himself an anthropologist, Professor Singer arranges the papers of the book in historical sequence. We begin with the *Bhāgavata* itself. Thomas J. Hopkins, while emphasizing the devotionalism of the poem, finds in it an ethics that one might almost call democratic and a scorn of wealth and status that, if not revolutionary in a political sense, is revolutionary at least in its attitude. J. A. B. van Buitenen, on the other hand, is concerned with the orthodoxy of the poem. In language, certainly, it is more than orthodox. In seeking causes, van Buitenen points to what has lately been called Sanskritization, that is, the adaptation of new movements to Brahmanic patterns; but he assigns to that process a motivation deeper than the status seeking that most users of the new term have had in mind. The next historical papers move to a world eight or nine centuries later. In some areas the pattern remains much the same; in others it has changed. To judge from the paper of S. M. Pandey and Norman Zide, Sūrdās was among the most faithful followers of the *Bhāgavata*. True, he leaves out here and he adds on there; his descriptions are more realistic, more popular. But the love of children is precisely in the spirit of the *Bhāgavata,* as is the sensuous mysticism of the *rāsa*. In Bengal, as Edward C. Dimock, Jr., shows, matters took some new turns. We have a new theology, combining Rādhā with Krishna in the one body of Caitanya. And we find social cleavage: between scholars and popularists, between orthodox and unorthodox. We skip two or three more centuries and come to four papers which deal with the present time. The editor himself gives us a careful account of *bhajana* celebrations of Krishna in the city of Madras. He is interested not only in what sort of persons take part in these rites and in what texts they sing and recite—a subject to which T. K. Venkateswaran's paper adds useful information—but also in what social uses these rites fulfill. The effects that he finds, the temporary removal of caste barriers and the easing of social tensions, may well have been manifested in the ninth century as well as in the twentieth. The historian should listen to the songs of the present just as intently as he reads his Sanskrit libretto. And surely one may project back into the past much of that acculturation to Hinduism, effected by means of the Krishna songs and the Krishna cult, that Surajit Sinha finds among the Bhūmij of Barabhum, a modern group that has recently passed from tribalism to peasant culture.

A difficulty remains. How does one bring the diverse facts of literature, of society, of religion, as one finds them in different ages and areas, into a single understandable system? What system shall we use for the evaluation even of contemporaneous phenomena? It may be said, of course, that systematizing is just what we should not yet do, for it has been the experience of the sciences, social as well as natural, to begin with description and to come to systems only when they are full grown. Let us first, then, gather the facts. But still, one must be aware of an ultimate goal, and one yearns for it. Personally, I tend to think of such a goal as a system of history, for such has been my training. But I recommend to the reader the very different systematization offered by McKim Marriott. Although the author is a scholarly man, his is the least academic of the contributions. And yet, from the disreputable phenomena of the Holī festival he builds, in bold strokes and in a very American way, a system that seems to me not inapplicable to much that is Indian, old as well as new, noble as well as mean.

Two thousand years ago, a Roman poet sang of an ever-youthful god who had conquered the East:

> Tu puer aeternus, tu formosissimus alto
> Conspiceris caelo . . .
> . . . Oriens tibi victus, adusque
> Decolor extremo qua cingitur India Gange.[1]

1. Ovid, *Metamorphoses* IV. 18–21.

Here it is sober historians and social anthropologists who write of such a god. By their writing they have shed light on the land of his conquest, on "dark India, even to where it lies girdled by the farthest Ganges."

Daniel H. H. Ingalls

Cambridge, Massachusetts, 1964

EDITOR'S PREFACE

Many a student of Indian culture on his first visit to India has been astonished and enchanted, as I was, to find so much of the epic and Purāṇic mythology and legends alive in contemporary oral traditions. Wherever he turns, he finds represented the legendary gods and heroes and the episodes from their stories on temple towers and as temple images; on lithographic posters; in dance, music, poetry, and song; and even in the "modern" theater, in film, and on radio. One is tempted on first exposure to interpret this phenomenon as simply a religious expression in the field of art. And the vocabulary of sophisticated Indians as they talk about these "performances," in the idiom of "concerts," "ballet," "dance drama," "art music," certainly lends plausibility to this interpretation. On a closer study of the "performances" one quickly finds that there is more to them than aesthetic forms and values—an essential component in many—and that they express, as well, social structure, moral ideals, and theological doctrines of salvation. Family and caste genealogies are traced to those given in epics and Purāṇas, and claims to the status of Brahman, warrior, or general high caste are thus validated.

For many Indians, the *Rāmāyana* is not merely a legendary epic, but a sacred scripture that, among other motifs, tells the story of the ideal dutiful wife, Sītā; the ideal faithful servant, Hanumān; and the divine warrior, Rāma. Draupadī and the Pāṇḍavas in the *Mahābhārata,* Krishna in the *Bhāgavata Purāṇa,* and countless other characters in these and other classics have a similar moral and theological significance.

These characters, moreover, are not only exemplary models but objects of living devotion, adoration, and identification. They are presences in the minds and hearts and actions of living Indians. And it is probably as expressions of devotion (*bhakti*) that the "cultural performances," which charm the visitor, gain their deepest significance for

Indians. The values of the "performances" as art productions, or "morality plays" or as dramatizations of cultural traditions are also recognized, but these values are secondary, so far as most Indians are concerned, to the religious meanings.[1]

One of the most popular of all the legends is that associated with the god Krishna. His pranks and "sports" as a child and a youth are familiar everywhere in India, in the villages and in the cities, to the traditional-minded as well as to the modern and highly educated. Episodes from the Krishna legend are endlessly enacted, recited, sung, and danced in every available medium of cultural expression.[2] The chief textual source of the story, the *Bhāgavata Purāṇa,* is regarded as a kind of New Testament and is frequently read or recited for religious merit. In its origins, this text and the Krishna cult may have been exclusively associated with the Vaiṣṇava sects, but they have long since spread, as some of the present studies show, far beyond the boundaries of any particular sect, caste, or region. Although all Hindus are not Krishnaites, the Krishna cult and familiarity with the Krishna legend have an all-India spread.

How are a legend and a cult so ancient, so varied, and widespread in their cultural expression, so profound in their significance, to be studied? No one of the scholarly disciplines in the humanities or social sciences seems qualified to undertake the task unaided. Perhaps a number of different disciplines in co-operation may prove adequate. The present volume, in any case, is an experiment in such a project of interdisciplinary collaboration; it includes a historian of religions (Thomas J. Hopkins), two Sanskritists (J. A. B. van Buitenen and T. K. Venkateswaran), a historian of the literature and culture of Bengal (E. C. Dimock, Jr.), two historians of Hindi literature (S. M.

1. A wide range of "cultural performances" is described and analyzed in a symposium on *Traditional India: Structure and Change,* which I compiled and edited for the American Folklore Society (Philadelphia, 1958–1959) and the *Journal of American Folklore* (LXXI [1958], 191–518).
2. A valuable study of the Krishna legend in poetry and painting is that of W. G. Archer, *The Loves of Krishna* (New York: Grove Press, 1957). Radhakamal Mukerjee's *The Lord of the Autumn Moons* (Bombay: Asia Publishing House, 1957) gives a theological interpretation. A useful brief summary of the Krishna legend and of Indian mythology is W. Norman Brown's "Mythology of India," in S. N. Kramer, ed., *Mythologies of the Ancient World* (Garden City, N.Y.: Anchor Books, 1961), pp. 277–328.

Pandey and Norman Zide), and three social anthropologists (Surajit Sinha, McKim Marriott, and myself).

Each of us has approached the subject, within the frame of a discipline, a region, and a personal outlook, more or less independently. As we exchanged early drafts—discussed formally in a seminar at the University of Chicago during the summer of 1962, and informally before and since—we came to take more and more account of one another's papers in writing our own later versions. The collaboration has been especially close between Professor Venkateswaran and myself in the Madras study. Because he himself, along with his father and family, is a devotee of the Rādhā-Krishna *bhajana* tradition, and has had some training in anthropology, his co-operation was of great value to my study, not only for his knowledge of the Sanskrit texts, but equally so for his firsthand knowledge of the movement and his anthropological insights.

A preliminary report of the results, in abbreviated form, of the entire project was presented in a special panel on "The Krishna Legend: Variations on a Theme" at the meetings of the Association of Asian Studies, March 1963. This report has not been published. Through the kind interest of the editor, Mircea Eliade, two of the papers, Dimock's and mine, have been published in the journal *History of Religions*.[3]

It must be left to others to judge the value of our interdisciplinary effort to study one major theme in Indian culture. Professor Ingalls, in his Foreword to this volume, discusses the results in relation to Indological studies. I should like to call attention to several implications of such collaboration for the anthropological study of civilizations. It is probably true, as Dr. van Buitenen remarks, that social anthropologists who try to study a civilization such as India's are handicapped by their disposition to concentrate on small, relatively isolated communities in the present. The more familiar they become with a civilization, however, the more they recognize that these communities are part of a wider context of culture and society, and that even the small communities cannot be adequately understood without a knowledge of the civilization's cultural and social history in its wide sweep.[4] These social

3. II (1963), 183–226; III (1963), 106–127.

4. I have discussed recent social-anthropological studies in "The Social Organization of Indian Civilization," *Diogenes* (Winter, 1964), 84–119.

anthropologists—perhaps they are not yet as numerous as they should be—are also beginning to appreciate the relevance of the textual scholars' analyses of texts for their own "contextual" studies.[5] This relevance is double: (1) In a civilization as "textual" as India's, the "texts" and ideas taken from them turn up everywhere—in the tribal villages of Bengal, in the peasant villages of Uttar Pradesh, and in the metropolitan center of Madras, as well as in other Indian regions. A knowledge of the literary and cultural traditions of these regions and of India in general becomes indispensable to the social anthropologist. (2) The relevance of the textual scholars' knowledge extends beyond this. As is evident from their contributions to this volume, they have a good deal to say about how the very processes the social anthropologist studies in the present have operated in the past. The interactions of little and great traditions, such processes as Sanskritization, parochialization, and universalization, take on historical depth and meaning from the textual discussions of Hopkins, van Buitenen, Dimock, Venkateswaran, and Pandey and Zide. These discussions also help the anthropologist to make his understanding of these processes at once more precise and more general. Dr. van Buitenen's extension of Professor Srinivas' concept of Sanskritization to the archaism of the *Bhāgavata* is an excellent example of this, for his analysis not only shows in precise detail how a literary text may be Sanskritized but also suggests that the motivation for the process may be more complex than the desire to rise in the social scale, although this motivation did play a role.

Some social anthropologists are apt to consider an inquiry finished if they can reduce the subject of the inquiry to a description of social structure and social organization. They would be inclined, therefore, to accept those parts of Hopkins' analysis of the *Bhāgavata* text which stress the social and economic side of the Krishna *bhakti* movement, its significance as a kind of Śūdra protest against the wealthy and high castes. But the same social anthropologists would be less likely to accept the analysis in Dimock's and Venkateswaran's papers of the philosophy of devotion as a philosophy both of love and of salvation, unless they could show that the philosophy and practice of devotion

5. See my "Text and Context in the Study of Contemporary Hinduism," *Adyar Library Bulletin* (Madras), XXV (1961), 274 ff.

are but a "reflection" of a structure of social relations, e.g., that master-servant *bhakti* is a "projection" of the servile status of the Śūdra.

This is not the place to debate the proper way to do social anthropology.[6] Let me conclude by pointing out that the social anthropologists in this volume are not "reductionists" in this sense. We have collaborated with textual scholars, not merely out of a spirit of good fellowship, but because we believe that a knowledge of the texts, and of social and cultural history, helps us to a better understanding of social behavior and social relations in the present. The reader can test the value of the textual studies of the Krishna legend for the contextual type of study in a simple way: by imagining this volume without them. I am sure he would regret the loss, and so would the social-anthropological contributors.

I am indebted to Donald Nelson for standardizing the transcription of Indian words, preparing the index, and for help with proofreading. The Committee on Southern Asian Studies of the University of Chicago has contributed a partial subsidy toward publication of the volume. The editor and contributors are grateful for this support.

Milton Singer

The University of Chicago
December 15, 1963

6. Some of the issues of an anthropology of civilization are discussed in Robert Redfield's *Peasant Society and Culture: An Anthropological Approach to Civilization* (Chicago: University of Chicago Press, 1956) and *Human Nature and the Study of Society: The Papers of Robert Redfield,* M. P. Redfield, ed. (Chicago: University of Chicago Press, 1962–1963), 2 vols.; A. L. Kroeber, *An Anthropologist Looks at History,* T. Kroeber, ed. (Berkeley: University of California Press, 1963); C. Geertz, "Studies in Peasant Life: Community and Society," in *Biennial Review of Anthropology:* 1961 (Stanford: Stanford University Press, 1962), pp. 1–41; D. G. Mandelbaum, "The Study of Complex Civilizations," *Current Anthropology* (Chicago, 1956); M. Singer, "The Social Organization of Indian Civilization," *Diogenes* (Winter, 1964), 84–119; P. Bagby, *Culture and History: Prolegomena to the Comparative Study of Civilization* (Berkeley: University of California Press, 1959).

CONTENTS

TRANSCRIPTION OF INDIAN WORDS

In the transcription of the various languages quoted in the papers of this volume the current scholarly conventions have been employed. For the Tamil fricative, retroflex sonant, which was variously transcribed by earlier writers, the letter "l" with a subscript hyphen (ḻ) has been used—thus Āḻvār. An effort has been made to standardize spelling throughout the volume by following the Sanskrit model, usually at the expense of dialectical and Anglicized forms—thus, *svāmī* for *swami,* Ekanātha for Eknath, *ācārya* for *acharya.* The nasalization of a preceding vowel is indicated by ṃ—thus, Śaṃkara, Gosaīṃ. The two words "Krishna" and "brahman" have everywhere been employed in their Anglicized forms, except where context demanded otherwise, e.g., *Kṛṣṇalīlātaraṅgiṇī.* Regional and dialectical spelling, where it seemed relevant in context, has been left intact—thus, *subarṇabaṇiḳ* for *suvarṇavaṇiḳ, biṛya* or *vīrya.* Generally, geographic names and the proper names of contemporaries have been used in their popular or dialectical spelling. However, where a geographical name (e.g., Vṛndāvana, Vraja) is used in its historical context, the Sanskritic spelling has been employed.

D.N.

Krishna: Myths, Rites, and Attitudes

I. THE SOCIAL TEACHING OF THE *BHĀGAVATA PURĀṆA*

by Thomas J. Hopkins

The *Bhāgavata Purāṇa* is among the latest productions of the Hindu Purāṇic literature and is undoubtedly the most famous and widely used of the Purāṇas. The Purāṇic writings as a whole are a heterogeneous collection of material varying greatly in date and origin. Purāṇic literature was in existence as early as the fourth century B.C.,[1] and Purāṇas were still being produced at the end of the first millennium A.D. The early Purāṇa material consisted of genealogies, records of dynasties and kings, legendary stories, and mythical accounts of the creation and population of the world—material that had been preserved by a class of bards, or *sūtas,* through many centuries.[2] In the early centuries of the Christian era Purāṇic literature was appropriated by various groups as a vehicle for popularizing their teachings. Primary among such groups were the developing Śaiva and Vaiṣṇava sects, who were also responsible for many of the changes in the *Mahābhārata* and *Rāmāyaṇa* during the same period.

Using the old Purāṇic material as a framework, these groups created over a span of several centuries a number of individual Purāṇas—all preserving to some extent the earlier character of the Purāṇic literature, but differing from one another in the use of new material and viewpoints. By the end of the tenth century A.D. there were some eighteen or nineteen major Purāṇas in existence, most of them identifiable at least in part as Śaiva or Vaiṣṇava works. These writings vary greatly in quality and content. Most of the Purāṇas are encyclopedias of material from many sources and periods. They document the great diversity within Hinduism over a period of centuries, but before the material can be used for historical purposes an almost impossible task of textual analysis must be achieved.

The *Bhāgavata Purāṇa* is thankfully free from most textual difficulties. It contains a variety of material from a wide range of sources, but a successful attempt has been made to resolve the resulting conflicts. The *Bhāgavata* is "the one Purāṇa which, more than any of the others, bears the stamp of a unified composition." [3] It is thus an invaluable historical document, since it is the only one of this important group of writings that represents the consistent viewpoint of a single group at a given point in their history.

The date of the *Bhāgavata* has not yet been definitely determined. It is included in al-Bīrūnī's list of the Hindu Purāṇas and was thus in existence well before this list was compiled in A.D. 1030. It contains a much more detailed version of the biography of Krishna than that given in either the *Harivaṃśa* or the *Viṣṇu Purāṇa,* both of which date from the third or fourth century A.D., and is thus probably several centuries later than these works. From these considerations, it is fairly certain that the *Bhāgavata* was written no earlier than A.D. 500 and no later than A.D. 950. As to the exact time within this period, however, there is considerable difference of opinion.

R. C. Hazra places the composition of the *Bhāgavata* in the first half of the sixth century, on the grounds that it is "earlier than the Viṣṇuite *Kūrma Purāṇa* [A.D. 550–650], which was, unlike the *Bhāgavata,* much influenced by Śākta ideas." [4] Most other scholars, however, prefer a date at least two centuries later than this. F. E. Pargiter assigns it to the ninth century on the basis of textual evidence.[5] Radhakamal Mukerjee believes it is a product of the Ācaryan period of South Indian Vaiṣṇavism, from the middle of the ninth through the tenth century.[6] J. N. Farquhar dates it around A.D. 900, on the basis of al-Bīrūnī's evidence and the fact that it presupposes the development of Vaiṣṇava devotionalism by the Āḷvārs, the South Indian ascetic poets of the seventh, eighth, and ninth centuries.[7] C. V. Vaidya places the *Bhāgavata* after Śaṃkara (*ca.* A.D. 788–850) and in the tenth century, on the basis of its acceptance of the Buddha as an *avatāra* of Viṣṇu and its revision of the Sāṃkhya philosophy to counteract the criticisms of Śaṃkara.[8] K. A. Nīlakaṇṭa Śāstrī puts the *Bhāgavata* in the tenth century because of its use of the Advaita theology championed by Śaṃkara.[9] M. Winternitz, citing Vaidya, Pargiter, and Farquhar, also believes that there are "good grounds for assigning it to the 10th century A.D." [10]

There is more general agreement on the question of where the *Bhāgavata* was written. The consensus of scholars who have expressed an opinion on this point is that the Tamil country of South India is the only likely place for its composition. Farquhar refers to passages in the *Bhāgavata* and in the appended *Bhāgavata Māhātmya* that praise Drāviḍa for the quality of the devotion displayed there.[11] These passages, plus the known activity of the Āḻvārs in the Tamil area, lead him to conclude that "the *Bhāgavata* was written about A.D. 900, in the Tamil country, in some community of ascetics belonging to the Bhāgavata sect who felt and gave expression to the *bhakti* characteristics of the work."[12] Vaidya summarizes the detailed references in the *Bhāgavata* to South Indian sacred places and concludes that this detailed knowledge of the area and the partiality shown in the praise of Drāviḍa make it "very likely that the author of the *Bhāgavata* lived in the Drāviḍa country."[13] Nīlakaṇṭa Śāstrī states that the "*Bhāgavata* was composed somewhere in South India," since it "combines a simple surging emotional *bhakti* to Krishna with the Advaita philosophy of Śaṃkara in a manner that has been considered possible only in the Tamil country."[14] Mukerjee believes that the *Bhāgavata* is a direct product of the devotional movement in South India that produced the Āḻvārs and the Ācāryas. He discusses the evidence of Krishna-worship in South India in the centuries preceding the *Bhāgavata,* the influence of the Āḻvārs on the religion of that area and the references in the *Bhāgavata* to South Indian culture, history, and geography, and he suggests that the *Bhāgavata* was most likely produced in the country of the Pāṇḍyas or in Kāñcīpuram—as South Indian tradition assumes.[15]

The evidence presented by these scholars fails to establish definitely either the date or the place of composition of the *Bhāgavata,* but it does suggest some reasonable assumptions. There seems to be no logical alternative to the Tamil country of South India as the place of composition, since the necessary developments leading to the production of the *Bhāgavata* are not known to have existed anywhere else in India at that time. The *bhakti* movements in the northern Deccan and in North India took place several centuries after the latest possible date for the *Bhāgavata* and for the most part were dependent on the influence of the *Bhāgavata* or of the Śrī-Vaiṣṇavas—also of South Indian origin. The internal evidence of familiarity with South India and admiration for its qualities serves only to strengthen this point.

As to the date of composition, the bulk of the evidence points to a time after the impact of the Āḻvārs on South Indian religion. Hazra's argument for an early date based on the absence of Śākta material in the *Bhāgavata* is certainly not strong enough to prove that it was composed some four centuries before the latest possible date, *ca* A.D. 950—for which there is no earlier evidence than that provided by al-Bīrūnī in A.D. 1030. The various arguments for placing the *Bhāgavata* after Śaṃkara are unconvincing. The theology of the *Bhāgavata* does have Advaita elements, but it differs too much from that of Śaṃkara to prove any reliance on his system. It is much more likely that both the *Bhāgavata* and Śaṃkara reflect the same development in South Indian thought, which possibly was due at least in part to the influence of Buddhist metaphysics.[16]

The single most important feature of the *Bhāgavata* is its emphasis on *bhakti,* or devotion, directed to Viṣṇu and his various incarnations. Any determination of the origin or significance of the *Bhāgavata* must ultimately depend on this element, which gives the work its purpose and consistency. Just as the area in which the *Bhāgavata* was composed must have been one where a high form of devotionalism had been developed, so the time and circumstances of its origin must also have depended on this factor. If we assume that the *Bhāgavata* was composed in the Tamil country, the Āḻvārs must also be considered in determining its date. Very little is known of their history, but the most reliable estimates place their main activity in the period between the middle of the eighth and the early ninth century.[17] This date would coincide with the reigns of the Pāṇḍyas and Pallavas, when Vaiṣṇavism enjoyed real patronage, before Śaiva Cōḻas gained ascendancy in South India. The ninth century, probably around A.D. 850, would thus seem to be the most likely time for the *Bhāgavata* to have been written.

With these considerations out of the way, we can turn to the content of the *Bhāgavata* itself.

The principal concern of the *Bhāgavata* is to illustrate, explain, and promote devotion to Viṣṇu in his incarnation as Krishna, referred to variously in the *Bhāgavata* as Vāsudeva, Hari, Mukunda, Acyuta, and Bhagavān. Devotion, or *bhakti,* was not a new element in Vaiṣṇavism; it held a major place in the *Bhagavad Gītā* and other earlier works, and it was already accepted as one of the ways of salvation along with *karma* (performance of acts) and *jñāna* (knowledge). In its earlier form, however, *bhakti* was primarily meditation or concentration of one's thoughts on the deity. In the *Bhāgavata,* as for the Āḷvārs, it is a passionate devotion of one's whole self in complete surrender to the Lord, a total way of life that is not one way among many but the only way to true salvation.

This type of devotion is described at length in the *Bhāgavata,* as in the following instructions of Viṣṇu:

> That which has the name of *bhaktiyoga,* by which—passing over the three qualities [goodness, passion, and darkness]—one may arrive at my being, is called *Ātyantika* [endless, eternal].
>
> By unmotivated attendance, by greater performance of one's duties, by repeated employment of rites, by constantly avoiding too much slaughter,
>
> By seeing, touching, worshiping, praising, and respectfully saluting my image, by contemplation of me in beings, by truth, by disassociation,
>
> By great respect for noble persons, by compassion for the miserable, and by friendship for those equal to oneself, by self-control and restraint,
>
> By rectitude, by association with honorable persons and by renunciation of individuality, from hearing discourse relating to the soul and from glorification of my names,—
>
> By these qualities, the mind of one whose *dharma* is mine is completely purified, for when my attributes are merely heard the mind of a person reaches me.[18]

Many of the same features of *bhakti* are described in a later section, where the characteristics of those who practice devotion are discussed:

> That person is the best Bhāgavata who sees his own affection for Bhagavān in all creatures, and sees [all] creatures in Bhagavān Himself.
>
> . . . .
>
> He is the best Bhāgavata who, apprehending objects with the senses, neither hates nor rejoices, seeing this world as the *māyā* [the power of illusion] of Viṣṇu.
>
> He is the foremost Bhāgavata who, by the recollection of Hari, is unconfused by the established characteristics of *saṃsāra* [the round of rebirths], consisting of birth, passing away, hunger, desire for prosperity, and pain in body, senses, vital breath, mind, and thought.
>
> He truly is the best Bhāgavata whose sole refuge is Vāsudeva and in whose consciousness there is no occurrence of the seeds of desire and actions.

He is truly the favorite of Hari for whom there is no pride attached to the body because of either birth and actions or because of *varṇa, āśrama,* or *jāti* [i.e., class, stage of life, or caste].

He is truly the best Bhāgavata who is tranquil, to whom all beings are equal, and for whom there is no distinction in self or acquisitions such as thinking "mine are different [or better]." [19]

For the *Bhāgavata,* the only permanent state worth attaining is devotion to Viṣṇu. Earthly pleasures and even heavenly rewards pass away with time, but once true *bhakti* is acquired it endures forever and protects the devotee from all misfortune:

If a person abandoning his own *dharma* and revering the lotus feet of Hari, but not mature [in his religious development], should fall from this [status] to any other [i.e., to a lower status], what misfortune would there be for him? Or what advantage would be gained from their own *dharma* by persons not revering his feet?

A wise person should strive for that which is not obtained by those wandering up and down [through the round of rebirths]; pleasure, like pain, is always obtained elsewhere in the course of time, whose speed is profound.

A person attending on Mukunda never in any way returns to the cycle of *saṃsāra* like others; remembering again the embracing of the feet of Mukunda and grasping that pleasure he does not wish to be deprived of it.[20]

The purpose of *bhakti* is to destroy men's attachment to the world by shifting their affection and desire from the world to the Lord. As attachment and devotion to Bhagavān increase, attachment to the world decreases, and release from *saṃsāra* is possible:

Even though its value is nonexistent, the cycle of *saṃsāra* does not cease for one contemplating the objects of the senses, like the attainment of useless objects in a dream.

Thus one should gradually, by *bhaktiyoga* and an intense change of affection, control thinking that is intent upon the course of the unrighteous.

. . . .

When contemplating what is effected by the sense organs, one repeatedly accumulates actions; there being ignorance with respect to action, there is bondage of the body to action.

Therefore, revere Hari with your whole self for the purpose of refuting this [bondage], seeing the universe as belonging to Him from whom are its maintenance, origination, and disappearance.[21]

Devotion that will bring about the necessary change of affection must occupy the whole self and absorb all of one's energies. The distinctive nature of the new Vaiṣṇava devotionalism is described by the devotee Prahlāda:

Hearing about, praising, remembering, and attendance on the feet of Viṣṇu, honoring Him, saluting Him respectfully, service to Him, friendship with Him, and offering oneself to Him,—

If *bhakti* fixed by a person on Viṣṇu and having these nine characteristics is directed to Bhagavān, then certainly the Highest is attained in thus thinking of Him.[22]

Such devotion represents a significant change from the *bhakti* of the *Bhagavad Gītā.* For the *bhakti* must be far more than quiet contemplation; it must be a transfer to the Lord of all the emotion and desires that are ordinarily expended on the world and its pleasures. *Bhakti* without this emotional fervor cannot purify, as Krishna explains:

Without the bristling of the hair of the body, without the mind dissolving, without being inarticulate because of tears of joy, without *bhakti,* how can the heart be purified?

He whose voice is stammering [from emotion], whose thought dissolves, who repeatedly weeps and sometimes laughs, who, shameless, sings and dances,—such a person, attached by *bhakti* to me, purifies the world.[23]

The activity of the devotees, stimulated by emotional attachment to the Lord, is continually directed into more general cultic activities in His service:

One should worship me in idols, etc., whenever and wherever there is faith; I am the soul of all, stationed in all beings and in the soul.

Thus worshiping by the ways of discipline of Vedic and Tantric performances, delighted because of these two [kinds of performance], a person acquires the desired fulfillment.

Establishing an image of me, one should make a permanent temple and pleasant flower gardens to be used for worship, processions, and merriment.

Giving fields, shops, cities, and villages for the sake of continuity of worship, etc., at major festivals and moreover every day, one may obtain equality of rank with me.

By erecting [images] one may acquire sovereignity over the whole world, by temples he may acquire the three worlds, by worship, etc., he may acquire the world of Brahmā, and by all three he may acquire equality with me.

He who thus worships me obtains *bhaktiyoga,* and with disregard [for the world] by *bhaktiyoga* he finds me.

. . . .

Seeing, touching, and honoring my images and persons devoted to me; attendance; praise; humbly proclaiming my qualities and acts;

Faith in the hearing of conversation about me; meditation on me, O Uddhava; the offering of all acquisitions; the offering of oneself by service;

Reciting my births and acts; approving of my festivals; merriment in my temples with songs, dancing, musical instruments, and meetings;

Processions and offering of oblations at all annual festivals; Vedic and Tantric consecration; keeping my vows;

Faith in erecting my image and, having joined together voluntarily, exertion in work on parks, groves, gardens, cities, and dwelling places;

Approaching me sincerely like a servant in temple service with cleansing and anointing [my image], with libations and going around in circles [i.e., circumambulating the idol];

Modesty, absence of deceit, and not boasting of what is done; seeing my light, should one not employ what has been given? [24]

Devotion as a way of life thus demands selfless dedication to the Lord of all one's actions, ceremonies, and duties. The sincerity of this activity is more important than the status of the worshiper or the size of his offering:

An offering to me in images, etc., by one who is free of illusion and devoted [to me] may be with perfected articles, with whatever has been obtained, or even with [only] affection in his heart.

Still, with respect to an image, bathing and decorating, accurate arrangement on a piece of open ground or an oblation covered with clarified butter in the fire are very well liked.

Or worship to the sun with water and so forth in water is well liked; even water offered with faith by one devoted to me is well liked.

But an abundance of things offered by one who is not devoted is not suitable for my satisfaction; how much less so are perfume, incense, flowers, a lamp, or food!

. . . .

Even a minute gift offered by those devoted to me through love becomes an abundance for me, but an abundance of things offered by one who is not devoted is not suitable for my satisfaction.

I enjoy that offered out of devotion by one whose nature is piously disposed, who with devotion presents to me a leaf, a flower, fruit, or water.[25]

From the above passages, we can get a fair idea of the major features of the religion supported by the *Bhāgavata.* Its most obvious feature is, of course, the importance of devotional activity. This activity is carried out in a number of ways, but it revolves basically around the worship of the forms and images of the Lord. Devotion is carried out by seeing, touching, worshiping, praising, and saluting these images, by cleansing, anointing, and decorating them, and by the offering of oblations and gifts. At least some of this activity is performed in temples, and great merit is attached to the establishment of temples, the erection of images, and the giving of donations for the support of worship. Much of the devotional activity is carried out in groups. There are processions, festivals, and temple gatherings, at which the devotees dance, sing, play musical instruments, recite stories about the Lord, and chant His glories. Besides participating in these festivities, they work together on parks, groves, and gardens surrounding the temples.

High standards are set up for the individual devotees. In addition to performing the various rites and ceremonies of devotion, they should have superior personal characteristics. Their activity should be unmotivated by any desire for personal gain; they should be tranquil and self-controlled, viewing all things with equanimity and neither hating nor rejoicing in the things of the world; they should have respect for honorable and noble persons and compassion for those who are miserable; they should be free from any pride in their birth, wealth, or accomplishments, and should recognize no distinctions between themselves and others; and, above all, their worship and all their actions should be sincere, based only on faith and devotion to the Lord.

Two main points stand out in this description of the religion of the *Bhāgavata:* the almost complete break with the traditional religious ceremonies based on the Vedas, and the absence of the qualifications based on birth and status that restricted participation in orthodox ceremonies. These features of the new *bhakti* religion are by no means unintentional. The *Bhāgavata* meets the minimum requirements of

Hindu orthodoxy by not denying the authority of the Vedas, but Vedic religion is generally damned with faint praise when it is not openly criticized. Some effort is made to preserve continuity with the Vedic tradition by the identifying of the Vedas with the manifested Lord; thus it is said that "the Veda is Nārāyaṇa in person" [26] and that "the learned Brahmans, cattle, Vedas, religious austerity, . . . and sacrifices are the form of Hari." [27] There is for the most part no criticism of the Vedas or their teachings where they do not conflict with *bhakti*. But where there is conflict, or where it is necessary to show the distinctive value of devotion, the *Bhāgavata* does not hesitate to point out the weaknesses of orthodox Vedic religion.

The Vedas, the *Mahābhārata,* and the earlier Purāṇas are all criticized for not sufficiently proclaiming the glories of the Lord,[28] and Krishna says that "an intelligent person should not endure that barren speech in which there may indeed be neither my purifying action—the creation, inspiration and destruction of this universe—nor my desired birth in incarnations for sport." [29] The basic criticism of the Vedas and orthodox religion, however, is that they are ineffective:

What [is accomplished] by what is heard [i.e., the Vedas] or by religious austerity, by commands or the activities of thought? What by skilled intellect, strength, or the power of the senses?

Or what by Yoga, Sāṃkhya, or even by abandonment [of worldly concerns] and recitation of the Veda to oneself, or by other auspicious things in which there is not Hari offering Himself?

. . . .

The lords of speech down to the present time, even seeing by means of religious austerity, knowledge, and meditation, do not see the highest Lord Who is seeing [i. e., omniscient].

Wandering in the Veda, which is difficult to get through and is extremely extensive, and worshiping intermittently with ceremonies having the sacred texts as their characteristic feature, they have not known the Highest.

When Bhagavān, self-created, favors a person, that person lays aside thought that is thoroughly dependent on the world and on the Vedas.[30]

This position is repeated even more decisively by Krishna:

Yoga does not bring me under control, nor Sāṃkhya, nor indeed *dharma,* nor recitation of the Veda to oneself, nor religious austerity, nor abandonment, nor the merit of sacrifices, nor a donation to a priest,

[Nor] penances, sacrifice, sacred hymns, places of pilgrimage, restraint or self-control, as does attachment to the good that destroys all attachment [to the world].

. . . .

O Uddhava, Yoga does not subdue me, nor Sāṃkhya, nor *dharma,* nor recitation of the Veda to oneself, nor religious austerity, nor abandonment, as does strong devotion to me.

I am overcome by *bhakti* alone; I myself am the friend of good persons because of [their] faith; *bhakti* intent on me purifies even Śvapākas from [the sins of] their birth.

Dharma accompanied by truth and compassion or knowledge accompanied by religious austerity cannot together cleanse a soul free of devotion to me.[31]

The *Bhāgavata* thus not only recognizes the significant differences between *bhakti* religion and Vedic or orthodox religion, but also repeatedly stresses the independence of *bhakti* from all alternative means of salvation. Criticism of orthodoxy does not stop at the theological level. Dissatisfaction with the *status quo* extends beyond the strictly religious sphere and includes all the traditional socioreligious system. Here the primary objective is to refute the idea that a person's birth, social status, or caste membership is of any significance with respect to salvation by means of devotion. The *gopīs,* or cowherd girls, in Krishna's boyhood village are primary examples of true devotion in the *Bhāgavata* despite their low caste status, and it is said of them:

These wives of the cowherds, in whom affection has developed for Govinda, the soul of all, strive after that which is better than the maintenance of the body in the world—[the same thing] that we and the saints strive after because of fear of the world. What [is gained] by birth as a Brahman for one whose pleasure is in conversation about the Eternal One?[32]

In contrast to the *gopīs,* the Brahmans of Vraja originally rejected Krishna:

Thus having heard Bhagavān's request, they whose desires were mean, whose acts were many, fools whose pride was great, did not listen.

Because of seeing [Him as] human, these stupid mortals did not honor Bhagavān Adhokṣaja, that highest Brahman in person,

Of Whom consist place, time, various articles, prayers, Tantras, priests, fires, divinity, sacrificing, worship and *dharma.*[33]

Throughout the *Bhāgavata,* true devotees without wealth or status are contrasted with wealthy or high-caste persons who reject *bhakti* and denounce its followers. The pride of the latter in their wealth, family, or learning blinds them to the truth, and they cut themselves off from the salvation that can come only from *bhakti:*

Unfortunate persons, by whom that which is food for dogs [i.e., the body] is pampered by its own nature with clothes, garlands, ornaments, and ointments, because of their ignorance ridicule the behavior desired by Him whose pleasure is in His own self.

. . . .

Hari, fond of those persons destitute of wealth, whose wealth is Himself, and knowing their affection, does not accept the worship of evil-minded persons who, by their conceit about their Vedic learning, wealth, family, and deeds, bestow harm on good people who are poor.[34]

Most severely condemned are the twice-born members of the three upper classes who have had all the advantages and have misused them:

Moreover, having reached the vicinity of Hari's feet by their [second] birth, produced by knowledge of the Veda, Brahmans, kingly persons and Vaiśyas are bewildered because of discoursing on the sacred texts.

These persons—unwise in action, arrogant, stupid, thinking themselves clever—utter flattering words, confused by the sweet speech with which they are anxiously striving.

Dreadfully desirous by means of the quality of passion, lustful, wrathful like serpents, hypocritical, proud and vicious, they ridicule those devoted to Acyuta.

. . . .

Those mischievous persons whose understanding is blinded by pride in their birth, by wealth, prosperity, family, knowledge, gifts, appearance, strength, and action despise the good people devoted to Hari—together with the Lord.

Those ignorant ones do not hear about the desired Lord celebrated in the Vedas, the soul eternally existing in all bodies like ether; they talk about things whose vehicle is the mind [i.e., only about dreams, ideas, or fantasies].[35]

In contrast to the unmotivated devotion practiced by the Bhāgavatas, their opponents, hoping for personal gain, follow the practices of orthodox religion.

Persons devoted to the qualities of passion, goodness, and darkness worship the gods, etc., whose chief is Indra, who are [themselves] fond of the qualities of passion, goodness, and darkness; thus they do not worship me.

[They think:] "Having worshiped the divinities here with sacrifices, going to heaven we shall enjoy; at the end of that, we should become ones whose houses are big and whose families are important here [in this world]."

Talking about me is thus not agreeable to men whose minds are carried away by flowery speech and who are proud and highly arrogant.[36]

The *Bhāgavata* is particularly critical of those who devote their time and energy to the acquisition, protection, spending, and enjoyment of wealth—a process that constitutes the "exertion, fear, anxiety, and confusion of men."[37] It is implied that the conflict between wealth and devotion is so great that only a poor person can be a true follower of *bhakti.* Krishna says to his wife Rukmiṇī, "We are poor and are always the favorites of poor persons; therefore rich people generally do not resort to me."[38] The advantage of poverty in the achievement of devotion is indicated in Krishna's description of how men are won to Him:

I gradually remove the wealth of him whom I favor; then, when he is destitute of wealth and distressed with difficulties, his own kindred abandon him.

I grant my favor to one who has formed a friendship with those for whom I am the chief object, whenever that person—whose endeavor is futile—becomes disgusted with exertion for the sake of wealth.[39]

In his instruction of some youthful disciples, the saintly Nārada discusses this point in more detail:

Poverty is the best ointment for an unrighteous person blinded by the intoxication of wealth. A poor person considers beings completely by analogy to himself.

As one whose body is pierced by a thorn does not desire that pain for [other] creatures, having attained impartiality toward living beings by means of their characteristics [i.e., by sharing their suffering], so one in whom a thorn has not been stuck does not have this attitude.

A poor person, freed from the arrogance of his ego and released from all conceit in this world, by chance obtains hardship; indeed that is for him the highest religious austerity.

The sense organs of a poor person, whose body is constantly emaciated by hunger and who is longing for food, gradually dry up and even injury ceases.

The righteous ones, seeing impartially, are suited for a poor person; he destroys that thirst [for wealth] by means of good people and immediately becomes pure.

What is accomplished by unrighteous people proud of their wealth, whose refuge is falsehood, by the disregarding of the impartial-minded righteous persons whose desire is for the feet of Mukunda?[40]

The generally critical attitude of the *Bhāgavata* toward the well-to-do extends not only to persons who are wealthy and secure but also to the institutions that support them. The most important of these institutions is, of course, the system of caste privileges in which status and power are determined by birth. The *Bhāgavata's* attitude toward the caste system is consistent with that toward wealth, although the pressures for conformity in this case are much stronger. The *Bhāgavata* does not, in fact, criticize the caste system as such with the same vigor it directs against orthodox religion or the abuses of wealth. It follows instead the policy that can be seen in some of the sectarian portions of the *Mahābhārata:*[41] acceptance of the concept of class divisions having definite distinguishing characteristics, but rejection of the idea that membership in these classes or possession of their characteristics is the inevitable result of one's birth.

The traditional class divisions and their features are set forth several times in the *Bhāgavata,*[42] following the general pattern of the *Mānava-Dharma-Śāstra.* Elsewhere, however, the *Bhāgavata* attempts revisions to bring the system more into line with the standards of *bhakti.* It is clear from what we have seen that the *Bhāgavata* does not acknowledge the superiority of even Brahmans simply on the basis of their status by birth. Whatever the value of the traditional Brahmanic characteristics, many Brahmans fall far short of these standards. Brahmans who are devoted to Bhagavān are said to be the highest of men,[43] but they must be persons "whose conduct is virtuous, who are free from jealousy, falsehood, hypocrisy, envy, injury, and pride"[44]—defects that, as we have seen, are characteristic of those who reject *bhakti* and condemn its followers.

In contrast to members of the higher classes who fail to meet the standards set for them, many persons of low social status exhibit those characteristics of attitude and behavior that are most important for devotion, and they may even have some advantages over the upper classes in this respect. Pride and arrogance, the defects most damaging to the practice of devotion, are not so likely among persons of low status as they are among the wealthy or learned upper classes. Just as a poor person has few possessions to tie him to the world, so the lower classes, born for service, have fewer reservations about devoting themselves to the service of the Lord. Those with wealth, power, and knowledge are accustomed to being masters and cannot give themselves to service with the same willingness. Among the characteristics of a Śūdra are said to be humility, purity, truth, and service to his master without guile,[45] all of which make him ideally suited for devotion, as well as for his traditional servile role. The *Bhāgavata* says, in fact, that when the four classes were created there was brought forth from the feet of Bhagavān "service for the fulfillment of *dharma,* for which in former times was born the Śūdra by whose conduct Hari is pleased."[46] Śūdras and other lowly persons, by virtue of their servile status, are thus closer to meeting the standards of *bhakti* than are many of the more fortunate members of society. And no matter what the advantages or achievements of the latter may be, they are useless without the service and devotion that are possible for even the lowliest person:

> I consider that wealth, family, beauty, religious austerity, Vedic knowledge, vitality, splendor, power, strength, courage, intelligence, and yoga do not serve for the propitiation of the Supreme Soul, for Bhagavān was satisfied with the leader of the elephant herd [only] by means of his devotion.
>
> I consider a Śvapaca whose mind, speech, activity, purpose and life are fixed on the lotus feet of the Lotus-navelled One [i.e., Viṣṇu] to be better than a learned Brahman possessed of the above twelve qualities who has turned away from His feet. The former purifies his caste, but the latter, whose pride is great, does not.[47]

It is obvious from many examples that character and devotion are not necessarily dependent on birth. The most desirable characteristics are those compatible with devotion, and these are independent of class. Thus when Nārada lists the thirty features of the highest *dharma* and includes many characteristics traditionally associated with Brahmans, he specifically states that these are for all men.[48] Krishna, for the same reason, uses the standards of devotion to reinterpret many of the traditional upper-class characteristics and omits any reference to specific classes or to orthodox religious practices.[49] After describing the various class divisions and their characteristics, Nārada adds that a person should be identified by the class whose characteristics he possesses, even if that class is not his own by birth.[50] And in the same set of instructions he makes the completely unorthodox provision that "a man belonging to the lowest class may always, in time of distress, resort to the means of livelihood of every class with the exception of the ruling class." [51]

Both the religious and social teachings of the *Bhāgavata* appear to have two related purposes. The primary purpose is to establish *bhakti* religion against opposition from any source. The major opposition, judging from statements in the *Bhāgavata,* comes from persons committed to the defense of their traditional religious and social status. The "good people devoted to Hari" are ridiculed and despised by Brahmans, Kṣatriyas and Vaiśyas who are confused by the Vedas and blinded by pride in their wealth, family, and knowledge. The nature of this opposition leads the *Bhāgavata* to the defense of those who suffer most from the established socioreligious system. This secondary purpose is not a plea for social reform, but a claim for recognition of those who have both the need and the ability for salvation by devotion. It points out, however, the nonreligious factors involved in the conflict between the followers of *bhakti* and the supporters of orthodox religion.

The *Bhāgavata* does not provide a direct or detailed description of the devotees in social or economic terms, but there is an abundance of indirect evidence from which we can derive a fairly accurate understanding of these factors. As we have noted above, the followers of *bhakti* are persons who consider poverty and service as positive virtues for the promotion of character and devotion. They are acquainted with the hardships of poverty and with the arrogance and pride of the wealthy. They stress understanding of the misery of others, compassion, and impartiality toward all persons regardless of class. Their standards include modesty, absence of deceit, and freedom from pride in birth, actions, class, caste, wealth, or status. They are opposed to ostentation, hypocrisy, self-indulgence, conceit, and acquisitiveness, which are seen as the qualities of those who support orthodox religion and ridicule the poor devotees. They admire tranquillity and self-control, but singing, dancing, laughter, and tears are an important feature of their devotional life. The devotees use Tantric as well as Vedic ceremonies in their worship, and in addition to formal rites—or in place of them—they perform service to the Lord by bathing, anointing, decorating, and honoring his forms and images. They stress simplicity and faith in worship, and deny the effectiveness of costly ceremonies in which faith and devotion are secondary to personal desires.

The attitude toward the socially and economically distressed is an important factor in any attempted description of the devotees. The *Bhāgavata* considers the poor and miserable as objects of compassion, not as persons who are reaping a just reward for past sins. The Lord is spoken of as one who is "fond of those who are distressed," [52] and righteous persons are said to be "kind hearted to those who are pitiable." [53] Devotees are reminded to show generosity and to recognize that "the pleasing of Viṣṇu is when all the distressed, the blind, and the pitiable have eaten." [54] Not only is compassion in individual acts encouraged, but *bhakti* religion itself is considered an act of compassion on the part of the Lord by which women, Śūdras, and those who have fallen from their twice-born status might be brought to a better condition.[55]

It is said that by studying the *Bhāgavata* and reciting its stories the twice-born may obtain the goals of their respective classes, but a Śūdra "may be purified from that which causes him to fall [i.e., the impurities of his caste]" [56] or "may obtain the highest status." [57] The emphasis on the gains to be made by Śūdras is hardly accidental. Similar statements are made throughout the *Bhāgavata,* extending the advantages of devotion not only to Śūdras but to the even lower castes of Śvapacas, Pulkasas, and Antevasāyins. Hari's fame is said to "immediately purify the world as far as the Śvapaca." [58] From hearing and celebrating the name of Bhagavān, from bowing down to Him and remembering Him "even a dog eater [i.e., a Śvapāka] immediately becomes fit for a Soma festival." [59] The Lord is often directly praised in similar terms:

O Bhagavān, it is not impossible that the destruction of all the sins of men is from seeing you, from once hearing Whose name even a Pulkasa is released from *samsāra*.

. . . .

Ah! A Śvapaca on the tip of whose tongue your name rolls is thereby extremely important to you.

. . . .

O Lord, Antevasāyins ["those who live on the outskirts of the village," i.e., the impure castes] are purified because of hearing, celebrating, and meditating on you who are the form of Brahman; how much more so are those seeing and touching you purified! [60]

Even allowing for the use of such statements as exaggerated praise, there is no reason for doubting the sincerity of the *Bhāgavata* in extending the advantages of devotion to even the lowest members of society. Apart from claims and praises, there is the even more significant evidence of the principal devotees who appear in the *Bhāgavata*. We have already noted the *gopīs,* the wives of herdsmen, of whom it is said that "for these women there is neither the purification of the twice-born, nor even residence in the home of a preceptor, nor religious austerity, nor knowledge of the soul, nor purity, nor auspicious rites; but still there is resolute devotion to Krishna." [61] Sūta, the narrator of the *Bhāgavata,* is himself born of a lowly mixed caste.[62] Prahlāda, one of the prime examples of true devotion, was the son of a sinful Daitya king and describes himself as "of inferior birth." [63] The most important figure in the *Bhāgavata* apart from Bhagavān himself is the saintly ascetic Nārada, the prime expositor of *bhakti* religion and one of the best examples of the devotional life. Significantly, although in his previous life he was a Gandharva (a class of demigods), in the *Bhāgavata* he appears as a Śūdra, the son of a servant girl, who obtained devotion from hearing the praises of Hari celebrated by the scholars whom he and his mother served.[64]

Aside from these major figures, the *Bhāgavata* mentions many others who have been saved by devotion to the Lord in spite of their lowly status. Vaiśyas, Śūdras, women, the low-caste Antyajas, merchants, and hunters are said to have attained the place of Viṣṇu by their association with righteous persons.[65] Low-caste Pulkasas and Andhras, persons from the Kirāta, Pulinda, and Ābhīra tribes, and even Huns and Greeks are mentioned as taking refuge with Viṣṇu.[66]

Krishna and Balarāma, entering Mathurā to battle King Kaṃsa, are given clothes by a weaver and flowers by a garland maker and are worshiped by a group of merchants.[67] Parikṣit notes the status of other devotees when he asks why those who worship Śiva are usually wealthy, while those who worship Hari are not.[68] And Krishna reflects the experience of the lowly followers of *bhakti* when he teaches the proper attitude and behavior for a distressed person who is "reviled, despised, cheated, or perhaps envied by the impious, beaten or bound or deprived of subsistence, spit upon or covered with urine by ignorant people, and thus shaken in many ways." [69]

Can we construct a picture of the social and economic character of the Bhāgavatas from these various pieces of evidence? Such an attempt must certainly be tentative in view of the lack of external historical evidence. Certain conclusions, however, would seem to be unavoidable. The *Bhāgavata* definitely does not represent the viewpoint of the established orthodox social and economic groups. On the contrary, the wealthy, learned, and influential supporters of the *status quo* appear as the prime opponents of devotional religion as it appears in the *Bhāgavata.* The wealthy ridicule the standards of behavior of the devotees, and those who are proud of their social, economic, or religious status despise and even persecute the poor but righteous people devoted to the Lord.

Praise of poverty and compassion for the distressed characterize the social teachings of the *Bhāgavata.* From these emphases, as from the evidence of conflict with the wealthy and secure, we can assume that the devotees in general were poor—either by choice or by circumstance. The extension of salvation through devotion to Śūdras and even to the lower unclean castes indicates a definite attempt to bring members of these groups into the *bhakti* movement, and one would suspect that they made up a large part of its mass support. The break with orthodox rituals and their social restrictions and the establishment of image worship and temple ceremonies would have opened *bhakti* religion to the lower classes in practice as well as in theory, and we may assume that many participants in the festivals and processions were from these depressed groups.

The literary quality of the *Bhāgavata* and the evidence of familiarity with a wide range of earlier literature point to learned Bhāgavatas who could not have been ordinary members of the lowest classes. They were certainly not priests or scholars within the established socio-religious system but were probably ascetics who devoted their scholarship to the promotion of *bhakti* religion. This assumption is supported by the references in the *Bhāgavata* to scholarly ascetics, such as Nārada, who were committed to devotion to Bhagavān. These ascetics may or may not have been Brahmans; if we consider the Āḻvārs as legitimate examples, we find a variety of class backgrounds which was probably also characteristic of the Bhāgavata ascetics.

Based on these assumptions, we get a sketchy but useful picture of the devotional movement represented by the *Bhāgavata*. It was probably led by devoted ascetics whose learning and prestige gave the movement its structure. It drew its support from social and economic groups that were despised by the rest of society, but their poverty and distress made them naturally sympathetic to a devotional religion based on faith and simplicity and led by persons who were themselves poor. The establishment of temples and the various group activities indicate that the movement probably was urban rather than rural and drew its support from members of the depressed urban classes that would be present in sufficient numbers to give the movement stability. Appealing as it did to the needs of these people, it could offset the opposition of established orthodox groups by its popular appeal.

II. ON THE ARCHAISM OF THE *BHĀGAVATA PURĀṆA*

by J. A. B. van Buitenen

It is one of the paradoxes of the cultural history of India, where the final norm of orthodoxy is the acceptance of the authority of the Veda, that even the most doctrinaire texts of Brahmanistic orthodoxy betray hardly any trace of Vedic archaism. Although in cultures far less traditionally oriented a mock archaic language could lend to a verse or a prose text the vague prestige of an irrelevant past, the definite prestige of an admittedly relevant past was rarely invoked in India by language meant to suggest it. Except in some incidental and quite early cases (as in the later portions of the *Maitrāyaṇīya Upaniṣad,*[1] the *Suparṇādhyāya,*[2] the apocryphal hymn to the Aśvins in the ancient *Pauṣyaparvan*),[3] Vedic archaism in classical Sanskrit is conspicuous by its absence.

The reason is clear. When we disregard the epic language and its continuation in the Purāṇas, the norm of correct Sanskrit is Pāṇini's grammar. The entire point of writing Sanskrit at all is writing it correctly. Inaccuracies, deviations from the given norm, are not countenanced—unless their context clearly proves them to be *ārṣa,* deriving from the Ṛṣis, or *chāndasa,* hymnal, that is, in both cases, Vedic. But even this decree one might expect to find transgressed in the Brahmanistic culture, which endlessly reaffirms that its roots are in the Vedas.

The Vedas, however, were not read; they were recited. Those who knew the Vedas were primarily ritual specialists, not literati. Of any literary influence of even the *Ṛgveda Saṃhitā,* traditionally the most prestigious one, on later high Sanskrit literature, whether in vocabulary or, more telling, in exceptional nominal or verbal forms, there is very little trace.

This point, well known though it is, deserves stress, because it shows how completely the Sanskrit language, as codified and described by the three sages Pāṇini, Kātyāyana and Patañjali, had supplanted the ancient Vedic as a cultural language and how little in later times the

Veda was actually known, except by rote. By the time that Sanskrit became cultivated, the Veda was present, in a symbolic fashion, as an eternal document; it was more actively present in the erudition of Mīmāṃsā and the practice of oblations, but most pertinently present —by however indirect an affinity—in the *smṛtis* that the orthodox lived by. The archaic language, which in the fifth century B.C. already stood in need of a glossary,[4] was no longer a productive presence in the culture.

It is therefore a unique phenomenon that far later in the history of literature, when Sanskrit letters were in fact on the decline, a text purporting to belong to the Purāṇic tradition consciously attempted to archaize its language. This peculiarity of the *Bhāgavata Purāṇa* has long been recognized by scholars, but, apart from a useful philological study by F. J. Meier,[5] it has not been made the object of further investigation.

Meier, after perhaps too hastily discarding the classically permitted imperatives in *-tāt,*[6] offers two partial explanations for the archaizing tendency of the *Bhāgavata, "dieser eigentümliche Charakter, der es nicht nur aus den andern Purāṇas, sondern überhaupt aus der indischen Literatur heraushebt."* He suggests that certain archaic forms may occasionally be explained by the exigencies of the meter, and that, in some other cases, archaisms may have been mediated by Middle-Indic.[7] However, though some cases can thus be accounted for, their number is negligible. Meier rightly points out, as Michelson[8] did before him, that on occasion Vedic forms are borrowed along with Vedic context, as in the Purūravas legend and the Śunaḥśepa story.[9] The results of this often ill-informed archaistic effort are picturesque: *"die Analyse solcher barocker Verse zeigt uns—und darin besteht ihr Wert—mit welcher unglaublichen Unkenntniss der Verfasser der vedischen Sprache gegenüberstand."*[10] I would dispute, however, that this is its only value.

This unique tendency of the *Bhāgavata,* which is displayed with equal density throughout the text, irrespective of style or context, still stands in need of explanation. The question briefly stated is: Why did the author or authors responsible for the final version of the *Bhāgavata* want the book to sound Vedic?

The question is the more challenging, since the Purāṇa has a somewhat ambivalent attitude toward Vedic orthodoxy. On numerous occasions, as Thomas J. Hopkins has ably shown elsewhere in this volume,[11] the empty and conceitful formalism of the Vaidikas is unfavorably contrasted with the simple and sincere devotions of the *bhakta*. In such criticisms of Brahmanism our Purāṇa is of course not alone; it is almost a refrain in epic and purāṇa. One might go back as far as *Ṛgveda* I.164.39: "What can he bring about with the hymns who does not know the *Akṣara* in the supreme heaven where the gods are seated? Only those who know it are sitting together here."[12] This is echoed by Yājñavalkya: "If one does not know this *Akṣara,* then one's oblations, sacrifices, and austerities for many thousands of years will come to an end; and when one departs from this world without knowing the *Akṣara,* one is miserable."[13]

The interesting passage (*Bhāgavata Purāṇa* XI.21.32–34) referred to by Hopkins, is unmistakably modeled on the *Bhagavad Gītā* II.42–44:

> This flowery language [i.e., the Veda], which they proclaim without wisdom, being bent upon discussions of the Vedas and maintaining, O Arjuna, that there is nothing else to know, inspired as they are by desires and intent on heavenly pleasures—this flowery language, productive of fruits of action that spell rebirth and abounding in a variety of rites to secure joy and power, robs those who are bent on joy and power of their senses.

But, in recalling these *Gītā* stanzas, the Purāṇa does not discard the Vedas, for the text goes on:

> The Vedas deal with both Brahman and Ātman and with the three rubrics:[14] the Seers speak in mystery and mystery is dear to me. The Brahman which is Veda, very hard to know, consists in breath, senses, and mind;[15] like an ocean, its shore is boundless and its deeps are unfathomable" (XI.21.35).

In fact, the orthodox formalists do not know their Veda; for in reality the Vedas celebrate the Lord; and in despising the Lord and those good people who are devoted to him, they show the depth of their ignorance.[16]

The exact date of the *Bhāgavata Purāṇa* is still unsettled, though in its case closer approximation can be achieved than in that of any other Purāṇa. The *terminus ante quem* is roughly 1000, as it was known by name (but barely) to al-Bīrūnī,[17] and was quoted by Abhinavagupta.[18] The *terminus post quem* is the *Vaiṣṇava bhakti* movement of South India. In a *post-factum* prophecy, the *Bhāgavata Purāṇa* (XI.5.38–40) reads:

In the Kali Age there will be devotees of Nārāyaṇa, O King, in great numbers everywhere in Tamil country, where the Tāmraparṇī River, abundant in water, fashions a garland, where the holy Kāverī and the westerly Mahānadī flow, whose waters, O king of men, are drunk by the people, devotees of pure heart generally to the blessed Lord Vāsudeva.

Until fresh evidence turns up, it is better not to push back the date of the final version of the *Bhāgavata* too far, nor too uncompromisingly to insist on the southern origin of our text. No quotations from the *Bhāgavata* have been identified in Rāmānuja's work, although this theologian of *bhakti* cites the *Viṣṇu Purāṇa* profusely. Nor have I been able as yet to identify citations from our text in the works of Yāmuna. Both Rāmānuja and Yāmuna were South-Indian Vaiṣṇavas deeply concerned with the orthodoxy of their faith. Their reticence needs explanation, if evidence from al-Bīrūnī and Abhinavagupta is admitted. That neither appears to quote from our text may mean either that in their days it was not sufficiently known or that it was not sufficiently respectable for their orthodox purposes. But *argumenta e silentio* are never conclusive; besides, Yāmuna is incompletely and fragmentarily preserved, and Rāmānuja was very exclusive in his sources.[19]

If then, with others, we prudently prefer to keep to the tenth century as the final date of the *Bhāgavata Purāṇa,* we have in the works of Yāmuna a most interesting control. Here we have a South Indian—equally inspired by the *bhakti* movement, and neither in time nor in ambience nor, probably, in space too far apart from the authors of the Purāṇa—who presents some other aspects of Bhāgavatism, of how Bhāgavatas thought of themselves and how they were thought of by others whom they had to accommodate. For, however interesting it may be to know what the Bhāgavatas thought of orthodox and well-to-do Brahmans, it is assuredly of no less interest to see what the Brahmans thought of the Bhāgavatas. Yāmuna, our source, is unimpeachable. Here we have not a sectarian text speaking in pious and traditional platitudes about wicked adversaries, but a Bhāgavata with a fine mind who seeks to enumerate, and subsequently to invalidate, very precisely the traditional arguments of the Smārtas against the less-than-respectable Bhāgavatas.

The context is Yāmuna's *Āgamaprāmāṇya,* a treatise meant to demonstrate the Vedic validity of Pāñcarātra. The text merits a full translation.[20] In the present passage[21] the Smārta Brahman is speaking.

Furthermore, we do not find that those who observe the rituals enjoined by scripture, like the *agnihotra,* etc., in the same manner as they observe such [Smārta] rites as mouth rinsing, initiation, etc., also follow the customs of the Tantrists. On the contrary, Vedic experts condemn those who do so. Hence, the validity asserted of the several traditions,[22] because they all have the same performers, cannot apply to heterodox traditions like Pāñcarātra, etc. For the exemplary people[23] of the three twice-born classes do not accept the content of the statements of such systems.

Objection. But Bhāgavata Brahmans, who wear the hair tuft, the sacrificial thread, etc., in accordance with the precepts of scripture and tradition, do observe the contents of Pāñcarātra day after day. Since it therefore may be deemed probable that these contents are based on Vedic injunction, how can we then assume that this tradition has its origin in error, deceit, and the like, which are the very antithesis of validity?

Reply. Well! One who argues like this renders beautiful proof of his "authority," if Bhāgavatas, who are hated by the three twice-born classes, are indeed considered to be "exemplary"!

Objection. Aren't the Brahmans, the foremost of the twice-born exemplary?

Reply. You miss the point. The Bhāgavatas are not even in the twice-born classes, let alone Brahmans! We do not hold that the Brahman is a different species, distinguishable from the human species, with defining characteristics that are found to persist in certain bodies while they are absent in others. No, the hair tuft, sacrificial thread, etc., which are enjoined upon Brahmans, etc., cannot make a man a Brahman. Nor do they convey that a man is a Brahman, for we see them inconclusively worn by crooks, Śūdras, and the like. Consequently the sole criterion of whether a man is a Brahman, is traditional nomenclature that is proved right beyond dispute.

Now, common usage does not apply the title of Brahman to a Bhāgavata without hesitation. Different appellations are used: one may be called a Brahman, or, in contrast, one may be called a Bhāgavata.

Objection. I'll grant that. Still, Brahmans may be called "Bhāgavatas," "Sātvatas," or similar names by some kind of metaphorical usage, just as they may be called "hermits"[24] and the like.

Reply. That is not the point. . . . A Sātvata[25] is, by definition, a member of the lowest class, descended from a tramp Vaiśya and excluded from the sacraments of initiation, etc. As Manu [26] says: "From a tramp Vaiśya issues . . . a Sātvata." It cannot be disputed that the word "Bhāgavata" denotes a Sātvata. A *smṛti* has it that "the fifth, Sātvata by name, worships the sanctuaries of Viṣṇu by royal decree; [27] he is traditionally known as a Bhāgavata." Similarly there are *smṛtis* to the effect that precisely that way of life which the Bhāgavatas are seen openly to pursue is the profession of the issue of the said tramps. Thus Uśanas: [28] ". . . offering worship to a god is the occupation of *ācāryas* and *Sātvatas*." Likewise in the *Brahma Purāṇa:* "[The Sātvata] shall worship the sanctuaries of Viṣṇu by royal decree." Elsewhere the same: "It is the occupation of the Sātvatas to keep clean the sanctuary of the god, to clean up the eatables offered to the god, and to guard the idol." And, likewise, to dispel all doubts about what kind of people they are, the statement of Manu: [29] "Whether they reveal or conceal themselves, know them by their deeds."

Besides, their conduct proves that they are non-Brahmans. Occupationally, they offer *pūjā* to a god, undergo a special consecration, consume the eatable offerings, observe a series of sacraments that deviate from the traditional series, which begins with the planting of the seed and ends with the cremation, fail to perform the scriptural rituals, avoid intercourse with Brahmans: these and other practices quite convincingly prove that they are not Brahmans.

The *smṛtis* hold that they are disqualified from performing Brahman duties, because they offer *pūjā* to a god. For example, "those who by heredity idolize a god by way of profession are disqualified from learning [the Veda], sacrificing or having a sacrifice performed." Likewise their own declaration in the *Parama Saṃhitā:* [30] "Whether in emergency or disaster, in terror or in straits, one must certainly never professionally offer *pūjā* to the god of gods." The very fact that they do wear the offered garlands and do eat the offered eatables—practices abhorred by all exemplary people—plainly illustrates that they are not Brahmans.

To continue: we are puzzled by the claim that the behavior of these people—at the very sight of whom all exemplary persons undergo expiatory rites like the *cāndrāyaṇa* [31]—can prove that their system is based on the scriptures. For the *smṛtis* have it that expiation is required when one has set eyes on a "godlinger"; [32] and "godlingers" are those who live off a god's treasury and offer *pūjā* for a living. Thus Devala: "One is called a 'godlinger,' when one lives off a god's treasury." Also: "A Brahman who offers *pūjā* to a god for a period of three years is called a 'godlinger' and is condemnable in all his actions." Those, on the other hand, who are found to worship a god by way of hereditary profession are automatically regarded as "godlingers." The *smṛtis* lay down the expiatory rite: "A Brahman while eating should not lay eyes on . . . a 'godlinger'; if he does, he must perform the *cāndrāyaṇa*." Atri likewise shows very clearly that they are not Brahmans: ". . . 'godlingers' . . . and those who are professional

Bhāgavatas are sub-Brahmans."[33] And, similarly, the venerable Vyāsa: ". . . the 'godlingers' are pariah Brahmans."[34]

Thus, the very fact that Bhāgavata folk—folk who are apostate from the way of the Veda—accept the Pāñcarātra scriptures is sufficient ground to deny them validity.

There is no reason to distrust Yāmuna's evidence as to the esteem, or lack of it, in which the Bhāgavatas of his time were held by orthodox Brahmans. As is clear from our lengthy quotation, the Bhāgavatas laid claim to being Brahmans; it is also clear that those who made the claim were the priests among the Bhāgavatas. The Smārtas vehemently disputed their claim, because Bhāgavatas/Sātvatas were traditionally (i.e., by *smṛti*) known to be very low class: the issue in fact (according to the usual *Dharmaśāstra* system, by which caste hierarchies are made intelligible by degrees of evolution from mixed *varṇas*) of a Vaiśya Vrātya. And not only does the Bhāgavata stand condemned by his heredity but his lowliness is compounded by his sacerdotal occupation; priest to his idol he lives off his priesthood, and, whatever his social pretensions, he is a common *pūjārī*.

Before we enlarge on the relevance of Yāmuna's *Āgamaprāmāṇya* as an explanation of the archaism of the *Bhāgavata Purāṇa* we should do well to reflect on his own background. He was the second great man in the *Śrīvaiṣṇavasaṃpradāya,* after Nāthamuni, whose grandson he is supposed to have been. At the end of his *Āgamaprāmāṇya,* Yāmuna adds a stanza glorifying the "impeccable scriptures, whose spirit has been increased by the glorious Lord Nāthamuni." These scriptures are not the Vedas of orthodoxy, but rather the Tamil *prabandham* of the hymns of the Vaiṣṇava saints of South India, the Āḻvārs, whose devotional lyrics Nāthamuni had collected and introduced into temple worship. Therefore, to conclude his treatise with such praise must have seemed most appropriate to Yāmuna. For Yāmuna had but continued Nāthamuni's work. As he now claimed validity for a class of texts that had not before been acknowledged by orthodox tradition—and claimed it by analogy to the main sources of orthodox tradition—so Nāthamuni had claimed authority for the *prabandham*. Within a couple of generations the canon of Vaiṣṇavism had been increased immeasurably. And it is of utmost significance to the cultural history of South India that Brahmanistic orthodoxy continued to be claimed for this Vaiṣṇavism. We observe here a process of Brahmanization, or, as we shall prefer to call it, Sanskritization.

Both Nāthamuni and Yāmuna were temple priests at the recently founded Raṅganātha temple of Śrīraṅgam. P. N. Srinivasachari [35] remarks that Nāthamuni's effort in incorporating the Tamil scriptures, the "Tamil Veda," into the temple service at Śrīraṅgam introduced an "innovation [that] effected a silent revolution in temple worship, as it raised the status of the *prabandham* to the level of the Veda, and liberalized the meaning of Revelation." It is, however, doubtful whether this "revolution" was all that silent.

It is worth while to recall here that it had been the *bhakti* movement which produced the Āḻvārs and that the momentum of this same movement kept their adulation of iconic representations of the God alive among the common people. The incorporation of the Tamil *prabandham* into the sacred scriptures that served in temple worship had two effects: a *soi-disant* "orthodox" tradition in Vaiṣṇavism was thus enabled to ally itself with popular movements that had a distinct tendency to break away from Brahmanism; [36] and these popular movements themselves were given the discipline and direction that only Sanskritic tradition could impose. In the efforts of the three *ācāryas,* Nāthamuni, Yāmuna, and Rāmānuja, we discern three phases: (1) acceptance of non-Sanskritic religious literature and institutionalization of it in traditional temple worship; (2) acceptance and traditionalization of Pāñcarātra; and (3) Vedānticization of Vaiṣṇavite *bhakti.*

Yāmuna's apologia at once raises the question of how orthodox the Bhāgavatas really were. But we should change our terminology: in view of the kind of objections leveled against them, the "orthodox" were hardly, if at all, concerned with ortho*doxy,* but with ortho*praxis,* as the norm for Hinduism generally is better described by orthopraxis than by orthodoxy.

Characteristically, Yāmuna's first argument concerns the Vedic affiliation of the Bhāgavatas who observe Pāñcarātra ritual. They belong, he emphasizes, to the *Ekāyanaśākhā* [37] of the Vājasaneyins, who themselves represent the White *Yajurveda* (69). And "when one sees learned people, who day after day study the *Ekāyanaśākhā* of the Vājasaneyins, wear prominently their sacred threads and upper garments and hair tufts, impart teaching, offer sacrifices, and receive priestly stipends [38] does one not know instantly that they are Brahmans?" (70).

If, moreover, the recollection of Brahmanic *gotras* makes one a genuine Brahman, so "the Bhāgavatas have the tradition: 'We are descendants of Bharadvāja, of Kaśyapa, of Gautama, of Aupagava.' [39] Nor," he hastens to say, "is their recollection of *gotra* descent unfounded or a recent matter: for the same can be argued for all *gotra* traditions. If doubt about descent were admissible, just because error could conceivably have crept in, this would confuse everybody about the authenticity of his Brahmanhood. After all, anyone might fear that he really is a *cāṇḍāla,* if he suspects his mother of having had a lover. And how, my eminent opponent, can you yourself be quite sure that your birth entitles you to Veda study! Therefore, as the Brahmanhood of the Bhāgavatas is entirely proved by their recollection of their respective *gotras,* which has been passed on from generation to generation in uninterrupted transmission and therefore stands unchallenged, there is nothing to differentiate between the Brahmanhood of Bhāgavatas and that of others."

The evidence of Yāmuna is significant, because it suggests a theory to account for the archaism of the *Bhāgavata Purāṇa.* In both cases, neither in time nor in ideology too far apart,[40] we have a conspicuous concern to persuade others, if not oneself, of one's orthodoxy, which is proved to be orthodoxy because it is based on the Veda. Briefly, Yāmuna's point is: we are orthodox on Vedic and Smārta terms, and we can prove it. The Bhāgavata's point is: I am not only orthodox in the Vedic tradition, I even sound like the Veda.

Even though much by the wear and tear of time unavoidably must escape us, neither Yāmuna's work nor the Purāṇa is alone in its Vedicism. It would be worth while investigating the suggestion that a similar concern in proving Vedic orthodoxy, reaching back beyond the Smārta or Vedānta traditions, motivated a Madhva, the founder of dualistic Vedānta on Vaiṣṇava religious principles, to compose the *Ṛgbhāṣya,* a commentary on a number of *Ṛgvedic* hymns. He was the first to take the *Ṛgveda* seriously as a source of metaphysical truth in the history of Vedānta. And would a similar concern contribute to an explanation of why in the Vijayanagara Empire a Sāyaṇācārya [41] arose to set himself to the gigantic task of commenting on the entire Vedic corpus?

The *bhakti* movement had rung in a new period in religion as well as in the philosophical formulation of it. No one who reads either the *Bhāgavata Purāṇa,* or the *Āgamaprāmāṇya,* or any one of Rāmānuja's works, can fail to sense the utter difference of spirit that prevails. In order to bring out the contrast, the best example is not Śaṃkara; his concern with the world of process was minimal; and the *bhakta's* world is the world of process. Another Vedāntin, chronologically later than Śaṃkara no doubt, but ideologically far more naïve and old-fashioned, impressively demonstrates the social conceit that Smārtas [42] could carry over into their soteriology.

In a most revealing introduction by Bhāskara to his commentary on the *Bhagavad Gītā,*[43] the learned author passes such judgments as:

It is forbidden to impart to the Śūdra, etc., knowledge of unseen things, to instruct him in *dharma* and the like. Besides, when a Śūdra, out of his own foolish desire, bypasses the instruction by Brahmans and either from a written text or from a commentary thereon learns its import and performs the rites, the rites he performs will not be of any benefit to him. On the contrary, the knowledge acquired by one who is forbidden it and who is not initiated only creates distress for him. . . . Since the higher and the lower classes are not equal, they likewise do not have the same *dharma.* As has been said, "If women and the Śūdras were qualified for release, the caste eminence of the Brahman would serve no purpose." . . . The norm of good conduct in the land of the Āryans is conveyed solely by the Brahman's action. . . . In the line "wisdom, knowledge and orthodoxy are the natural functions of the Brahmans," our text will demonstrate that the Blessed *dharma* is only for Brahmans a way to Release. [How typical, his expression *bhagavān dharmaḥ!*] The Śūdra, etc., cannot be elevated . . . nor can iron be made into gold by heating it some more. . . . Even the Kṣatriya and the Vaiśya do not have the same qualification for release as the Brahman. Therefore, only the Brahman has it. No release is possible for Śūdras, no more than it is for animals. . . . Since the Śūdra etc., have no release and lack qualification for the three pursuits of *dharma, artha,* and *kāma,* which are the goals of man, it follows that they may also not learn the doctrine of the *Bhagavad Gītā.* . . . Just as a bilious man who, in order to cure himself, takes medicine that is intended for a phlegmatic not only fails to be cured, but suffers even worse from the onslaught of his ailment, so indeed is it in the case of Śūdras, etc.

In Bhāskara we have a spokesman for an old-fashioned Vedānta, in which the desire of knowing Brahman is compatible only with the performance of appropriate Vedic ritual,[44] which excludes all but the Brahman. This attitude was only *partly* reformed by Śaṃkara. Although he relegated all ritual performances to the realm of *vyavahāra,* or the provisional truth of process, he did not alter the spirit of exclusiveness associated with Vedānta. Precisely this uncompromising dichotomy between the realms of supreme truth and relative process encouraged an attitude summed up in the well-known dictum: *vyavahāre Bhāṭṭaḥ, paramārthe Śāṃkaraḥ* "in *vyavahāra,* a follower of Kumārila Bhaṭṭa; in respect to the supreme truth, a follower of Śaṃkara." But to be a legitimate follower of Kumārila,[45] the Mīmāṃsaka had in theory to be twice-born, in practice to be a Brahman.

It would not be difficult to multiply quotations in line with Bhāskara's views. They are important inasmuch as they show, for the age with which we are concerned, the mentality of those who traditionally regarded themselves (and, however reluctantly, were regarded by the others) as the final arbiters of *dharma* and *mokṣa.* Against their spirit of exclusiveness, in society as well as in soteriology, the rise of the *bhakti* movement placed a spirit of catholicity. This catholicity was predetermined by the movement's popular character, which gave the prime role of expression to the vernacular languages.

In spite of the long prehistory of *bhakti* (not in all respects as clear as one could wish), the southern *bhakti* movement was something new—not perhaps per se but for the first time a consistent effort was being made to place it in the Brahmanistic tradition. In the labors of a Nāthamuni, a Yāmuna, a Rāmānuja, we observe a consistent effort to promote the Sanskritization of the *bhakti* religion. The God of the *bhakta* is equated with the supreme principle of the Upaniṣads; the adoring contemplation of God in his heaven by the worshiper is equivalent to *mokṣa;* the acts of worship and veneration are on a par with the rites prescribed by scripture and tradition. Similarly, in the archaistic emphasis of the *Bhāgavata Purāṇa* we find an attempt at Sanskritization of the popular Krishna legend. Krishnaism no longer is merely a popular mythology, with its rather womanly idyl of the little boy who is also a lover, set in the rustic scene of pastures, cows, cattle tenders and their wives. Purāṇic rather than epical, let alone Vedic in provenience, it now speaks, or at least tries to speak, in the solemn language of the Vedic seer.

Sanskritization, in the sense in which I want to use it here, is a term for a conception recently evolved by certain cultural anthropologists who are studying the factors that are active in cultural change in contemporary India. M. N. Srinivas [46] was the first to introduce the term into anthropology, and it has since been taken up by others. Its principal disadvantage is, of course, that it is a misnomer. It does not mean what it means to the Indologist—a "rendering in Sanskrit" (e.g., the Sanskritization of the Paiśācī *Bṛhatkathā* in the *Kathāsaritsāgara*), or "adoption of Sanskrit as a literary language" (e.g., the Sanskritization of Mahāyāna Buddhism since Aśvaghoṣa). More precisely the term corresponds to "rendering Sanskritic." This again is a term easily misunderstood, if it is derived from Sanskrit as the name of a language. But Srinivas is an Indian; for him Sanskrit is more than the name of a language, it is the summation of a way of life. His use, and that by others, of "Sanskrit" and "Sanskritic" has reference to a rather complex notion of normative self-culture, of which it is more or less consciously felt that the Sanskrit language was its original vehicle. It carries with it associations of a sacral character. One is *saṃskārya* (to be perfected or "sacralized" by appropriate ceremonies), one observes *saṃskāras* (sacramentals)—words derived from the same root *kṛ-* with the prefixed verb *sam*. In such words a meaning of "refining or perfecting one's nature and conduct by ritual means" becomes central. Other characteristic connotations help to widen the comprehension of the concept. "Sanskritic" is that which is the most ancient, therefore the most pure, and therefore hierarchically the most elevated; it thus provides a norm for exclusive personal or group conduct—exclusive for its purity and elevation—that most effectively proves itself in securing correct descent, backward by relating oneself to an ancient lineage or an ancient myth and forward by safeguarding the purity of future offspring. It is in this comprehensive Hindu, if not in fact Brahmanistic, sense that Srinivas seems to use the term; and in this sense the term describes a significant context of cultural notions that should not be reduced too rashly. It is in this sense, too, that the term can legitimately be applied to describe processes that took place in what the non-Indologist would tend to call "Sanskritic" culture,[47] known to us solely from Sanskrit texts.

Sanskritization, then, refers to a process in the Indian civilization in which a person or a group consciously relates himself or itself to an accepted notion of true and ancient ideology and conduct. His criterion for judgment of orthopraxis is likely to be the practice of those in his community whose prestige has continued to hallow their way of life. If they are Brahmans, they are likely also to be normative for orthodoxy, but here a far greater variation of norm is possible. When the person's or group's own ideology significantly diverges from the norm set by those who regard themselves as models, either a conciliation is effected, at least in orthopraxy, or a separation of tradition is accepted. Social scientists tend to find this active confrontation and the consequent change of conduct to be motivated primarily by a desire to raise one's social status. This may well be the case. But it seems to me desirable not to build this limited motivation into the conceptualization of the whole process, since other motivations may be recognized.

Despite the confusion it may create, it is worth while to retain the term "Sanskritization." More than other terms employed in varying, though related, contexts of conceptions—e.g., traditionalization, generalization, universalization, Brahmanization, Hinduization—it has special overtones that ought to be heard and recorded. Most audible among them is the one that rings of the past.

Central to Indian thinking through the ages is a concept of knowledge which, though known to Platonism and Gnosticism, is foreign to the modern West. Whereas for us, to put it briefly, knowledge is something to be *discovered,* for the Indian knowledge is to be *recovered.* Although doubtless a great many other factors have contributed to the reputed traditionalism of the Indian civilization, one particular preconception, related to this concept of knowledge concerning the past and its relationship to the present, is probably of central significance: that at its very origin the absolute truth stands revealed; that this truth—which simultaneously is a way of life—has been lost, but not irrecoverably; that somehow it is still available through ancient life lines that stretch back to the original revelation; and that the present can be restored only when this original past has been recovered. Phenomenologically, this belief is no doubt akin to that of an original paradise on earth; but the paradise is not irretrievably lost.

One may find this belief, enacted as an attitude toward life, reflected in many different but coherent ways: metaphysically, in the assumption of the self's original universal consciousness before its implication in transmigration; ritually, in the preservation of a Vedic tradition, "continued" in Purāṇic and Tantric traditions; ethically, in the conservation of *dharma,* which itself was the way of life of the original seers who saw the light; educationally, in the teacher's pledge to transmit in full and intact his knowledge to his pupil; sociologically, in the Brahman's self-identification with the *gotra* of an ancient *Ṛṣi;* societally, in the maintenance, against all historical and contemporary fact, of a sacral prototype in the four-class system; linguistically, in the acceptance of one ancient language; and religiously, in the notion of a progressive revelation.

There is an image here of a supraculture, not to be discovered in an eventual future, but to be recovered from an available past. History, from this point of view, is not a horizontal development from event to event, with its beginnings nebulous and its end not in sight, but a vertical development, a ramification—deterioration no doubt, but with the pure roots still in sight.

Sanskrit is felt to be one of the lifelines, and Sanskritization in its literal sense, the rendering into Sanskrit, is one of the prime methods of restating a tradition in relation to a sacral past. So it was in the *bhakti* movement. Before the rather sudden rise into textual view of the great religions in the epic, *bhakti* was absent from the emerging Sanskritic tradition. The contexts in which it then arose—and the *Bhagavad Gītā,* in this respect overrated on the strength of later traditions, is certainly no exception—clearly show that the kind of religious attitude and devotion to which the term *bhakti* is more and more applied is essentially a popular one, an everyday religion of immediate existential needs, for sufferings to be alleviated, for prayers to be heard, for grace to be the only thing left, for joy to be shared, and for royal worship obediently to be demonstrated. A human dignity, a pride in achievement and in certain hope, is absent from it and the use of Sanskrit is secondary to it.

It is useful to remember that, in the Sanskritic tradition, the use of Sanskrit was always secondary. The first language of anyone always was the vernacular, even if his language of preference was to become Sanskrit. The *śiṣṭa,*[48] the Indian, or rather Sanskritic, literatus, was always bilingual, speaking in a regional vernacular and in Sanskrit. And his bilingualism implied a biculturalism. Just as the bilingual man is the mediator of loans between two languages, the *śiṣṭa* was the mediator of "loans" between his vernacular culture, as small as a village or as wide as a nation, and the Sanskrit culture. On his capacity of absorption depended the free interflow. The Sanskrit culture itself is of course the product of early stages of such an interflow. But by the time the epic was concluded, to put an arbitrary date to it, a definite Sanskrit culture had constituted itself, and the future became the commentary on a basic text. This text has a context, and this context differs from region to region and from date to date. And this context is the way of life that local *śiṣṭas,* rooted in their subculture, hold to be Sanskritic.

I borrow the terms "text" and "context" from a recent article by Milton B. Singer,[49] who uses them to draw a distinction between the interests of "textualists," the philologists among the Indologists, and the interests of the "contextualists," those investigators, mostly drawn from the social sciences, who are primarily interested in the twentieth-century function of the "text" as part of a larger "context" of the social and cultural realities of those who make use of this "text."

These terms and distinctions are equally applicable to the Indian culture itself, which happens to be very textual, in the sense that a fairly limited corpus of texts was considered to be authoritative—to such an extent that thought and practice of later centuries held validity only if and when they could be shown to be in accordance with these texts.

For Bhāskara the "context" to the Vedānta "text"—literally the *Brahmasūtras* and the *Bhagavad Gītā*—is his own traditional Smārta way of life. But for Yāmuna (if we care to consider him already a Vedāntin), and certainly for Rāmānuja,[50] as later on for Madhva, the "context" was the Vaiṣṇava *bhakti* way of life. In so far as the commentators must justify their own contexts in their text, this text must make appropriate sense. And in the explication of the text we find, if the context is new, continuous Sanskritization of the context. Thus, given the "text" of the Veda, we find that the new context of the Āgamas of Pañcarātra are Sanskritized as Veda-based, like the *smṛtis;* the Bhāgavatas are Sanskritized as Brahmans; the Viṣṇu of personal devotion, as the Brahman of the Upaniṣads; the acts of the *bhakta,* as Vedic or Smārta rites, and so on.

In this Sanskritization, some violence has to be done to reigning orthodoxy and orthopraxy. It is to be shown that the dominant norms are either not right, not really Sanskritic, or not exclusively right. In orthopraxy, the prestige of these dominant norms is often insuperable: nowhere does Yāmuna suggest that the Smārta *saṃskāras* are superseded by the Tantric ones. In other, less "textual," fields of action, the dominant orthopraxy can more easily be adapted to or accommodated. In matters of orthodoxy there is wider scope. One can go beyond the accepted norm, as Yāmuna goes beyond the *smṛtis* to the authorship of God, who in omniscience is at least equivalent to the Veda or else, as the same author does, show that one's dogma and practice are Vedic by pointing out the Vedic lifelines of the tradition (the *Ekāyanaśākhā* of the Vājasaneyins, the *gotras* that trace Bhāgavata prestige back to the *ṛṣis*). Rāmānuja writes exclusively on the level of orthodoxy (from which he silently omits Pañcarātra, only acknowledging it in passing —a further Sanskritization), and, by widening the scope of his original texts to encompass the Vaiṣṇava *bhakti* contexts, he proves the correctness of his system. Madhva, as the first of the school founders, reaches all the way back to the *Ṛgveda* for his sources, but significantly also brings in a far greater variety of Purāṇic and Tantric materials.

I should like to suggest that in the archaism of the *Bhāgavata* we have the expression of the same concern. The Krishna legend has to *sound* Vedic because it *was* Vedic. There is a similar reaching back to the most ancient sources—however imperfectly known—to make the old foundation support the new edifice. Here Sanskritization once more takes a linguistic form. Writing in Sanskrit was not enough; to the faithful the supremacy of Krishnaism was hardly in doubt, but the high-sounding language (which often must have been unintelligible) gave appropriate notice of its Vedic orthodoxy.

The above inquiry was undertaken in order to see what precise application the "textual" Indologist can make of concepts that field workers in anthropology are evolving on the basis of contemporary materials. If their concepts help to understand contemporary processes in cultural change, they may help the historian to understand previous processes. Although it is, of course, true that the materials brought together by cultural anthropologists observing present-day facts can have no documentary bearing on ages and countries beyond the time and region in which the evidence was observed, nevertheless their theories concerning cultural and social changes (sometimes, for the Indologist, too hastily hypothesized from the evidence) may have a heuristic value in general for the history of Indian culture. The historian has always taken for granted such processes as Sanskritization and cultural universalization, but the frustrating lack of "contextual" detail, in Singer's sense, often dooms attempts at specific theorizing to futility—at least for the early and classical periods.

There is, however, more hope for the middle period. Then, in greater detail of sculpture, monuments, and vernacular literature, the sects arose, or, to put it more cautiously, crossed the threshold of respectability into Sanskrit. Simultaneously, the "Sanskritic" tradition itself became the issue. In this little-studied period, the canons of what is "Sanskritic" became codified from place to place. In the process, the role of the original Sanskrit culture had become negligible. After the *śiṣṭas,* the clerics had taken over. Their knowledge is secondhand, a prestige-making product of limited erudition and no originality. It is par excellence the age in which the interflow between supraculture and subculture ceases, when the supraculture gets translated, adapted, adulterated, to conform to the subcultural standards of the clerics concerning what is deemed Sanskritic.

Before "textualists" and "contextualists" can effectively work together, greater clarity must be brought to this middle period. Sanskritists will have to modify their beliefs that much that is Sanskritic quietly persists, whereas anthropologists ought to discriminate more clearly between the various higher traditions that too frequently are lumped together as "Sanskritic," and placed in some kind of contradistinction to littler traditions.

In spite of an increasing sophistication on the part of anthropologists in dealing with textual materials, their traditional disciplinary orientation toward a here-and-now of isolable contemporary communities renders unfeasible their leisurely investigation into the significance of the texts, and the continuous feedback of this significance into the reality of here and now. The Indologist, often too uncompromisingly insisting on the primacy of a Sanskrit education, rarely gives expression to the well-known fact that the further we progress—or retrogress, as the case may be—into middle ages and modernity, the less relevant is the living Sanskrit culture of, say, the Gupta Age. Despite a growing good will on both sides, there are still to be broken down unspoken prejudices that have nothing to gain from companionable assurances of good-fellowship.

Practically, both Indologists and social scientists ought to engage in a concerted endeavor to expose the middle period. It is there that the modern "traditions," whose age is always overrated, find their origin; it is there that the Sanskritic tradition, whose pertinacity is always overrated, finds its conclusion. It would be instructive for the textualist to accompany the anthropologist to the field, however arbitrary the choice of the location may seem to him, in order to gain an understanding of the special conditions under which the material is gathered, and find out what is invisible to him. At the same time it would be most salutary for the Sanskritist to find the contextualist sitting next to him in the quiet of his study and pointing out, with similar confidence, what is inexplicably invisible to *him*.

III. DOCTRINE AND PRACTICE AMONG THE VAIṢṆAVAS OF BENGAL

by Edward C. Dimock, Jr.

A full treatment of an extensively documented religious movement is not possible within a few pages. The Vaiṣṇava [1] movement of Bengal is such a religious movement, with its own well-defined doctrinal, literary, and ritual peculiarities.[2] In some ways it typifies, in some ways complements, and in some ways is quite divergent from, the great *bhakti* (devotional) religious movement which swept across northern India in the fourteenth to seventeenth centuries and the older *bhakti* movements of the south. Since full treatment is impossible, the remarks that follow will deal, somewhat sketchily, with three aspects of the Bengal Vaiṣṇava movement that are relevant to the purposes of this volume. After an introductory sketch, I shall attempt to treat the views of the Vaiṣṇavas of Bengal regarding the relationship of man to God and the relationship of man to man and then to discuss the symbolism in the expression of these views. My hope is that these three brief sketches will suggest enough of the salient features of the Bengal Vaiṣṇava movement to indicate its nature and its relationship in both time and space to other *bhakti* movements in India.

1. Introductory Sketch

The Vaiṣṇava movement in Bengal probably had its rise in the eleventh or twelfth century A.D.[3] In some respects, its doctrine and history are peculiar among the *bhakti* movements of medieval India. Claims have been made that not only his followers, but Caitanya (1486–1533) himself, the most significant figure of the Bengal movement, belonged to the school of the great South Indian dualistic philosopher Madhva. This, however, was probably not the case. It was probably not until the relatively late (eighteenth-century) philosopher Bāladeva Vidyābhūṣaṇa [4] that such a relationship between the Bengal and Madhva schools became established; Caitanya himself, it is almost certain, was a member of a Śaṃkara Advaita order of *saṃnyāsins.*[5] It has also been claimed that the emphasis that the Bengal school places upon the cowherd manifestation of Krishna and on the *gopī* Rādhā indicates a connection with the Nimbārka school of Vaiṣṇavism. Although there are indeed similarities between the two schools of thought on the matter of Rādhā and the *gopīs,* this tradition must have developed in Bengal at about the same time as Nimbārka lived in the south.[6] On present evidence, perhaps the best we can do is to postulate an unknown, possibly an oral, source for the tradition as manifested in both areas. Other peculiarities of the doctrine of the Bengal school include the unique position of Caitanya; the contention that Krishna is himself the supreme deity and not a mere incarnation of Viṣṇu; the device of phrasing religious experience in terms of knowledge of the beautiful, as in esthetics; and, perhaps most important, a formalized sublimation of human sexual and emotional erotic experience as a means to the experience of the divine. All these peculiarities will be discussed in some detail below.

But, despite these peculiarities of the Bengal school of Vaiṣṇavism, there is one all-important tie with other *bhakti* movements in India, namely the *Bhāgavata Purāṇa,* which has been discussed in detail by Thomas J. Hopkins.[7] This text is the foundation of the doctrine—and in some sense, as we shall see, of the enthusiastic practice—of the Bengal Vaiṣṇavas. Jīva Gosvāmin, perhaps the most significant theologian of the Bengal school, categorically rejects all the traditional types of theological proofs and arguments (*pramāṇa*) except that of *śabda* (word)—direct revelation. Among the texts that fall into this category of revelation, the primary ones are the Vedic texts and the Purāṇas. Of these two types of texts, according to Jīva, the Purāṇas are the higher: they are the completion (purāṇa) of the Vedas, and are to be used exclusively in this present age. And, of all the Purāṇas, the *Bhāgavata* is the greatest; it reveals all the Vedas, all *itihāsa* (tradition), and all the Purāṇas; it is Vyāsa's own commentary on his *Brahmasūtra,* which others hold to be itself the ultimate revelation of truth.[8]

Insofar as the *Bhāgavata* is their basic text, then, the Vaiṣṇavas of Bengal are directly in line with the *bhakti* tradition that the *Bhāgavata* represents, and with which Hopkins has dealt. At the same time, however, it must be remembered that the *Bhāgavata* is the immediate expression of a group of devotees. The Bengal school is a school in the strict sense of the term; that part of its thought which deals with the *Bhāgavata* elaborates and classifies the doctrines suggested by that text. The position of the Bengali scholastics is arrived at by exegesis. By exegesis one can easily find oneself at a point fairly distant from the intention of the original.

I suggested above that there is a distinction in the Vaiṣṇava movement of Bengal between doctrine and enthusiastic practice. This distinction was a formal one. Beneath the doctrine lay the *Bhāgavata;* the leader of the enthusiasm was Caitanya.[9] Details of Caitanya's life and character can be found elsewhere.[10] Suffice it to say here that the revival of devotional religion that he inspired was so powerful that during his lifetime and shortly after his death it encompassed the greater part of eastern India.[11]

Caitanya was the revivalist, not the originator, of Krishna-*bhakti* in eastern India. It is said that he read "with great delight" Vaiṣṇava texts by writers from Bengal and elsewhere who had preceded him. These texts included the lyrics of Vaiṣṇavas Vidyāpati and Caṇḍīdās (fourteenth to fifteenth century) and the Sanskrit *Gītagovinda* of Jayadeva (twelfth century); they also included the *Brahma-Saṃhitā* and the *Kṛṣṇa-karṇāmṛta,* which he had brought back with him from South India (thus allowing for speculation on the extent to which the South Indian forms of *bhakti* influenced his own thought).[12] But, though he was not the originator of the *bhakti* movement of Bengal, Caitanya was certainly the single most effective force in its development. So powerful was the force of his religious personality that even in his lifetime he was looked upon by some as an *avatāra* (incarnation) of Krishna, and by others as Krishna himself.[13] He was thought by some to be the ultimate form of the divine: Rādhā and Krishna in a single body, thus tasting in as intimate a way as possible the sweetness that is the highest characteristic of the divine pair; he was the earthly representation of the principle of *acintya bhedābheda,* the theory that postulated simultaneous and incomprehensible difference and nondifference between human and divine.[14]

Caitanya was not himself a theologian. He wrote, as far as we know, a total of eight verses in his lifetime, and these are devotional, not theological, verses.[15] But he was evidently not so absorbed in his devotions that he did not foresee the potential power of the movement he led. For he deputed men who were theologians and philsophers to go to Vṛndāvan, the holy place of the Krishna of the *Bhāgavata,* to establish there an *āśrama* for Vaiṣṇavas and to shape the formal doctrine of the Bengal Vaiṣṇava sect. These six theologians, the "six Gosvāmins," as they are called, were Rūpa, Sanātana, Jīva, Gopāla Bhaṭṭa, Raghunātha Bhaṭṭa, and Raghunātha Dāsa.

Rūpa, Sanātana, and Jīva were members of a single family; Rūpa and Sanātana were brothers, brilliant men who had held high positions at the court of Husein Shāh (1494–1525), Muslim ruler of Bengal at the time. Jīva was their nephew. The caste affiliation of the three is somewhat in doubt. By Sanātana's testimony, the family had originally been a Kārnāṭa Brahman one that had settled in Bengal.[16] The question is whether or not the brothers had been converted to Islam while in the service of the Muslim ruler. Some feel that there are indications that this was indeed the case, others that it was their father who had been converted.[17] But whether or not they were actually Muslims, it is clear that the brothers had lost caste by their Muslim associations.[18]

Of the calling of Rūpa and Sanātana, the most famous biography of Caitanya, the *Caitanya-caritāmṛta* (*Madhya-līlā* I:25 ff.) says:

> Then Caitanya sent Rūpa and Sanātana to Vṛndāvana; upon the order of Prabhu [i.e., Caitanya], the two brothers came there. They preached *bhakti* . . . and spread the service of Govinda-madana-gopāla [i.e., Krishna]. Having brought many books of *śāstras,* they wrote many works on *bhakti,* thus being the cause of salvation to all deluded people.

Jīva Gosvāmin, the son of Rūpa and Sanatāna's younger brother Anupama (or Vallabha), was the most brilliant theologian of the school. He was much younger than the other Gosvāmins, and the chances are that he never met Caitanya. It is recorded that he did meet Nityānanda, Caitanya's righthand man, though this was probably after Caitanya's death.[19]

Gopāla Bhaṭṭa was called by Caitanya while the latter was on a pilgrimage through the south. On that pilgrimage, Caitanya stayed for four months at the Bhaṭṭa house. The *Bhakti-ratnākara,* a historical text, says that Caitanya was impressed by the devotional capacities of the young Gopāla. It is, however, not specifically stated that he directed Gopāla to go to Vṛndāvan.[20] Gopāla Bhaṭṭa was a Brahman.

Raghunātha Bhaṭṭa, also a Brahman, was the son of Tapana Miśra, with whom Caitanya stayed in Benares.[21] Raghunātha visited Caitanya in Puri, and was deputed thus:

My command, Raghunātha, is that you should go to Vṛndāvana; stay there with Rūpa and Sanātana. Read the *Bhāgavata* constantly; repeat the name of Kṛṣṇa, and soon Lord Kṛṣṇa will shed his grace on you.[22]

Raghunātha Dāsa, although he spent much time with Caitanya in Puri and obviously knew him intimately[23] did not depart for Vṛndāvan until after Caitanya's death. He was a Kāyastha by caste, the son of a wealthy landowner of Saptagrāma. It is recorded that from his earliest childhood he showed great devotional capacities.[24]

These six Gosvāmins,[25] then, played the major role in the codification of the doctrine and ritual of the sect. They were learned men, scholars, and they wrote in Sanskrit. And here can be seen the primary division in the Bengal Vaiṣṇava sect. The Vṛndāvan Gosvāmins knew the *śāstras* and based their doctrinal formulations upon the texts, especially the *Bhāgavata;* they were eager to prove, by the testimony of the *śāstras* themselves, that the Krishna of the *Bhāgavata* is himself the full God, not a mere *avatāra* of Viṣṇu. It is of considerable significance that the Gosvāmins rarely mention Caitanya except in formal ways, and then usually in devotional rather than theological contexts. They ignore completely the matter so vital to the other main branch of the movement—Caitanya conceived as both Rādhā and Krishna bound in a single body.

For, while these developments were taking place in Vṛndāvan, others were occurring in Bengal itself and in Puri in Orissa. In these places, the devout followers of Caitanya were not always scholarly men; they were characterized more often by passionate devotion than by cool analysis. They wrote, significantly in Bengali, religious lyrics and biographies of an intensely devotional nature, celebrating Caitanya as himself the living Krishna or as Rādhā and Krishna in one body.

While Caitanya was alive, devotion to him allowed his followers no thought of anything else. But when he died, his memory was not enough. No leader came forward who had enough strength to hold Caitanya's followers together. The Bengal group again split into two. One branch followed the lead of Caitanya's friend and intimate companion, Nityānanda, the "casteless Avadhūta";[26] the other followed

Advaita-ācārya, an early and leading devotee of Caitanya, a Brahman of Santipur. The significance of this split we shall see shortly.

Even after splintering, first into Vṛndāvan and Bengal factions, and the Bengal faction again into Nityānada and Advaita-ācārya factions, the movement continued to spread rapidly during the sixteenth and seventeenth centuries. Such great Vaiṣṇava apostles as Narottamadāsa and Śrīnivāsa-ācārya carried both devotion and theology into the far corners of the land. But somehow, after the seventeenth century, the stream of creative thought and literature loosed by Caitanya seemed slowly to dry up. Except for Bāladeva Vidyābhūṣaṇa and Viśvanātha Cakravarti in the eighteenth century, the line of powerful Vaiṣṇava theologians and poets had run out.

The most obvious cause of this, of course, is that neither Nityānanda nor Advaita inspired the same emotion as had Caitanya. But there were other contributing factors. The Gosvāmins of Vṛndāvan, reflecting both devotion and intellect, were too much cut off by both geography and inclination from the lifeblood of the movement, the enthusiasm of the devotees of Bengal.[27] Without this lifeblood, the intellect withered; without the intellect, the devotional movement lost direction. The *bhakti* which Caitanya preached is far from dead in modern Bengal. On the contrary, Vaiṣṇavism is still a strong social and intellectual force. But there is only a remnant of the vigor and enthusiasm that the earlier texts reflect. With a few exceptions, the missionary spirit, the intense conviction that only Krishna-*bhakti* is justified and true, seems no longer there.

2. *The Concept of Bhakti: the Relationship of Man to God*

According to the thought of the Vaiṣṇavas of Bengal,[28] the divine has a threefold aspect, three gradations of reality. These three gradations are known as Brahman, Paramātman, and the Bhagavat. Of them, the Bhagavat is the highest, and the "true form" or "true essence" (*svarūpa*) of the Bhagavat is Krishna. In contradiction to the Advaita or non-dualistic systems, the Bhagavat is conceived as possessing infinite qualities and infinite energizing powers, called *śaktis.*

The divine *śaktis* also have three basic gradations: *svarūpa-śakti, jīva-śakti,* and *māyā-śakti.* Of these, the *svarūpa-śakti,* the *śakti* of the true essence, is the highest. The *jīva-śakti* is neither fully essential (*antarāṅga*) nor fully extraneous (*bahirāṅga*) to the Bhagavat; it relates to the *jīva,* the creature, the individual, who is neither fully within nor fully without the divine. *Māyā-śakti* relates to the material world and is the cause of the pleasure and pain of worldly life and thus is the power which hides from the *jīva* the basic truth that the *jīva* is by its nature a part (*aṃśa*) of the divine. *Māyā-śakti* is felt only in the lower planes of existence; if *māyā-śakti* is felt, the *svarūpa* of the Bhagavat cannot be perceived. Yet, although *māyā-śakti* is extraneous to the Bhagavat itself, it is a power of the Bhagavat; therefore its effects are real.

The *jīva* is part of the Bhagavat. The *jīva* shares with the Bhagavat some of the Bhagavat's infinite qualities, the highest of which is *ānanda,* absolute bliss. If the *jīva* can gain release from the power of *māyā,* he can realize his true *ānanda*-relationship with the Bhagavat. This release can be gained by *bhakti,* devotion. Released, the *jīva* is no longer affected by *māyā-śakti,* but is affected only by the *svarūpa-śakti* of the Bhagavat.

Bhakti is selfless dedication to the Bhagavat, the *svarūpa* of which is Krishna. *Bhakti* brings release from *māyā-śakti,* but it must not be prompted by desire for such release. If there is in the *jīva* any desire for his own satisfaction, either positive (i.e., desire to taste the absolute bliss of the deity) or negative (i.e., desire for release from the pain of earthly life), there can be no true *bhakti.*[29] Further, *bhakti* is the only means of gaining the right relationship to the *svarūpa.* The path of works and ritual leads only to the insignificant pleasures of heaven (*svarga*), and the path of knowledge leads only to the lesser Brahman, not the full Bhagavat.[30] These paths are useless unless they are sanctified by *bhakti. Bhakti* itself, on the other hand, is not a state of inactivity; it is a state of active worship of the deity, as we shall see.

Of all the qualities of the Bhagavat, the greatest is "belovedness" (*priyatva*). Because of this quality, the whole being of the *jīva* is drawn toward the Bhagavat, as man by his nature seeks that which is most beautiful and most satisfying. All men seek love on earth and are ready to give their lives for the objects of their love. But this phenomenal earthly love, transitory and imperfect, can never be entirely satisfying. Fully satisfying love, for both lover and beloved, is love for God. Such love is also satisfying to God, for as the *jīva* is a part of the Bhagavat, the *jīva* shares in the quality of belovedness; and since this quality attracts man to God, it also attracts God to man.

There could be no such love as this if the lover and beloved were the same. Although the *jīva* is part of the Bhagavat, and therefore contains at least partial bliss and other qualities, *jīva* and Bhagavat are not the same. There is a quantitative distinction between the two. The *jīva* shares in the qualities of, yet is eternally distinct from, both the Bhagavat and other *jīvas*. This simultaneous difference and nondifference (*bhedābheda*) is essentially incomprehensible (*acintya*) to the human mind. Thus, when by *bhakti* the *jīva* gains release from *māyā*, he is "near" the Bhagavat, in a perpetual attitude of worship of the Bhagavat; but he is not, as the Advaitins say, the same.

Worship in the love-relationship of *bhakti* is wholly and eternally satisfying both to Krishna and to the *bhakta*, the devotee. The *śakti* of the *ānanda* aspect, the blissful aspect, of the Bhagavat is *hlādinī-śakti*, which by its nature gives bliss both to the Bhagavat and to his worshipers, "as a lamp reveals itself and those things that are around it." The *bhakta* needs Krishna as the object of his own natural bent toward a satisfactory love relationship, but Krishna needs the *bhakta* just as much. For it is through the *bhakta*, the same yet different from himself, that Krishna realizes his own blissful nature. Krishna knows his own beauty and sweetness, but he cannot taste it unless it is objectified in another person toward whom he can direct his love. So he manifests the *śakti* of his own blissful nature, the *hlādinī-śakti*, as Rādhā and the *gopīs*. By their dedication and love for him he tastes his own sweetness; he knows his own beauty and sweetness through them, who are projections of himself, and he knows his own beauty and sweetness through himself in his love for them. So the *bhakta*, emulating the love of the *gopīs* for Krishna, gives Krishna pleasure, and Krishna in his turn gives pleasure to the *bhakta*, as he did to the *gopīs*.

The term *bhāva* in Sanskrit poetics indicates an intense personal emotion that becomes transformed by the qualities of poetry into a *rasa*, an impersonalized condition of pure esthetic enjoyment. The Bengal Vaiṣṇavas adapted this poetic theory to their concept of religious realization.[31] To the Bengal Vaiṣṇvas, *bhāva* is the worshipful attitude that the *bhakta* assumes toward Krishna; *rasa* is the experience of the pure bliss of the love relationship between the two.

Krishna is eternal, but has manifested himself upon the earth in many ways, at various times, and in varying degrees. But it is his manifestation as the dark-colored, two-armed cowherd boy of the *Bhāgavata Purāṇa* that is fully real: the dark cowherd is the true form of Krishna in his eternal existence. The stories of the *Bhāgavata* that deal with the *līlā*[32] of Krishna in Vṛndāvan and Mathurā are filled with people who have various relationships and degrees of intimacy with Krishna. There are, for example, his family, his friends, and, closest of all, the cowherd girls, the *gopīs,* with whom Krishna carried on love play. In assuming a *bhāva,* the *bhakta* assumes the attitude of one of these intimates toward Krishna, one that is suitable to himself. Through this *bhāva,* the worshiper experiences the love relationships that the people of *Bhāgavata* stories eternally feel toward Krishna. Nor is this merely a formal transformation. Caitanya in his *bhāva* of Rādhā becomes Rādhā, and knows all the depth of emotion experienced by Rādhā in her love for Krishna.[33]

The *bhāvas* that a *bhakta* can assume are of five basic kinds:

1. *Śānta-bhāva,* the emotions a worshiper feels when he considers Krishna as the supreme deity: awe, humbleness, and insignificance.[34]
2. *Dāsya-bhāva,* the emotion that a servant feels toward his master: respect, subservience, dedication.
3. *Vātsalya-bhāva,* parental or fraternal affection, such as the parents and brother of Krishna feel toward him.
4. *Sākhya-bhāva,* the love that a friend feels for a friend, that the cowherd boys felt for Krishna.
5. *Mādhurya-bhāva,* the highest and most intimate emotion of love, of lover for beloved, the love that the *gopīs* felt for Krishna.

The complex analysis of how these *bhāvas* are raised to the condition of *rasa* would be somewhat out of place here. Suffice it to say that beginning with a natural inclination toward one or another of these emotional relationships, the *bhakta* by increasing discipline conditions his attitude so that he actually becomes the servant, parent, friend, or lover of Krishna. Of the five, the most intimate and intense, and therefore the *bhāva* leading to the most blissful state, is the *bhāva* of the *gopīs*.

It should be noted that not all *jīvas* need to discipline and condition themselves in order to become transformed in *bhāva*. There are two types of *bhaktas*, those who by their nature are immediately able to cast off the bonds of *māyā* and to realize their natural state of intimate relationship to Krishna (i.e., to be under the influence of *svarūpa-śakti* alone), and those who need to be led to the path of *bhakti*. The second category includes, however, the great majority of people.

Before the *jīva* starts upon the path of *bhakti*, if he is one of the great majority, he is enmeshed in *māyā*. He needs assistance to extricate himself from this, for while he is under the influence of *māyā-śakti* he does not realize his potential as a part of the Bhagavat. Krishna does not grant him grace directly, for Krishna himself is beyond *māyā*, and therefore cannot feel the need for dispensing grace. The grace of Krishna, which allows the *jīva* to release himself from *māyā*, is dispensed through the *siddhas*, *bhaktas* who have obtained release while still alive. Although themselves released from *māyā*, these *siddhas* have a recollection of the pain of *māyā*, and thus can be motivated and sympathetic. The *bhakta*-to-be must take such a one as *guru* (preceptor). The *guru* helps the would-be *bhakta* through the preliminary stages to the point at which pure love for Krishna, through *bhāva*, is possible. This preliminary *bhakti* is called *vaidhi-bhakti*[35] and has several stages:

1. *Śaraṇa-pattiḥ*, feeling Krishna to be one's only refuge.

2. *Guru-sevā*, service to one's *guru*.

3. *Śravaṇa*, listening to the accounts of Krishna, listening to the reading of the *Bhāgavata*, to the praises of Krishna, etc.

4. *Kīrtana*, singing the name and praises of Krishna;[36] this is the most powerful means of bringing about an attitude proper for *bhakti*, and should be universally adopted in the present (Kali) age.

5. *Smaraṇa*, thinking constantly on the name, form, and *līlā* of Krishna.

6. *Pada-sevā*, "serving the feet" of the deity, seeing, touching, and circumambulating the image, following the image in procession, etc.

7. *Ācaraṇa,* rites learned from the *mantra-guru,*[37] ceremonies which are especially applicable for householders: putting the Vaiṣṇava signs on one's body, taking the remains of an offering to the deity as *prasāda,* drinking the water used to wash the feet of the deity, etc.

8. *Vandanā,* making *namaskāra,* which in Vaiṣṇava terms means prostration, before the image.

These eight acts are designed to bring about the proper feeling of humility and self-surrender, the "harmony between body and mind,"[38] which is essential to *bhakti.* Jīva Gosvāmin lists three more, which however are more properly states than actions:

9. *Dāsya,* as in the *bhāva,* the feeling that one is subservient, as well as in actual service to the deity.

10. *Sākhya,* as in the *bhāva,* friendship toward the deity.

11. *Ātma-nivedana,* complete self-surrender, dedication of one's whole being to Krishna. When one has surrendered oneself completely to Krishna, one is prepared to realize his true relationship with Krishna, through *bhāva.*

3. *The Concept of Bhakti: the Relationship of Man to Man*

Who then is the *bhakta?* The *bhakta* has no desire for material things or for the gratification of himself. He is the true lover, who seeks only the happiness of his beloved: when the beloved is happy, the lover is also happy—even in separation, if the beloved is content, so is the true lover, who then has pleasure even in his own pain of separation.[39] The *bhakta* emulates the *gopīs,* who gave up home and family, good name, respect, and social position, to give themselves to Krishna; they cared only for him, not for society or for the opinions of others. The *bhakta's* only object is the pleasure of Krishna; he is indifferent to the pain and pleasure of the world, for he is beyond *māyā,* which is its cause: "Their own pleasure and pain were not matters of concern to the *gopīs.* The happiness of Krishna alone was beneath all desires of body and of mind."[40]

The true *bhakta* is as humble and unassuming as a blade of grass. He respects and honors others. He is patient and forbearing as a tree, and he never censures or reproaches anyone for any cause:

[The *bhakta*] is as humble as a blade of grass; he will take the name of Hari [i.e., Krishna] incessantly. He will himself be modest, but will honor others. The Vaiṣṇava will be patient as a tree; though he be cursed and beaten, he will say nothing, even as a tree says nothing when it is cut. A tree does not beg for water, even when it shrivels and dries in the heat of the sun.[41]

The true *bhakta* is merciful, and harms no one; he is truthful and dispassionate; he is pure and "free from sin"; he is charitable, gentle, lowly, and humble, he is a benefactor to all; he is calm; he has Krishna as his only refuge and is free from desire; he is moderate about his food, nor does he indulge in anything too much; he honors all things other than himself; he is humble, grave, compassionate, poetic, friendly, skillful, and silent. These are the signs of the true *bhakta*.[42]

It is obvious that many of these virtues are social virtues, and that they imply not only avoidance of offence, but positive actions and attitudes toward other people. This does not mean, however, either that the Bengal Vaiṣṇavas accepted the society in which they lived or that they were accepted by it. Hopkins has discussed the attitude of the *Bhāgavata* toward caste; the Bengal Vaiṣṇavas follow the Purāṇa in the matter.[43]

He who worships Krishna is not a Śūdra, he is a holy man among men; but he of whatsoever caste who does not worship Krishna, he is a Śūdra. All the *śāstras* witness this.[44]

Wherever there is caste, or pride in intellect, or fear—there *bhakti* cannot exist.[45]

Caitanya himself was not a social reformer, any more than he was a theologian. He was a devotee and religious leader of great power and depth, but I think it would be a mistake to assume that in the present context this implies a social consciousness. He preached to all castes, and believed that all castes had the right and duty to worship Krishna.[46] He approved positively of breaking down caste barriers for religious reasons, and frequently shocked his Brahman followers by doing so—for example, by embracing the Śūdra Rāmānanda Rāy.[47] But it is likely that such actions were "ritual," not "individual,"[48] and that he did not consider the social implications of his religious position. By taking no real stand on the matter of caste, he left it to be thrashed out by those who assumed the leadership of his movement after his departure.

We have already seen that in one branch of the movement, that of the Vṛndāvan Gosvāmins, at least three of the six leaders were non-Brahman: one was definitely a Kāyastha, and two, Rūpa and Sanātana, even if originally Brahman, had certainly lost caste by working for the Muslims. Furthermore, among the followers and students of the six Gosvāmins were other non-Brahmans, perhaps the most notable being Narottama, a Kāyastha who was a student of Jīva.[49] Narottama himself had both Brahman and non-Brahman students, a fact which was most disturbing to the socially orthodox, and which caused considerable controversy.[50]

These facts might seem somewhat surprising to those who are used to equating social and religious orthodoxy, for the Gosvāmins were certainly representative of Vaiṣṇava religious orthodoxy. The causes of their attitudes toward caste are, I suspect, two. First of all, the Gosvāmins were the inheritors, far more than were the Vaiṣṇavas of Bengal itself, of the *Bhāgavata* and its traditions, including, as Hopkins has shown, an antagonism toward certain types of Brahmanism.[51] Second, and perhaps related to this, the Gosvāmins inherited the social, and to some extent the ritual, if not the doctrinal, position of the Tantras, that little-known substratum of Indian religious life which had for centuries held an anticaste position.

Opposed to the doctrinally orthodox, but socially unorthodox, school of the Gosvāmins were the enthusiastic Vaiṣṇavas of Bengal itself. The Bengal branch was in some ways socially and doctrinally liberal, as Kabīr and other *bhaktas* were liberal, but in some ways it was quite conservative.

As we have already seen, after the departure of Caitanya for Puri and his ultimate death, the Bengal branch of the movement split, the two parts falling one toward Nityānanda and the other toward Advaita-ācārya. Nityānanda, unlike Caitanya, was decidedly conscious of the social significance of the *bhakti* doctrine. Not only was he himself casteless, as a member of an Avadhūta ascetic order, not only did he "stay with Śūdras,"[52] as indeed Caitanya himself had done, not only was he "apostle to the Bāṇyas,"[53] but he has been accused by tradition of allowing "degraded elements"—some thousands of Buddhist monks and nuns, presumably Tāntrics—into the Vaiṣṇava fold.[54] And one of the biographers of Caitanya, a partisan and apologist of Nityānanada, has Caitanya say:

> Hear, O Nityānanda. Go quickly to Navadvīp. It is my promise, made with my own mouth, that ignorant and low-caste and humble people will float upon the sea of *prema* [love] . . . you can set them free by *bhakti*.[55]

There are indications that there were differences of opinion on the issue of caste between Nityānanda and his colieutenant Advaita-ācārya. Advaita was a Brahman, and seems to have been very conscious of it.[56] Perhaps for this reason, among others, after Caitanya had left for Puri, Advaita deserted the cause of *bhakti* and returned to the monistic position (which his name indicates that he had held) and to the *jñāna-mārga* (path of knowledge) of the orthodox monist.

> Advaita-ācārya has abandoned the path of *bhakti*, and has taken *mukti* [release from rebirth] as his primary concern.[57]

> There are certain ones among the followers of Advaita who, because of their unfortunate fate, reverence Caitanya not at all.[58]

Thus it seems as if the primary division in regard to attitude toward caste was not between the intellectual Vṛndāvan and the emotionalistic Bengal schools, but was within the Bengal school itself.

In regard to caste, among other matters, then, the Bengal Vaiṣṇavas did not see eye to eye with the society in which they lived. Nor did the society in which they lived see eye to eye with them. Part of the reason for this, of course, was the antagonism that the Vaiṣṇava attitude toward caste aroused in orthodox society: we have seen, for example, that Narottama's taking Brahman pupils raised a storm. There are indications that antagonism existed for other reasons as well. It is clear that the Vaiṣṇava form of worship was not accepted by some others in Bengal:

> Hearing the *kīrtana,* many people gathered outside the house, burning with anger, and thought how they might bring pain to Śrīvāsa [in whose house the *kīrtana* was going on]. One day a Brahman named Gopālacapala, chief among these evil people, a foul-mouthed man, took the remnants of Bhavānī-*pūjā* and during the night scattered them at Śrīvāsa's door.[59]

In a sense, the Vaiṣṇavas brought this intolerance upon themselves. They were exclusive. Śiva and the other gods should not be worshiped as full gods; they could be worshiped only as aspects of Krishna.[60] The Vaiṣṇavas were missionary. Caitanya and his followers converted many Muslims (which antagonized the ruling power), as well as giving the Brahmans an opening to bring official complaint against Caitanya and his followers.[61] And, perhaps most important, the Vaiṣṇavas did not act as other men; they felt themselves apart from society. Those who are released from the power of *māyā* are no longer subject to the power of *māyā,* which includes the laws of men and of society. This does not mean that they necessarily deliberately broke such laws—the description of the characteristics of the *bhakta* which we have seen would not allow for that. But they danced ecstatically and sang; they were as if mad. Their sure knowledge of release gave them no compunction to heed the thoughts of other men regarding them. The laws of society and custom have no bearing on one's progress along the path of *bhakti.* Caitanya rejoiced when he had persuaded Vāsudeva to take *prasāda*—remnants of food-offerings to the deity—without first having washed his hands. "Now," said Caitanya, "you have truly broken the ties with your body." [62]

4. The Expression of Bhakti: Literary Symbolism

A. THE DOCTRINE

High in the canon of the Bengal Vaiṣṇavas are the *Bhāgavata* itself, as we have seen, and the *Gītagovinda* of Jayadeva. The tenth book of the *Bhāgavata* tells of the love of the *gopīs* in Vṛndāvan for Krishna, and the *Gītagovinda* tells of the love of Rādhā, chief among the *gopīs,* for him. These stories are full of the imagery of passion. They are often beautiful and charming, but the idea of trysting with the wives of other men is not one acceptable to most of Indian society. The Vaiṣṇava exegetes took several courses.

The first was in terms of Sanskrit poetic theory, which, as we have seen, makes several unique contributions to this theology. According to this poetic theory, women are divided into two basic classes: *svakīyā* or *svīyā,* she who is one's own, and *parakīyā,* she who is another's. *Parakīyā* women can be those who are unmarried and those who are another's by marriage. In the *Bhāgavata* story, the *gopīs* are in the latter category. But Jīva Gosvāmin and others contend that this cannot be meant literally, for two reasons. In the first place, a *parakīyā* woman is not recognized by standard poetic theory as acceptable for a primary role in drama; therefore the *gopīs* cannot be *parakīyā*. In the second place, the *gopīs* had never really consummated their marriages. By the *māyā*-power of Krishna, shapes like the *gopīs,* not the *gopīs* themselves, had slept with their husbands. Furthermore, the *gopīs* are really *śaktis* of Krishna, essential to and in some way identical with him. Therefore they are really *svakīyā,* really his own.

Although these are fascinating bits of exegetical gymnastics, the second set of attitudes which the Vaiṣṇavas took toward the stories in question is perhaps more significant. It accepted the *parakīyā* interpretation of the *Bhāgavata* stories and justified it in various ways.

First, Rūpa Gosvāmin, in his *Ujjvala-nīlamaṇi,* says that the relationship of Krishna to the *gopīs* is beyond ordinary standards of morality, that Krishna cannot be considered an ordinary *upa-pati,* lover, and judged accordingly. This is a justification anticipated by the *Bhāgavata* itself. In response to a question from Parikṣit, who asks how Krishna, the "upholder of piety," could have indulged in love play with the wives of others, Śuka replies:

> O Lord, for those who are free of egoism there is no personal advantage here by means of proper behaviour, nor any disadvantage by means of the opposite; how much less is there a connection with proper or improper [behaviour] on the part of the ruler of all that is to be ruled? [63]

This is an attitude of extreme importance for the later Vaiṣṇava-Sahajiyās, for whose ritual as well as doctrine the *parakīyā* interpretation is central, and who felt themselves, like Krishna, beyond the standards of ordinary society.

But perhaps a more important interpretation, for both Vaiṣṇavas and Vaiṣṇava-Sahajiyās, is that the *parakīyā* condition of the *gopīs* made their love for Krishna more pure and real. For *svakīyā* leads to *kāma,* to desire for the satisfaction of the self; only *parakīyā* results in the *prema,* the intense desire for the satisfaction of the beloved, which is the characteristic, to be emulated by the *bhakta,* of the love of the *gopīs*. It is because the love of Krishna and the *gopīs* is a *parakīyā* love that it is so intense. The pain of separation, possible only in *parakīyā,* and the resultant constant dwelling of the minds of the *gopīs* on

Krishna, is their salvation. In the *Bhāgavata* (X:46–47) Krishna sends Uddhava to Vraja to see the *gopīs* with the following remark:

> Since I, primary among the objects of their desire, have been away, the *gopīs* have been greatly anxious because of our separation, and, thinking of me, are deeply grieved. Their minds are constantly in meditation on me, and they anticipate with pleasure my return. . . . Had their souls been left to themselves only, they would long since have been destroyed by the fire of separation from me.

Uddhava also stresses the value of the *gopīs*' longing, when he says:

> These wives of the cowherds, in whom affection has developed for Govinda, the soul of all, strive after that which is better than the maintaining of the body in the world—[that] which we and the saints strive after because of fear of the world.[64]

Their *viraha,* their pain of separation, draws their interest away from worldly concerns and leads to the meditation on Krishna which is the essence of *bhakti* and leads to attainment of him.[65]

And finally, some interpreted the stories of the *Bhāgavata* and the *Gītagovinda* as allegory.

B. THE POETRY

Students of Indian culture sometimes express a certain wonder that it can entertain at the same time such seemingly opposed views of love as that expressed, on the one hand, by the admirably athletic and frankly sensual figures on the temple friezes at Konarok and, on the other, by the equally frank shock often expressed by modern Indian society and literature on such matters; or, on the one hand, by the lusty Śiva of village poetry, who, like Zeus, "knew exactly what he wanted and set about efficiently to get it, without wasting time in introspection,"[66] and, on the other hand, by the austere Śiva of the Purāṇic texts, who is not only indifferent to the lady's charms but goes so far as to burn up the god of love when the latter inadvisedly tries to tempt him from his meditation. Western society has, of course, the same dichotomy between the values of simple and uncomplicated lust and those of the courteous and romantic love of the knight and troubadour. And Western society seems to think it has a pretty good idea of how these two sets of values are separated. We know, for instance, that spiritual and sacramental love is sacred; we know that carnal and nonsacramental love is profane. And we pass off any uncomfortable combination of these, such as Zeus taking the form of a bull in order better to carry out his purposes, or Śiva taking the form of a Muslim sentry in order to facilitate his rape of Pārvatī, as products of a primitive mentality. And yet, with almost perfect equanimity, we read the most carnal imagery of St. Bernard: "A completely refined soul . . . has but a single and perfect desire, to be introduced by the king into his chamber, to be united with him, to enjoy him." [67] We can accept this because we know that St. Bernard does not really mean it.

It is too obvious a notion to bear stress that poetry uses language and imagery which go beyond the symbolic level of normal usage. As Paul Tillich has written, "In the situation of revelation, language has an expressive power which points through the ordinary expressive possibilities of language to the inexpressible and its relation to us." [68] Or, putting it on a slightly different level, John Frederick Nims, in the notes to his book of translations of the poems of St. John of the Cross, after quoting Garcia Lorca to the effect that "metaphor links two antagonistic worlds by an equestrian leap of the imagination," goes on to say that "absorbed chiefly in the love between man and the supreme object of his desires, the poet may have wondered, What image for this ultimate delight? The poet's equestrian leap took him to the image of human love, as in the Song of Songs." [69] The leap did not have to be too equestrian. The essential problem of poetic expression is communication, through image and symbol, of those intuitions and perceptions which lie beyond. The assumption of the Vaiṣṇavas is that God is love. What more apt image could there be in human experience than that of the joy of human love, to express this? What better statement, in the situation of revelation, to express the longing of the soul for God than that of the longing of human lover for beloved?

For, in the acute observation of the Vaiṣṇavas, human love has these two essential phases: love in separation and love in union. The Bengali poets say that one is always latent in the other. Thus, a well-used sexual image calls both to mind. In St. Bernard's image, the soul *desires* to be united with the Christ; the emphasis is therefore on the fact that the two are separate, according to the doctrine. And the doctrine is reflected in Christian poetry and in social attitudes as to what human love should be.

It is said that this dualism, with the subsidiary notion of the sinfulness of the flesh, came to Christianity through Manichaeism.[70] Suffice it here, however, to say that the view in question is that the soul is a particle of light, longing always and by its nature for reunion with the source of light, with God. But the passion and lust of the flesh seeks to keep the soul trapped within dark matter; and thus arises the perpetual and all-consuming struggle between the spirit and the flesh, between true and carnal love, between the love of man for God and the desire of man for woman. Thus, in "true" human love, woman is God.

It has been suggested that love is an invention of the eleventh century.[71] While on certain grounds this is perhaps debatable, it is true that it was about that time that the Manichaean heresy, now in the form of the Church of Love, the Cathars, appeared in France. And it is true that with this reappearance of Manichaeism came the troubadours, who have left us their heritage of Romantic love, of love in separation, of the human and divine dualism transposed to that of man and woman. The troubadour Jaufre Rudel sings; is the song of a man separated from his beloved, or of the soul separated from God?

> When the days are long, in May,
> it pleases me—the song of birds, far-off.
> And when I no longer hear the song of birds,
> I remember a love. . . .
> And then I go, adverse and sad,
> and not the song of birds, nor scent of aubepine,
> pleases me as does the frozen winter.
>
> Both sad and joyous would I separate myself from her,
> if ever I could see my far-off love.
> But when? Our countries are so far. It's true,
> there are roads and ways from here to where she is,
> but I have not the strength. . . .
> What is to be is that which pleases God.
>
> Never shall I rejoice in love, if I rejoice not
> in her love. For woman more gracious and more gentle
> I have never known. So pure is she, and tender,
> that I could wish to be a captive there,
> in the country of the Saracens.

He speaks the truth, who calls me avid and desirous
for that which is apart. There is no joy
to please me more than this.
But to my vow it is an obstacle. For he who held me
at the font bequeathed me this:
that I should love; not that I should be loved.[72]

Such is true love. The difficulty is that some logical minds see the extension of this: that true love is love apart from marriage (*parakīyā*). For marriage implies not separation but union; and besides, in marriage there is always a touch of the carnal: *svakīyā* is *kāma.*

Although, as far as I know, it is questionable whether or not such things as Courts of Love actually existed in medieval Europe, it is a charming fancy which has some relevance here. The Courts of Love were supposedly places to which troubadours and others brought subtle questions of love and the conduct of affairs which were then decided by the noble lady who was president of the court and by her attendants. The following decision is said to have been taken by the court conducted by the Countess of Champagne in 1174:

We declare and affirm . . . that love cannot exercise its powers on married people. The following reason is proof of the fact: lovers grant everything, mutually and gratuitously, without being constrained by any motive of necessity. Married people, on the contrary, are compelled as a duty to submit to one another's wishes, and not to refuse anything to one another. For this reason it is evident that love cannot exercise its powers on married people.[73]

Whether or not the conclusion is that evident is not at the moment the point. The poetic conception has now come full circle, and is in direct conflict with doctrine:

	POETRY	*DOCTRINE*
Sacred	love in separation	sacramental union
Profane	sacramental union	love in separation

All of this is not as far from the point as it might seem. The following is a story which, it is said in a relatively early text, Caitanya loved:

There were two young people, the girl a princess, who were very much in love. Each day they met in the flower-grove behind the palace. One day the girl's father discovered the tryst and forced their marriage. Their bed of flowers turned to thorns, and their love faded away.[74]

Which proves, the text goes on to say, that true love cannot exist in marriage. To the orthodox Vaiṣṇavas also, then, true love is love in separation. And this true love is expressed in poetry of longing, in many ways like that of the troubadours, with undertones suggesting the joy of union:

O my friend, my sorrow is unending.
It is the rainy season, and my house is empty.
The sky is filled with seething clouds,
the earth with rain, and my love is far away.
Cruel Kāma pierces me with his sharp arrows:
the lightning flashes, peacocks dance,
the frogs and waterbirds, drunk with delight,
call constantly. And my heart is bursting.
A darkness fills the earth;
the sky lights restlessly.
"Vidyāpati" says,
how will you pass this night, without your lord? [75]

Like Christianity, orthodox Vaiṣṇavism posits a separation between man and God, and expresses it in love poetry. The notion of *viraha* is both poetic and doctrinal: not only is separation the most potent force in human love, but, as we have seen, it is a saving grace which fixes the mind on God. And separation is stated by the fact that the *gopīs* were married to other men when they were in love with Krishna. Thus, the relation of poetry to doctrine is just as it is in Christianity:

	POETRY	*DOCTRINE*
Sacred	love in separation	sacramental union (i.e., marital)
Profane	sacramental union (i.e., marital)	love in separation

The *gopīs* long for Krishna, and are deeply in love with him; man by his nature longs for union with God, though, by the nature of the two, actual union is impossible. Man seeks God because he is by his nature attracted to that which is of greatest beauty and sweetness, to a love which is most satisfying, and that is love for Krishna. The poet Yadunātha sings:

> Water to the creatures of the sea,
> and nectar to the *cakora* bird;
> night is companion to the stars,
> as is my love to Krishna.
> As the body to its image in the mirror,
> mine is with greedy love for him.
> My life is marked so deeply with his mark
> that like the moon it will be forever so.
> As day without the sun,
> so is my heart without my lord.
> Yadunātha says, Cherish this and keep it young,
> O lucky girl who deeply loves.[76]

But, as I tried to suggest, the sexual image is double-edged. It can be read as suggesting not that worshipful longing is the end of man but that if union with the divine could be attained it would reward one with the joy of human sexual union raised to the nth degree. And if, unlike Christians and orthodox Vaiṣṇavas, one were to hold that there is no qualitative difference between human and divine, such union would seem possible. And, under such conditions, there would no longer be a distinction between sacred and profane, between carnal and spiritual love. Longing for union then becomes not the end of man but the means to the end; sexual union becomes not denial of the ideal relationship between human and divine, but affirmation of it.

The Sahajiyā Vaiṣṇavas, having a Tāntric legacy, did believe in the identity of human and divine. They used the Vaiṣṇava poetic paraphernalia of human love, but read the basic image the other way. To both orthodox and Sahajiyā Vaiṣṇavas, the love of Rādhā and Krishna is the guiding principle of the universe. To the Sahajiyās, however, men and women are microcosms, and have within them the ultimate reality of the divine pair in both phases of their love: in separation and in union. Thus love between man and woman duplicates, not symbolically but actually, the love between Rādhā and Krishna, the nature of which is transcendent joy.

Both sets of Vaiṣṇavas accepted as valid, in poetry at least, the love of unmarried women and women married to others for Krishna: to both this is illustrative of true love. But while the orthodox interpreted the image in terms of separation of human and divine, with resultant longing, the Sahajiyās interpreted it in terms of union. To the Sahajiyās, the longing evidenced in the poems previously quoted is real enough, but is mere decoration which enhances the moment when union will be attained. As for the suggestion that the best kind of love relationship is with women married to others, the Sahajiyās said indeed, as Rādhā and the *gopīs* were married to others, so the human woman who has realised her true divine nature is also married to another. It works out something like this:

	POETRY	*DOCTRINE*
Sacred	love in separation	love in separation (or non-marital union)
Profane	marital union	marital union

The Vaiṣṇava lyrics are religious documents, but they are also love poetry. The poets found in Rādhā especially not only an aspect of divinity, but a real woman. Her affair with Krishna, with all the jealousies and pique, the angers and satisfactions of human love, is not only allegory but is marked with human passion. And this lends to it a quality of warmth not usual in religious poets of any time or place.

IV. VAIṢṆAVA INFLUENCE ON A TRIBAL CULTURE

by Surajit Sinha

From the seventeenth canto of *Śrī Caitanya Caritāmṛta* we learn that the great Vaiṣṇava reformer of Nadīya passed through "Jharīkhaṇḍa" on his way to Mathurā from Nīlācala and made converts. Thus we read:

> He came to Jharīkhaṇḍa on the plea of going to Mathurā
> There lived Bhil-like barbarians
> He saved them all by love and by the sacred name of God.
> Who can delve the deep mystery of Caitanya?
> This very forest looks like Vṛndāvan
> The hills look like Govardhan.

And again—

> All the living and stationary beings of Jharīkhaṇḍa
> He made them mad with the name of Krishna.
> Wherever he passes through, wherever he halts
> The people become infused with love and devotion.[1]

Although the exact territorial extent of Jharīkhaṇḍa cannot be clearly ascertained, it is taken to include roughly the area known today as the Chota Nagpur division. The route of Caitanya's travel in Jharīkhaṇḍa is not precisely known, but he must have given a powerful Vaiṣṇava stimulus to this jungle-clad country in the fifteenth century. Caitanya's missionary tour was repeated by other Vaiṣṇavas. S. C. Roy [2] writes about this early Vaiṣṇava influence among the Mundas of Rāñcī as follows:

> Subsequent [to Caitanya] Vaiṣṇava preachers appear to have made earnest attempts to convert the Mundas. One of them was Binondia Dās by name whose memory is still preserved in songs he composed in the Mundari language. . . . The elevated ideas expressed in the songs about *pāpa* and *puṇya* and about the vanity of earthly enjoyments, the style and composition and the characteristic mannerism of Vaiṣṇava poets in these songs, leave no doubt as to their Hindu origin. . . . The small number of Bhagats among the Chotanagpur Uraons and the Vaiṣṇavas among the Mundas of Bundu

and Tamar Parganas bear testimony to the partial success that attended the efforts of the early Vaiṣṇava preachers. And even among the unconverted Vaiṣṇavism has left its mark on songs and religious festivals. The Karma festival with its "Lahsua" songs can be clearly traced to Vaiṣṇava influence. . . . In genuine Munda villages, one is sometimes surprised to hear the Munda young men and women ending their songs with lusty shouts of "Rādhā Rādhā." . . . In Pañc Parganas, a number of well-to-do Mundas, ambitious of rising in the social scale, have adopted the faith of their more civilized Hindu neighbours, by preference—the Vaiṣṇava form of the religion. And it seems that if ever Hinduism once more earnestly seeks to bring the Mundas into its fold, the Vaiṣṇava sect will have a greater chance of success than any other sect of Hinduism.

What the searching mind of Roy detected among the Mundas of Rāñcī we find in a much more intensified form as we move farther east to Manbhum district and focus our attention on the Bhūmij tribe. The Bhūmij are an eastern offshoot of the Munda who have given up their original Mundari language in favor of Bengali, the language of the immigrant Hindus.[3] The Vaiṣṇavas themselves are much more numerous in Manbhum than in the Munda area, and the Vaiṣṇava tradition permeates the cultural atmosphere in rituals, songs, and general attitudes.

We shall follow the nature of the impact of the Vaiṣṇavas and of Vaiṣṇavism in this area by restricting our attention to one ethnic group, the Bhūmij, and to one *pargana,* namely Barabhum. Within this *pargana* we shall be concerned mainly with the situation in a single Bhūmij-dominated village, i.e., Madhupur. One of the first things that attracted my attention in this village was that there was a mud platform with the sacred basil, or *tulsī* plant, on it in every household courtyard. But then, although some families stated very proudly that they received the ritual service of Vaiṣṇava *gurus,* there were others who said, "The Vaiṣṇava *sādhus* are all bastards."[4]

The Various Orders and Sections of the Vaiṣṇavas

The Vaiṣṇavas are usually regarded as a caste rather than a sect, or *saṃpradāya,* and are called the Boiśtams. In the *pargana,* the Bhūmij number 37,947 (15.52 per cent of the population); the Vaiṣṇavas number about 4,203 (1.72 per cent). There are fewer Vaiṣṇavas than

Brahmans, who number about 8,412 (3.44 per cent). However, if we restrict our observations to the Taraf Pañcasardari, the traditional revenue area within which Madhupur is situated, the proportion of the Vaiṣṇavas becomes much higher than that of the Brahmans—1,245 (3.36 per cent) to 106 (0.29 per cent)—more than eleven times as many.

The majority of the Vaiṣṇavas in Pañcasardari belong either to the Mādhavācārī or to the Rāmāyat orders. I am labeling these groups as "sects" or "orders" in accordance with the popular convention; they actually operate in the area as endogamous subcastes within the Vaiṣṇava caste. A Rāmāyat Vaiṣṇava gave me the following information:

There are mainly five orders of Vaiṣṇavas in Pargana Barabhum. They may be ranked as follows, from the highest to the lowest: Nityānanda, Rāmāyat, Nimāyat, Mādhavācārī, and Viṣṇusvāmī. Of these, the Nityānandas are the *gurus* of the Rāmāyats and are, therefore, regarded as the highest. The *gurus* of the *rājā* of the *pargana* also belong to the Nityānanda order.[5] The Nityānanda, Rāmāyat, and Nimāyat employ Brahman priests in marriage and funeral ceremonies and put on the sacred thread in addition to the Vaiṣṇava marks. The Mādhavācārī, the largest Vaiṣṇava group in Pañcasardari, do not employ Brahman priests. They accept the Nityānanda, Nimāyat, or Rāmāyat Vaiṣṇavas as *gurus* who officiate in their rites of passage, and they do not cremate the dead, but bury them in a sitting posture. The Viṣṇusvāmī are the lowest of all the Vaiṣṇavas. They are the "fallen" class and include the issue of a Vaiṣṇava father and his concubine of a lower caste. The Rāmāyat would accept cooked rice from the Nityānandas and water and puffed rice from the Nimāyats and the Mādhavācārī, but none of these items from the Viṣṇusvāmī.

According to the same Rāmāyat informant, the Nityānandas are believed to have originated from the Brahman caste to which Śrī Nityānanda Gosvāmī, the founder of the order, belonged. The Rāmāyats are believed to have originated from the Kanauj Brahman caste; but the Nimāyats and the Mādhavācārīs are converts from the Śūdra castes.

When an old Vaiṣṇava of the Mādhavācārī order was interviewed at Tilla, he claimed that of the four orders of Vaiṣṇavas in the area, the Mādhavācārī were the highest. Then, in order of rank were the

Nimāyat, the Rāmāyat, and the Viṣṇusvāmī. Another Mādhavācārī informant from the same village placed the Nityānanda at the top, followed by the Nimāyat, the Rāmāyat, the Mādhavācārī, and the Viṣṇusvāmī.

When one collates the information gathered from the various Vaiṣṇava subcastes with that collected from the non-Vaiṣṇavas in the area, it becomes clear that there is a hierarchy in the area that is more agreed on than is apparent from the rival status claims of the various sects. This hierarchy is as follows:

Nityānanda	Regarded as Brahmans professing the Vaiṣṇava faith.
Nimāyat, Rāmāyat	Accept the service of the Brahman in rites of passage.
Mādhavācārī	Accept no service of the Brahmans.
Viṣṇusvāmī	Regarded as the degraded class.

The order of receiving religious initiation also gives a fairly reliable index of status hierarchy among the various sects: the Viṣṇusvāmī are initiated by the Mādhavācārī, the Mādhavācārī by the Rāmāyat, the Rāmāyat by the Nimāyat, and the Nimāyat by the Nityānanda.

We are not interested here in going into further details about the internal organization of the several orders of the Vaiṣṇavas.[6] Suffice it to say that the Bhūmij accept initiation (*dīkṣā*) from the Vaiṣṇavas of the Rāmāyat order, whereas the Mādhavācārī operate as *adhikārīs* in their funeral rites. And, although the ordinary Bhūmij accept initiation from a Rāmāyat Vaiṣṇava, the higher fief holders in the *pargana* and the Bhūmij-derived Rājput Rāja of Barabhum accept initiation only from the higher orders of the Vaiṣṇavas, namely, the Nimāyats and the Nityānandas, respectively.

Although I have labeled the Vaiṣṇava a caste, Vaiṣṇava affiliation transcends the caste limit. From this point of view, the Vaiṣṇavas may be classified as follows:

1. The Brahman Vaiṣṇavas. They retain their caste identity as Brahmans, restrict their marriages within the Brahman caste, and embrace the Vaiṣṇava religious doctrines. These Vaiṣṇavas are not endogamous and are, therefore, not subcaste groups.

2. Jāṭ Boiśtams, or the Vaiṣṇavas by caste. The Nimāyat, Rāmāyat,

Mādhavācārī, and the Viṣṇusvāmī subcastes belong to this category.

3. Bairāgī Boiśtams. These have left their formal ties with "this world" and move around as religious mendicants with their spiritual consorts, or *mātās,* and never beget children. They may have been converts from various castes, but, as Bairāgīs, they do not claim any caste affiliation. Such wandering Vaiṣṇavas are rather few in number in the *pargana.* But they have played a very significant role in the circulation of Vaiṣṇava religious traits among the tribals and the lower castes in the area.

The Bhūmij usually rank the Vaiṣṇavas as second only to the Brahmans and as higher than all the other castes, including the Rājpūt Kṣatriyas. This is also roughly the position accorded them by the other tribal and low-caste groups in the area. This is in sharp contrast to the rather low position of the Vaiṣṇavas in the more Hinduized areas of Bengal. H. H. Risley [7] places the Vaiṣṇava (the Boiśtam) in the fifth rank, along with the Sunri and the Subarṇabanik, in his generalized scheme of social precedence among the Hindu castes of Bengal.

Although I have described the various Vaiṣṇava sects in Barabhum as subcastes, Vaiṣṇavism as a way of life transcends the limits of these subcaste groups and extends also to other castes. Practically, the Vaiṣṇava way of life includes: the putting of sandalwood paste and mud marks on the face, the wearing of a wooden-bead necklace, the maintenance of a *tulsī mañca,* the avoidance of animal sacrifice and of food with animal protein (other than fish), and the singing of characteristic devotional songs to the accompaniment of *ḳhol* drums and *ḳartal* cymbals. It also involves some acquaintance with texts like the *Caitanya Caritāmṛta, Śrīmat Bhāgabat* (i.e., the *Bhāgavata Purāṇa*), and familiarity with the theme of celestial love between Rādhā and Krishna and with the concepts of heaven and hell, sin and merit, and the need for protection from evil influences through the blessing of the *guru* and the assistance of a guardian spirit whose sacred name is whispered into the ear by the *guru.*

The Role of the Vaiṣṇava Guru

Like the Brahmans of Barabhum, the Vaiṣṇavas live mainly by nonritual occupations. Like the Brahman, again, they do not till the land with their own hands, for such an act would make the entire region barren, since the wrath of the gods would fall upon all who allowed the sacred hands of the Vaiṣṇavas to do a menial's job. The Vaiṣṇavas farm with hired labor, sell sweets in the markets, and engage in other forms of trade. Here, however, I am concerned mainly with the ritual role of the Vaiṣṇavas in relation to the Bhūmij tribe. I shall begin with the roles of *grihi* Vaiṣṇavas, that is, those who live as householders rather than as casteless *sādhus*.

It has become customary for the Bhūmij of Madhupur and of the surrounding villages to be initiated before marriage to the sacred name of a guardian spirit. A Rāmāyat Vaiṣṇava presides over such an initiation rite. This process of *dīkṣā* was described to me by a Vaiṣṇava:

Last year I gave *dīkṣā* to the wife of C. Singh, a Bhūmij of the village of Burudih. Mrs. Singh and I went separately to the village tank to bathe. Mrs. Singh then drew *ālpona* designs in her inner cow shed with an emulsion of sun-dried rice powder. It was carefully insured that no one except the *guru* and the disciple would be present at the place of initiation. First, two earthen pots, one representing Nārāyaṇa and the other representing Lakṣmī, were placed on the ground. Both contained betel nuts, sun-dried rice, copper coins, and *haritaki* fruit, but the pot of Lakṣmī also contained coconut pulp. My disciple and I sat on separate seats facing each other, wearing wet clothes. First, I taught her the spells for "cleaning the mouth," "taking a bath," and for "drinking water kept in the right palm." Then I brought my mouth close to the ear of my disciple. Since she was a female, I whispered into her left ear the name of Tarak Brahmha. From then on, this sacred name, *Iṣṭa Nāma,* became her protecting deity. Then she placed flowers on my feet and offered me obeisance by lying prostrate on the ground. She also washed my feet and drank a portion of the washed water, *caraṇāmṛta.* I was offered a rupee and a white piece of cloth as gifts and was also given molasses, flattened rice, and curd to eat. We do not accept water, puffed rice, or cooked food from the Bhūmij disciples.

Whenever a Vaiṣṇava *guru* visits his client's family, the Bhūmij householder lies prostrate before his feet and literally licks the dust of his feet. He usually washes the feet of the *guru* and then sips a little of the water as "nectar of the sacred feet." The *guru,* while visiting the disciple's house, talks mainly on mundane affairs. He inquires about the physical well-being of his client's family, about the crops, and so on, but he may also say a few things on religious topics. A Rāmāyat *guru* told me:

We tell them, "If you drink the nectar of your *guru's* feet, all the accumulated sins in your body will be cleansed and all your desires will be fulfilled." . . . We also tell them, "Don't ever beat a Brahman or a Vaiṣṇava. That will be the worst of sins and will take you to hell and cause unending unhappiness. Give alms to the Brahman and the Vaiṣṇava and you will gain merit and go to heaven."

It is interesting to note here that the Rāmāyat Vaiṣṇava presses his claim of divinity in the sacred company of the Brahman. The Bhūmij feels uneasy about letting his Vaiṣṇava *guru* or for that matter, any wandering Vaiṣṇava mendicant, leave his house unsatisfied and without alms. The Vaiṣṇavas, in collaboration with the Brahmans in Taraf Pañcasardari, have succeeded in instilling into the mind of the Bhūmij a concern about the afterlife in relation to heaven and hell and to merit and sin that was not present at all in the aboriginal system.[8] These *gurus,* however, do not usually engage in elaborate theological discussions with their clients.

The main role of the Rāmāyat Vaiṣṇava is that of *guru* offering initiation, but the Mādhavācārī Vaiṣṇava has a different role to play—that of *adhikārī* in funeral rites.

On the eleventh day of mourning after the death of a person among the Bhūmij, the chief-mourner has to perform a rite known as *Ghaṭ Piṇḍa* beside a tank, under the guidance of a Brahman priest. The mourner must cook rice with milk and jaggery, make the paste into the form of balls, and offer these to the departed spirit. After this, his head hair, beard, and mustache are shaved by a barber. Then he takes his cleansing bath in the tank, and while he is still standing in the water, a Vaiṣṇava *adhikārī* of the Mādhavācārī order draws a *tilak* design with sandalwood paste on his forehead and also sticks *gulañc* flowers on the top of his ears. Just then the *Hari Bol Hari* (the calling on the name of Hari) is uttered by those assembled at the spot. The chief mourner then, proceeding back to his home, follows a number of Mādhavācārī Vaiṣṇavas who sing typical *nāma-saṃkīrtana* songs to the accompaniment of drums and cymbals. The wife of the chief mourner washes the feet of the Brahmans, of the Vaiṣṇavas, and of her husband as soon as they arrive at the household courtyard.

The Mādhavācārī Vaiṣṇavas have other functions to perform on the following day of *Śrāddha,* the end of the period of ritual mourning. The bulk of the rites of the *Śrāddha* ceremony is guided by the Brahman priest, but the Vaiṣṇava *adhikārī* is also present during the rites. After the Brahman-directed portion of the rites is over, the chief mourner takes off his *dhutī,* or cloth, and puts on a *gajī,* or loincloth, while a *cadar,* another piece of cloth, hangs around his neck. He is now ready for the *dadhi kado,* making-mud-with-curd, ceremony. The *adhikārī* holds an earthen pot containing an emulsion of curd and turmeric, and the chief mourner in his loincloth stands behind him with some rice in a new split-bamboo basket, while a few other Vaiṣṇavas with drums and cymbals follow him. They encircle the courtyard three times in a counterclockwise direction while they sing the name of Hari. The *adhikārī* then pours on the ground the curds from his pot in such a way that they fall in a straight line from north to south. The chief mourner is made to lie across this line of curd and is made to roll from the northern margin to the southern margin. The *adhikārī* then has to wipe off the marks of curds from the mourner's body, and his curd-soaked piece of cloth is carefully kept in a room. Then the *adhikārī* ties the hands of the mourner with the two ends of his cloth and says, "Now son, your dear father is no longer alive, and you have completed the *Śrāddha* rites. But your work is not over. Give us some cows or some land." To this the Bhūmij peasant answers: "We are passing through very hard days. Please do not insist on cows or land." After some mock haggling, it is customary for the *adhikārī,* after having received only a rupee, to release the client.

The Mādhavācārī Vaiṣṇavas from the village of Tilla occasionally visit Madhupur to beg alms; they sing the name of Krishna in various forms, to the accompaniment of cymbals. In contrast with their rather pragmatic way of dealing with the problem of evil by the rite of *caraṇāmṛta,* the mendicant Vaiṣṇavas communicate in many of their songs a message of otherworldliness and of the futility of the pleasures of this life:

> What wealth is there in this world without the name of Hari?
> Your days are flowing out.

After singing these otherworldly songs with much charm and feeling, the Vaiṣṇava mendicant eagerly looks forward to receiving this-worldly returns in the form of alms.

Offering feasts to the Vaiṣṇavas on the occasion of marriage and particularly on the occasion of funeral rites is considered to bestow *puṇya,* or merit, on the feast-giver and, in the latter case, on the departed soul. The number of Vaiṣṇavas and Brahmans invited to a funeral feast is a matter of social prestige. *Nāma-saṃkīrtanas* sung by a team of Vaiṣṇavas are prestige elements in the funeral feasts of the upper-class Bhūmij.

There is one more rite in which the Vaiṣṇavas play an important part. Agricultural production in this area depends in large measure upon the construction of small-scale irrigation dams, or *bandhs.* Such an important economic venture is usually accompanied by a ritual known as *bandh-biha.* This involves a re-enactment of the marriage ceremony of the sponsoring couple along the edge of the tank. At the conclusion of this ceremony it is conventional to have Brahmans and Vaiṣṇavas sit in a line on all four sides of the tank and take part in the feast of merit. This insures a perennial water supply in the tank. Nonstop singing of *nāma-saṃkīrtanas* for days by the Vaiṣṇavas is another feature of these *bandh-biha* ceremonies.

The Vaiṣṇava *gurus* do not ask the Bhūmij to give up their beliefs in their local gods, such as the hill gods Parsa Pat and Jambira Pat and the gods of the village's Sacred Grove. As a matter of fact, a Mādhavācārī Vaiṣṇava of Tilla told me:

> Our main festival is *Nāma-saṃkīrtana,* which takes place on different occasions. But we also join the villagers in the various local festivals as "customs of the region." We regard Gaurāṅgā Mahāprabhu, Krishna-Rādhikā, Kālī, and Durgā as the main gods and goddesses. But we also respect such local gods as Tirla Pat, Jahir Than, Gosāiṃ Era, Nāgera Budi, and Ban Kunārī. We have to obey these village gods if we are to live safely in the village.

The Vaiṣṇava *gurus* are, therefore, not concerned with replacing the traditional rituals of their clients; they are mainly interested in superimposing a few rituals of their own in order to make their presence as ritual specialists essential in the life of the Bhūmij. The Vaiṣṇava *guru* is not moved by a reformist's zeal to save the heathen souls of his clients, but he is very much interested in increasing the number of his clientele. With a view to achieving this end, he dwells on the theme of the divine magical qualities of the Vaiṣṇava (and of the Brahman) that could help the Bhūmij client avoid disasters in this life and in the afterlife. The Vaiṣṇavas are, however, conscious that their own religious beliefs and rituals represent a higher style of living than that of the Bhūmij. For their part, the Bhūmij do not look upon their contact with the Vaiṣṇavas as displacing their own rituals. But association with the Vaiṣṇavas and acceptance of their ritual traits convey to the Bhūmij an element of respectability. He looks upon a ritual association with the Vaiṣṇavas as a means of attaining prestige in the eyes of the Bengali upper castes in the area. After initiation by the *guru,* some Bhūmij may even give up eating chicken.

One typical Vaiṣṇava feature has been diffused rather widely among the Bhūmij, namely, the erection of a mud platform in the courtyard with a sacred basil plant on it. This platform, or *tulsa thān,* is cleaned and plastered with an emulsion of mud and cow dung. Every day, a circular design representing the sun is made in front of the *tulsa thān* by a female member of the house. The *tulsa thān* becomes a sort of household temple, or, rather, the seat of miscellaneous gods and goddesses. The lady of the house every evening offers obeisance to the *tulsa thān* with a lighted earthen lamp. On all major festive occasions, the *tulsa thān* is marked with vermilion dots, and such offerings as sun-dried rice, *gulañc* flowers, lamp soot, and *methi* seeds are made to the gods temporarily residing in the *tulsa thān*. These gods include such standard gods of the Hindu pantheon as Durgā, Kālī, and Śiva, as well as the local tribal gods, such as the hill gods, gods of the Sacred Grove, ancestral spirits, and so on. In a way, the *tulsa thān* replaces the traditional sacred tabernacle of the Bhūmij, where the soul of the departed was called back to be united with the *burha burhi,* or ancestral spirits. Such a displacement, however, has not been brought about by any conscious design.[9]

Sādhus of Two Kinds at Madhupur

Although the *grihi* or the Jait Vaiṣṇavas have not gone in for introducing elaborate rituals beyond the rites of passage or for instilling otherworldliness in the minds of their clients, the Bhūmij of Madhupur have also been exposed to the teachings of the wandering Vaiṣṇava *sādhus,* who have made the pursuit of otherworldly religious activities their only vocation in life. It appears, from their activities in the village, that the *sādhus* were concerned both with gaining economic support from the householders and with converting some disciples into *sādhus.*

We were told that the first Vaiṣṇava *sādhu* to settle for any length of time in the village of Madhupur came in approximately 1897. In 1896, or thereabouts, it is said that the widowed mother of the village headman requested B. Singh, an influential Bhūmij, to search for a Vaiṣṇava *sādhu* from whom she could accept initiation. It was known at the time that a young *sādhu* of the Vaiṣṇava order, who originally had come from the village of Parasa, was residing with his spiritual consort, or *mātā,* in the village of Duaridih, about twelve miles from Madhupur. B. Singh and his associates met the *sādhu* and, after great efforts, were able to persuade him to settle at Madhupur. However, the whole transaction had to be managed secretly, since it was feared the people of Duaridih would be reluctant to part with their favorite *sādhu.* It is said that Śrīnāth and his consort were brought to Madhupur under cover of darkness. The village headman offered one of his vacant huts as residence for the *sādhu.* The man had "a fair complexion and fine physical features," and his consort is reported to have been as beautiful as the goddess Durgā herself.

The *sādhu* explained to the Bhūmij the concept of sin, *pāp,* which causes men to suffer immeasurable torture in hell at the hands of assistants of Yama. His teachings were concerned with the ways and means of avoiding the path to hell. The discharge of semen was considered to be the root of all evil, and virtue was to be attained mainly by learning the secret art of withholding the discharge of semen at the time of sexual intercourse. This art is known as *rati sādhan.* Apart from the difficult art of *rati sādhan,* which will be described later, the path to hell could be avoided by various merit-earning devices, such as being instructed in the sacred spells by the *guru,* by giving reverence to the Vaiṣṇavas and the Brahmans, and by observing typical Vaiṣṇava traits and practices, e.g., wearing bead necklaces, painting the forehead with sandalwood paste and clay marks, and so on. This particular *sādhu* was somewhat puritanical in his preachings and asked his disciples to give up intoxicating liquor and chicken. He did not, however, interfere with the performance of the local cults.

Apart from imparting the fear of hell and placing some restrictions on behavior, the *sādhu* contributed to the joy of the village by introducing new forms and contents of aesthetic expression. He sang devotional songs very melodiously to the accompaniment of a one-stringed harp, or *tuila*. Along with the headman of the village, a large number of Bhūmij in his hamlet accepted initiation from the *sādhu* and spent a good deal of their leisure hours in his company. Some Bhūmij of the northern neighborhood in the same hamlet, however, refused to be initiated by the *sādhu* and said: "Who is going to believe that the Bhūmij is to become like the Vaiṣṇava or the Brahman? It will not suit us. If we take the sacred Five Names, our bodies will dry up and children will no longer be born to us."

In spite of such opposition, the rest of the Bhūmij population of the hamlet continued, with their headman, to gather around the *sādhu*. Every evening they had gatherings and sang devotional songs, accompanied by *ḳhol* drums and cymbals. Such sacred texts as the *Birat Gītā, Bhramar Gītā, Arjun Gītā, Kaiḳī Gītā, Śrīmat Bhāgabat,* and the *Mahābhārata* were recited in their Bengali versions with commentaries. The *sādhu,* in his expositions, dwelt at length on the stern punishment given to sinners by the god of death. He also explained the evil effects of wine and chicken. A few years thus passed in the spiritual intoxication afforded by the delightful company of the holy couple. The followers of the *sādhu* began to feel proud that they were leading a more "civilized" and "clean" life than that of the average Bhūmij in their own and neighboring villages. A song was sung by the neighboring villagers, half mockingly and half admiringly:

> Some of them have put on *tulsī* necklaces and painted marks
> on the face and the forehead.
> O brother, Madhupur-Bhangat is not the same as it used to be.

Śrīnāth Sādhu was presented with three acres of good cultivable land by his disciples, and they also took the trouble to till his land.

I was told that the people of the neighboring villages became jealous of the religious display of the people of Madhupur and their *sādhu*. Singh, of Makula village, is said to have stated: "If your *sādhu* is so gifted, let him cross a tank in wooden sandals." Without asking the consent of the *sādhu,* he announced at the weekly market, with the beating of drums, that on a particular date Śrīnāth would walk on the water of a tank at Madhupur. The *sādhu* became terribly nervous on hearing this. But his disciple B.S. consoled him by saying, "Master, do not worry. Let them first of all test the power of the disciple." As many people assembled around the tank, the hands and feet of B.S. were tied with rope, and he was thrown into the water. Much to the wonder of the spectators he is said to have floated at ease for a long time. This convinced the assembled people of the merit of initiation by the *sādhu*. About 1910, when his brother died in the village of Parasa, Śrīnāth left Madhupur and finally settled down at Parasa. However, he visited Madhupur every year and spent a few days with his disciples. For several years there was no other resident *sādhu* in the village.

About 1914, the people of Madhupur heard about the *sādhu* Kiśtodās, who frequently visited the neighboring village of Makula. This *sādhu* came from Burda, a village in Pargana Baghmundi, and originally belonged to the Bhūmij caste. His spiritual consort, Rādhā Mātā, was originally Vaiṣṇava by caste. J. S. and Gm. S. of Madhupur approached him about settling in their own village. The *sādhu* agreed, and he finally took up residence in a temporary shed near the courtyard of the village headman. Kiśtodās derided the doctrine of puritanical asceticism preached by Śrīnāth and propounded a hedonistic cult. He used to sing—freely translated:

> Sing the name of Hari.
> Take fowl curry
> And the lap of a young woman.

The villagers, after a prolonged period of abstention under Śrīnāth, listened to the preachings of the new preceptor with a feeling of relief. The new *sādhu* became popular, sang the local *jhumur* songs, and even joined the Bhūmij in their mixed dances. In this relaxed atmosphere, most of the families that had abstained from fowl and wine under the influence of Śrīnāth reverted to their familiar practices. Both Kiśtodās and his consort drank wine and ate chicken.

A year later, when Śrīnāth came to Madhupur on a short visit, a debate was organized between him and Kiśtodās on the interpretations of the scriptures. It is said that Śrīnāth was defeated and, being somewhat disheartened, left Madhupur. Kiśtodās reigned supreme until his death in about 1928. Although Kiśtodās differed from Śrīnāth in dietary and drinking taboos, his teachings were otherwise essentially similar. He also placed great emphasis on the importance of reverence for the *guru,* of initiation, and of *rati sādhan* as the means to avoid the path to hell.[10]

As noted above, the coming of the *sādhus* reinforced the major factions in the hamlet—the group following and the group opposed to the headman.

I shall now describe some of the practices that the Vaiṣṇava *sādhus* teach their initiates.

G.S., who attended some of the musical parties at the shed of Kiśtodās Sādhu, narrated the following account:

> One day the *sādhu* asked me why I had not yet taken initiation from a Karṇadhār *guru.* His consort Rādhā Mātā was willing to initiate me. The rite was rather simple. I sat facing the east and opposite to the *mātā,* and she covered me with a piece of cloth so that the rite could not be observed by anyone else. She whispered a sacred spell three times into my right ear. This spell became my protecting spirit, *iṣṭa devatā.* I then offered obeisance to her, lying prostrate at her feet, and drank the water washed from her feet. She became my *dīkṣā-guru.* . . . After a few days I began learning sacred spells, or *mantras,* from the *sādhu,* who became my *śikṣā-guru,* or teacher of spiritual lore. The spells I learned were all related to purification of various kinds of *āśauca,* or pollution. But they did not impose any restrictions on my diet.

The various spells, or *mantras,* may be categorized and translated as follows:

1. After urination:

   A golden penis and silver flow.
   O Earth Mother, I salute you.

2. On ablution after evacuation (while saying the following one must strike the left hip with the left palm three times):

   My hands are pure; my feet are pure;
   Two and a half hand measures of the earth are pure.

3. Before washing the mouth in the morning (while saying the following, the tooth twig, which should be exactly twelve finger breadths in length, is offered salutation and is then put into the mouth):

Golden tooth twig and silver vessel,
Dear Rādhā is washing her face.

4. While taking one's bath in the morning:

Gaṅgā Jamunā Sarasvatī Bhāgīrathī Godāvarī Triveṇī
The tortoise averts sins.
Bless my body
Sins will be averted,
Hari Viṣṇu, Hari Viṣṇu.

5. Prayers to the sun while taking one's bath:

O luminous sun of Kaśyapa, you are like the *jabā* flower.
I salute you, giver of daylight.

6. While pouring water from the joined palms into the water of the tank:

Salutations to the *guru,* to Śiva, to Gaṇeśa,
To father, grandfather, and to the great-grandfather

7. While coming home from the tank:

(reciting the name of Hari Krishna and chanting the rosary beads)

8. While offering water to the *tulsī mañca:*

O Mother Tulsī, you take the water.
You give me reverence for Krishna.

9. Spells for purifying the food at dinnertime:

(not recorded)

10. At dusk, with an oil lamp in one's hand, at the base of the *tulsī mañca:*

The light of the lamp is Brahmā himself.
The light of the lamp is Janārdana.
The light of the lamp cleanses sin.
Salutations to you, goddess of the evening.

11. At bedtime:

Salutations to you, Padmanābha.

12. Before placing the feet on the ground in the morning, as one is getting out of the cot:

> The seas are your skirt;
> The mountains are your breasts.
> O wife of Viṣṇu,
> Please forgive the touch of my feet.

The above spells derive from an extremely mechanistic concept of pollution and sin, which must be removed with equally mechanistic rituals. The material elements that effect the cleansing are water, fire, and the earth; and then many benevolent gods and goddesses are invoked with spells. The spells, however, are essentially supplicatory and not coercive in nature. Most of the spells taught by the Vaiṣṇava *sādhus,* some of which are in Sanskrit, are essential elements of the Brahmanic rituals in Bengal.

G.S. seems to have transcended the pragmatic concern of his *guru* —averting the road to hell by the magical protection of ritual acts, spells, and supernatural blessings. He does share the *guru's* concern for augmenting the magical power of his personality, but he also has genuine love and devotion for Krishna, Rādhā, and the other gods introduced to him by the *guru,* and he looks up to these gods as guides for ethical conduct. The villagers look up to him as a strictly honest man, and he is held in very high esteem and is often addressed as *Ṭhākur* (Holy One). He procured brass images of Krishna and Rādhā, and every evening he worshiped them with incense and prayers. When his only son died in spite of prayers to the deities, G.S. threw the images into the village tank. But his faith soon returned and he now observes fasting at every new moon and full moon and offers prayers to Krishna, Śiva, Durgā, Kālī, Gaṇeśa, and Bhagavān, with incense, a lighted lamp, and *gulañc* flowers. A few years ago, he lived for a fortnight in the jungle, entirely on the green leaves and tubers while he was searching for God. He failed to meet God, but believes that this was because his search was not strong enough.[11]

While G.S. received ritual training in purification from the *sādhus,* J.S. is supposed to have learned the art of *rati sādhan* from Kiśtodās. I have written elsewhere[12] in detail about the concept of *rati sādhan:*

> *Bastu* or *birya* is generated inside the body of a man and *rati* is generated in the body of a woman after the intake of food. Food is converted into

blood, and from the blood itself are generated *birya* and *rati*. The circulation of *birya* and *rati* all over the body depends upon the phase of the moon. *Birya* is also known as *ojo,* and *ojo* is regarded as *brahmabastu* by the saints. As soon as a man becomes aware of the existence of a woman, his *birya* elements get excited and begin moving. The same is true for the woman when she becomes aware of the presence of a man. As Lord Kāmadeva was attached to his wife, the goddess Rati, so is the human male attached to his wife. The symbol of Kāmadeva is the human phallus, or *liṅga,* and that of Rati, the vagina, or *yoni*. The friction of the phallus and the vagina results in the discharge of *birya* and *rati* inside the vagina. *Birya* being the more powerful element, it rushes forth in great speed and mixes with *rati* inside the vagina. A good part of the male *birya* is unfortunately wasted, since it comes out of the vagina after the sexual act of *rati śṛngār*. The *sādhus,* concerned with the spiritual training of the body, place a good deal of importance on preventing this wastage of vital *birya*. They therefore prescribe that efforts be made to draw inside the channel of the penis the vaginal discharge, or *rati,* of the female. A person who attains this quality becomes immensely powerful and gains eternal youth and thereby becomes a *sādhu*. By repeatedly indulging in sexual union with their spiritual consorts in the above manner, the *sādhus* attain their spiritual salvation, just as Lord Krishna had ecstatic union with his beloved Rādhā. The heart of such a *sādhu* is ever full of joy. He sings *jhumur* songs depicting the celestial love of Lord Krishna and Rādhā, to the accompaniment of a *gupijantra,* stringed instrument. This is why the *sādhus* regard *birya* as *Brahma Bhagaban*. *Bhag* means *yoni,* or vagina, and *ban* means *liṅga,* or penis; that is why the word *"Bhagaban"* (or Supreme Being) actually means wholeheartedly enjoying the *bhag,* or vagina, with the *ban,* or penis.[13]

It appears from the above statement that although the cult of *rati sādhan* is not approached as a means of enjoying simple carnal love, it is also not geared so much to a spirit of devotion as to a drive for gaining magical power.

On January 10, 1957, and again on May 14, 1958, I met L.S., a Vaiṣṇava *sādhu,* who originally belonged to the weaver caste. He is a gifted composer of poems and songs and is also a talented acrobatic (*natua*) dancer. L.S. has taken a vow never to eat food with his own hands, and he is accompanied by one or two *mātās,* or consorts, who lift the food to his mouth. He is an expert in the cult of *rati sādhan*. In the house of one of his disciples, while he was taking food from the hand of the disciple's wife, he suddenly felt overtaken by the feeling that he was a baby Krishna or Gopāla, and took off his clothes and started crawling on the floor like a baby. Although some villagers felt that the *sādhu* was taking advantage of his role as the spiritual initiator of the family, no one dared to raise any word of protest. In my conversations with this *sādhu,* I found him to be rather keen in his awareness both of the trends of sociopolitical developments in India and of his own philosophy of life. This will be apparent from some of his remarks:

> I take food offered by the lowest castes, such as the Hari, Dom, Chandal, and Mussalman; but the food has to be brought to my mouth. My consorts, however, do not take food cooked by others. . . . If you ask me about God, I will say that I believe only in *ātmā,* in the soul that is here inside me, but is part of the *Paramātmā,* the Supreme Soul, and so my soul is indestructible. . . . Gandhiji failed in his mission because he tried to combine religion with politics. The path of religion is lonely and that of politics is with the crowds. And you cannot unite many people by religion as quickly as you can by force of arms.

Such intellectually alert *sādhus,* however, are rare in this area. But, like L.S., most of the *sādhus* take care to attain proficiency in some art, such as singing, poetry, dancing, or flute playing, in addition to the art of the exposition of religious doctrines. These aesthetic achievements add to their charisma and quite often aid in the winning of disciples.

The Impact of Rādhā-Krishna Themes in Songs

In addition to the participation of Vaiṣṇava *gurus* in the rites of passage and of the *sādhus* in the more incisive and elaborate ritual training in their sacred lore, the Bhūmij disciples are indebted to the Vaiṣṇavas for another influence. The minds of the indigenous people of Barabhum have been permeated by the attractive Vaiṣṇava theme of celestial love between Rādhā and Krishna. The Rādhā-Krishna theme is the central element of many folk songs and of accompanying dances. To a certain extent it also enriches and guides personal love between men and women. I have the impression that the immigrant theme of Rādhā-Krishna love has fitted in very nicely and effectively with the vigorous sensuality of a tribal world view in which there is ample sanction for love-making by the young.

One of the important channels for the cultivation of such a mood in a self-conscious way is the institution of keeping concubines, or *raḳhni,* who are quite often also dancing girls, or *nāchni.* This used to be a favorite pastime of the Bhūmij upper class, although the custom is today somewhat on the decline. A dancing girl is a woman who has lost her caste either by being the daughter of a dancing girl or by seriously transgressing taboos in sexual relations. The Bhūmij master of the concubine usually learns to become an expert dancer, or *rāsiḳ,* in typical *nāchni* dances. He may also become a composer of songs, or *ḳabi,* or he may patronize a composer. The famous composers of songs in this area were formerly attached to the chiefs of the *parganas* and their subordinate fief holders. Their elaborate songs served as models for lesser composers in the ordinary villages. These songs achieve wide circulation on festive occasions, of which *nāchni* dances are an attractive feature. Besides learning to dance with appropriate gestures and rhythms, the *nāchni* also learns the typical *nāchni saila jhumur* songs, whose themes are always the celestial love of Rādhā and Krishna—quite often the lamentations and intense love cravings of Rādhā. While dancing, the *rāsiḳ* plays the role of Krishna and the girl that of Rādhā. Both the audience and the performers become completely enraptured as the performance goes on throughout the night. The loud and vigorous beating of kettledrums and the impulsive gestures of the dancers impart a somewhat different mood from that inspired by the refined *ḳīrtanas* that are usually performed in more Hinduized villages of West Bengal. In my long years of acquaintance with the Bhūmij in the various phases of their rites and activities, I have had the feeling that the Vaiṣṇava-influenced songs, which are sung in such varied settings as agricultural work, group dances, and *nāchni* dances, have raised the Bhūmij to the peak point of their expressive life and thus have moved them very deeply indeed.

Some of these songs are simple love songs implicitly composed on the divine love of Rādhā and Krishna; others deal more directly with their love. One of the singers told me at the end of a song: "These are songs of raw emotions; there is no end to their flavor." A Bhūmij young man may sing some of these songs to attract the attention of a girl. If the girl responds with an appropriate song, she indicates that she has accepted the proposal for love-making. A few of these songs, freely translated, are given below:

1. Listen, my friend,
Listen to my sad plight.
So much did I desire
To unite with the beloved one.

With so great a craving
I placed my bed on the floor.
So much did I desire
The meeting of the two clever ones.

He has roused such passion in my life,
I can bear it no more.
My ribs are aching in pain;
I can live no more in separation.

What to do and where to go?
I can rest no more in my home.
What magic has he played?
I can rest no more in my home.

Rai Harirām [the poet] implores,
Do not burn my life any more.
Now that you have opened the door,
Don't cast me adrift.

2. I rest my eyes on the roadside,
I cannot sleep.
I keep awake in expectation, my beloved,
I cannot sleep.

I am angry,
I would like to scold you.
Now I see you,
I forget everything in joy.

I make the garland with such care,
I make it with such care, my beloved,
I keep it hanging just for your coming.
I keep it only for you.

With a smiling face
I will sit on your lap.
With such caresses I will sit on your lap.
I will hold your neck tenderly.

What else do I care for
If I get your love?
Just tell me, my beloved,
Tell me that you are wholly mine.

But you did not come to console my heart,
So says Rāmakrishna [the poet].
All my heart's dreams have been spoiled,
All that was in my heart.

3. You are the fine parting of my hair,
You are the necklace of my neck,
You are my favorite comb and mirror,
O pretty girl.

You are my *dhutī* and my shirt,
You are my slanting headdress,
You are the flower in my ear,
My friend, my pretty girl.

You are love itself,
You are the smile on my face,
You are the restless look in my eyes,
O pretty girl.

I am only a quarter rupee or one anna,
You are sixteen annas in a rupee.
Why are you looking aside,
My moonfaced pretty girl?

4. I have fallen in love with you.
What is my fault that you made me weep in midday?
Why did you make me weep, O friend,
Why did you make me weep?

With such tenderness and care
You have treated me so long,
With your pretty ways
You have charmed my heart.

You have intoxicated my mind.
Now I am in trouble,
So says Dīnabandhu [the poet]
With tears flowing down his chest.

5. Friend, who is standing there,
Who is standing there in such a fashion?
Who is he, who is he,
Who is he with a black face holding the flute?
Who is standing there, who knows?

His face is full of smiles;
His look is shameless.
Oh what shame, my friend,
He has winked at me.

So says Duryodhan [the poet],
With the garland around his neck.
You take him, you take him, you take him,
Take him in your life,
Take him in your heart.

6. What to do, my friend?
My heart is restless.
Look, the night is over—
Why hasn't my beloved come?

I have decorated my garden,
Waiting to welcome Śyām.
I have spread my bed with flowers morning to evening—
Why hasn't my beloved come?

With vermilion on the forehead
And face like the full moon
He has caused so much pain in my heart—
Why hasn't my beloved come?

Nandalālkiśore [the poet] says,
Was this my fate?
The lord did not fulfill my desire—
Why hasn't my beloved come?

7. Kalia, my beloved one,
Tightens his waistcloth,
Puts on a big turban,
Kalia, the beloved one.

I call Kalia, Kalia—
Day and night I am looking for him.

Who knows with whom he spends this night, too?
His *cadar* has the stain of betel.

The water of Jamunā is black.
It is no good to bathe in the morning,
My head reels as I move back and forth.
I fear my beloved one would get angry.

My friend becomes blind at night;
He moves by the backyard.
Don't go in the backyard, black Śyām,
Rats have sown there *gora* rice.

Besides these love songs of the *bhaduriya nāchni saila* category, there are other songs, like the *khyapar dhuā,* that do not have love themes, but dwell mainly on the futility of worldly life.

Gaurāṅga is the poisonous snake.
Can he rest at home who has been bitten by that snake?
He will become a homeless wanderer in a moment—
Gaurāṅga is the poisonous snake. . . .

But these songs are not among the most popular ones.

Decline of the Vaiṣṇava Influence

G.D., a Rāmāyat Vaiṣṇava of Gordih, told me:

Today the Bhūmij do not respect us as much as they did in the past. Now many would think, "He [the *guru*] is also a human being." Formerly no one would ever disobey the orders of the *guru*. Nowadays some disciples drink *caraṇāmṛta,* but others do not. B.S. of Madhupur, who is a clever person, does not take my *caraṇāmṛta;* he salutes me from a distance. Only a disciple who has had no education and is a fool takes our *caraṇāmṛta.*

B.S. of Madhupur, referred to in the above conversation, told me:

In our younger days, we were much more concerned with observing the correct Hindu rites. We never took water or food while we were putting on shoes. In the market place we would not sit on the same bench with a Muslim. Now we do not observe any of these rules. We used to pay great attention to the Brahmans and the Vaiṣṇavas.

The general decline of the Vaiṣṇava influence is apparent in the decreasing number of wandering Vaiṣṇava *sādhus,* of dancing girls, and of expert composers of poems and songs. It is also apparent in the decreasing number of Bhūmij who drink *caraṇāmṛta.* The Bhūmij, however, continue to take *dīkṣā* from Vaiṣṇava *gurus.* And these *gurus* are essential in the funeral rites and at the opening of irrigation tanks. The Vaiṣṇava-introduced *tulsī mañca* in the courtyard is still a most sacred center. In spite of a general decline, enough Vaiṣṇava influence is still alive in Barabhum to enrich the life of the people and to offer a background for revivalism if it should occur.

Discussion

The Vaiṣṇava impact on the Bhūmij represents a special kind of acculturation within the general context of the study of the emergence, persistence, and spread of Indian civilization. The Vaiṣṇavas are one among many of the "hinge groups" or "cultural brokers" that mediate between Hindu civilization and the tribal society.[14]

The flow of Vaiṣṇavism has been importantly aided by its association with the higher levels of power in the Bhūmij feudal structure. As cultural brokers, the Vaiṣṇavas facilitated the communication between the upper-class Bhūmij, who were seeking prestige and the relatively higher-powered aristocracy surrounding their jungle clad enclaves. Vaiṣṇava influences reaching the common Bhūmij were thus already charged with a prestige that flowed down the steps of the regional power hierarchy. From the activities of the Vaiṣṇavas today it appears that most of the Vaiṣṇavas have been motivated more by the consideration of economic gains than by the impulse to save the souls of the heathens, the original objective of Caitanya and his immediate disciples. Although recitals of the *Bhāgavata Purāṇa* and the *Caitanya Caritāmṛta* continue to convey the message of the futility of caste distinctions, the Bhūmij take part in these recitals with the feeling that they are leading a "civilized" order of life, one that will raise their caste status above the level of the uninitiated tribesman. The spirit of *bhakti* for Krishna is imbibed in the recitals of sacred texts and devotional songs, but the Bhūmij attitude toward Vaiṣṇavism is dominated by a concern for attaining magical power through typical Vaiṣṇava rituals.

The structural context of the power situation alone cannot explain the smoothness and the extent of the Vaiṣṇava impact. The spread has been importantly facilitated by the accommodating attitude of the Vaiṣṇavas and by the nature of their theological ideas—namely, the promise of success in this life and the avoidance of miseries in the afterlife. Vaiṣṇavism not only avoids directly threatening the tribal way of life, but also accommodates to the higher status of the Brahman and, ultimately, to the caste system itself. From the way the Rādhā-Krishna cult has permeated the life of the Bhūmij today, it appears that the cult's sensuous aesthetic charm, clothed in appropriate artful display, gave a great stimulus to the spread of Vaiṣṇava influence. In the lyrics, the love theme of Rādhā and Krishna carries with it the idea of the supramundane play, or *līlā,* of the gods and the attendant meanings for spiritual quest; but in the context of the performance of these songs, the love theme appears to be more earthbound than it is in the Sahajiyā poems of Vidyāpati and Caṇḍīdās, which these lyrics closely resemble in form and content. As a matter of fact, a student of medieval Vaiṣṇava lyrics would be thrilled to find the tradition so much alive in Barabhum, in spite of their slightly parochialized rustic vigor.

One should not, however, have the idyllic impression that the Vaiṣṇava influence faces no resistance at all in its spread. I mentioned that the villagers of Madhupur were divided into pro- and anti-Vaiṣṇava *sādhu* factions. Such resistance, however, is not offered to Vaiṣṇava-derived aesthetic forms, the songs and dances. Also, in the long run, resistance tends to lose force mainly on account of the association of Vaiṣṇavism with the higher power and prestige strata.

If we may digress for a while from the conventional strictures of anthropology and indulge in value judgments, the influence of Vaiṣṇavism on the Bhūmij may be evaluated.

To begin with the debit side, the Vaiṣṇavas added to the preexisting load of supernaturally slanted tribal "superstitions" and, along with the Brahmans, injected into the tribal mind a hitherto unknown feeling of guilt on account of sin and a fear of hell, which could be counteracted only by merit-earning ritual devices. They exploited this additional load of "superstition" to their own economic advantage and for the extension of their own socio-political influence. In spite of important egalitarian elements in their teaching, most of the Vaiṣṇavas in this area are loyal supporters of the higher castes and of the regional power hierarchy, and they contribute to the differential prestige consciousness of the Bhūmij. In other words, if we evaluate positively an egalitarian social arrangement and ethic, Vaiṣṇavism in this area has largely operated against this end.

On the credit side, the Vaiṣṇavas have substantially "enriched" the aesthetic cravings of the tribals by the remarkable spread of the Rādhā-Krishna cult in songs, dances, and in poetic moods. There is in the songs the added gift of otherworldly overtones which provide a special medium for the expansion of their expressive moods. Most importantly, the operation of the Vaiṣṇava influence offers a model for transforming and "enriching" the social and cultural horizon of a primitive, isolated people without violently disturbing the original social cultural structure. It is, of course, uncertain how much of this model can be adapted to meeting the current demands for fast, directed culture change toward set secular goals.

V. THE RĀDHĀ-KRISHNA *BHAJANAS* OF MADRAS CITY *

by Milton Singer

In Madras City a form of congregational devotional worship—called *bhajana*—is becoming popular and seems to be developing into a Hindu cult that links the cults of temple and domestic worship. Superficially, the *bhajanas* resemble the older devotional cults (*bhakti*) within Hinduism, emphasizing recitation of divine names and worship of personal deities. But the contemporary *bhajanas* show many features that are distinctive of the region within which they have developed, of the social groups that support the development, and of the problems confronting contemporary Hinduism as it tries to adapt itself to modern urban conditions. The *bhajana* programs followed in Madras today are probably derived from a codification and a philosophy attributed to three teachers who lived in Tanjore district near Kumbakōṇam in the seventeenth century. The names of these three *gurus* are invoked in some *bhajana* songs at the very beginning of a *bhajana* program. They are: Bodhendra, Śrīdhara Veṅkaṭeśa (or "Ayyaval"), and Sadgurusvāmī. It is quite likely that the use in the *bhajanas* of devotional songs by saints from different regions, the centrality of the Rādhā-Krishna story, and the general selection and sequence of songs go back to these founders. Influences from other individuals and regions, however, particularly from Bengal and Maharashtra, are also evident. In Madras City the movement is only about fifty years old and may have been brought in by leaders who came from Kumbakōṇam in Tanjore district. Since the end of World War II *bhajana* groups have multiplied rapidly in the city and have also become fashionable in smaller towns and villages. The meeting of a *bhajana* group usually takes place at a private home and is attended by a mixture of castes and sects, with middle-class professionals and Smārta Brahmans predominating. I have discussed elsewhere the relation of *bhajanas* to the

* This chapter was previously published in *History of Religions,* II, No. 2 (1963), 183–226. A few minor alterations in spelling, punctuation, etc., have been made for the sake of consistency within the volume.

full range of religious-cultural performances that may be found in Madras City.[1] In this chapter I shall discuss the different types of *bhajanas,* their social organization, transmission and leadership, and their meaning and function as cultural performances.[2]

I. Types of Bhajanas

While the word *"bhajana"* is in common use in South India, it does not have a very precise meaning. The usual translation is "prayer" or "devotional song." In North India *ḳīrtan* and *saṃḳīrtan* are used as rough synonyms. The meaning of the word can best be clarified by reference to the types of performances that are called *bhajanas* in Madras City. At least five different types are called *bhajanas* and may be observed in contemporary Madras: weekly, monthly, annual, morning, and occasional.

1. The first type is a weekly evening gathering of relatives, friends, and neighbors in a private home for about three hours from 7:30 to 10:30 P.M. Saturday night is the most popular choice, although some groups meet on Thursday or other nights of the week. The men of the group, usually about a dozen, sit in a circle or in rows on the floor and lead the singing, while the women and children sit to one side and join in the refrains. The standard pattern is for the leader of the singing to recite or sing a phrase, like "Let us sing the name of Govinda," and for the audience to respond by repeating the name, or by shouting *"Jai, Jai"* ("be victorious") or a similar phrase along with it. In the kind of refrain called *"nāmāvali"* (necklace of names), it is customary to begin slowly and then to speed up the recitation, and with each repetition to raise the pitch gradually to correspond to the seven pitches, or *svaras,* of the Carnatic system of music and then to lower it in the reverse order. These *nāmāvalis* are the emotional thermometers of a *bhajana.* When accompanied by cymbals and *chiplas* (a kind of castanet), a drum, and sometimes a harmonium, the *nāmāvalis* can become very intoxicating. However, if an audience tends to be carried away by too much repetition of *nāmāvalis,* the leader has a diplomatic way of returning to a slower pace of recitation or singing by interrupting the *nāmāvali* with a set phrase, such as "Let us remember the Lord who is the life of the *gopīs.*"

The opening refrains and *nāmāvalis,* starting with the chanting of "Hari Nārāyaṇa! Hari Nārāyaṇa!", invoke the names of various deities—Rāma, Govinda, Mahādeva, Viṭṭhala, Gaṇeśa—and famous devotees. These are usually followed by a recitation of fourteen or more Sanskrit stanzas that sum up a kind of "unformulated creed" of the *bhajana.*[3] Some of these stanzas honor the three *gurus* and other great devotees, such as Prahlāda, Nārada, and Arjuna. In other stanzas the underlying philosophy of the *bhajanas* is stated: namely, that singing about Krishna will bring salvation, that such singing is obligatory for Brahmans, and that people who have "fallen" or committed "sinful" acts can be saved in this way. This is followed by *Tōḍayamaṅgalam, Nāmāvali,* and *guru-stuti.* Then at least one song each is sung from *Gītagovinda, Krishnalīlā Taraṅgiṇī,* Bhadrācala Rāma Dāsa, Purandara Dāsa, Tyāgarāja, Sadāśiva Brahmendra, Kabīr Dāsa, Mīrābāī, Caitanya, and other devotees. Then comes the major ritual part of the weekly *bhajana:* a *pūjā* (religious offering) to Krishna and Rādhā. There are also *pūjās* at the very start and toward the end of the *bhajana,* but these are very brief—with offerings of flowers and food to the lithographs of Krishna and Rādhā on the wall, a recitation of 108 names, and the waving of a camphor or wick light (*ārati*). The *pūjā* that follows the stanzas is far more elaborate. This is performed by a leading devotee; other devotees participate in it to varying degrees, but all participate even if their favorite deities are not Krishna and Rādhā.

The major *pūjā* takes from about forty-five minutes to an hour and follows more or less the steps of domestic and temple *pūjās.* It differs from these in performing some of the steps mentally or symbolically—for example, the image of the deity is not actually bathed; the *bhajana pūjā* uses lithographs rather than metal or stone images; it changes the sequence of steps and introduces songs that are not part of domestic or temple *pūjās.* The sixteen "attentions" (*upacāras*) offered to a deity in the other *pūjās* are offered in songs in the *bhajana pūjā.* Miniature metal images, garlands, fans, etc., may be used if they are available. Some of the songs are addressed not to Krishna but to Rāma, but because of their appropriateness are sung anyway. Vedic *mantras* and Sanskrit stanzas that are used in domestic *pūjās* are also used with flower offerings. The first *mantra* of each Veda and the first *sūtra* of each Śāstra are recited as offerings. And there are stanzas to glorify sacred texts, sacred places, sacred trees, and sacred days. Tamil and Sanskrit songs of the Āḻvārs are sung, and the *pūjā* concludes with invocations of auspiciousness (*śobhanam* and *maṅgalam*) to Rāma and Krishna, and with some *nāmāvalis*.

In the next part of the *bhajana*, the three *gurus*—Bodhendra, Śrīdhara Veṅkaṭeśa, and Sadgurusvāmī—are praised in Sanskrit songs and stanzas. Most detail is given about Bodhendra, who is described as "the author of one hundred works on the efficacy of the Divine Name," as enjoying and sporting "in the sea of Rāma's name," and as having heroically repudiated the differentiation between Hari and Śiva. Śrīdhara Veṅkaṭeśa is said to be concerned with Śiva's name; only Sadguru Svāmī is said to be concerned with Krishna. "In his mind, the Lord of the Yadus, the lotus-faced Lord, Krishna, plays with Rādhā in an uninterrupted manner." These devotees and others, such as Tukaram and Nāmdev, are said to be "good men" who are "full of peace" and who "work for the welfare of the people like the Spring./ Having themselves crossed the fearful ocean of *saṃsāra,* / They help others to wade through with ease and spontaneity."

Following the praise of the *gurus* is a series of songs in many different languages about or by different regional saints, each followed by a *nāmāvali.* Jayadeva's *Gītagovinda,* a passionate medieval Sanskrit poem on the love of Rādhā and Krishna, heads this list. One *aṣṭāpadī,* or canto, is sung during each weekly *bhajana* until the entire work of twenty-four *aṣṭāpadīs* is finished; then the first *aṣṭāpadī* is repeated, and so on. The other songs include some from Nārāyaṇa Tīrtha's *Krishnalīlā Taraṅgiṇī,* a Sanskrit work about Krishna's pranks and "sports"; another Sanskrit song also about Krishna by Sadāśiva Brahmendra; a Telugu song about Rāma by Rāmdās; some of Purandaradās' Kannada songs to Krishna; Gopāla Krishna Bharati's Tamil song to Śiva; and one of Tyāgarāja's Telugu songs on Rāma. Except for Jayadeva, all the preceding composers were South Indian, but some songs from North Indian saints are also included: a Hindi song of Kabīr's on Rāma, a Hindi song of Mīrābāī's on Krishna, and a Marathi song by Tukaram on Viṭṭhala. Most of these saints' songs deal with the personal discovery of refuge in a particular deity. Mīrābāī's, which is perhaps the most personal, will serve as one illustration:

When the decorative stub on the *pādukā* [wooden sandal] of my great teacher touched me, I forgot the world. I obtained an inner peace and bliss.

Wherever I looked, I beheld only the feet of my teacher.
Everything else was *māyā* to me, like things seen in a dream.
Birth and death—this ocean of *saṃsāra* has dried up.
I have no anxiety about the seeking of a plan to cross it.
Govinda protected Gokula village by holding aloft a mountain.
When I sought refuge in him, he turned my vision inward.

After a short *pūjā* to Krishna and other deities come the concluding songs and stanzas of the *bhajana.* These consist of a verse and *nāmāvali* saluting and asking for the special protection of Gaṇeśa, Sarasvatī, Subrahmaṇya, Śiva, Pārvatī, Rāma, Sītā, Āñjaneya, Krishna, and Garuḍa or Vainateya. In these supplications, the supplicants' needs are rarely mentioned—only the qualities and deeds of the deity. Lines from a Sanskrit song by Bhadrādrivāsa will illustrate this peculiarity:

O joy-giver of the *gopīs,* of the festival of Gokula village,
O Govinda, glory to you. Do protect me.
O Son of Nanda, moon-faced one, your face is charming. Do protect me, . . .

The closing invocations of the *bhajana* (another *maṅgalam*) ask for auspiciousness for Krishna and his devotees, and also for all people:

All welfare and auspiciousness to the people. Let the rulers of the earth rule in the righteous way.
Let there be ever auspiciousness for the cows and the Brahmans.
Let all the people in different countries (*lokas*) be blessed with happiness.

Let there be rain in the proper season,
Let the earth be full of crops,
Let this *deśa* (country, nation) be free from poverty and misery,
Let the Brahmans be free from fear.

Of the last two invocations, one asks that Hari (Viṣṇu, or Krishna) be remembered in all places where devotees assemble and the other asserts that "Brahman alone is [ultimately] real," to which the audience replies, "*Oṃ.*"

At the end of the *bhajana,* the special food of the day, already offered to the deity in the *pūjā,* is distributed to all as a "favor" (*prasāda*) of the Lord. The sharing of the *prasāda* in a symbolic communion is as essential to the *bhajana* as is the singing together.

2. The second type of *bhajana,* called a *divya-nāma-bhajana,* or

dīpa bhajana, is generally a monthly affair. Once a month, usually on a Saturday night, a group of twenty to forty people meet from about 7:30 in the evening until about 6:00 the next morning to conduct this type of *bhajana.* Not everyone comes at the same time or stays throughout the night. Some of the children are taken home to sleep; others try to stay awake as long as they can until they fall asleep on their mothers' laps. Adults, too, come and go according to personal convenience. Many songs and stanzas from the weekly *bhajana* are also used in the monthly *bhajana,* but many others are added, particularly about Krishna's activities and "sports" (*līlās*) with the *gopīs,* or milk-maids. The heart of the monthly *bhajana* is the singing, dancing, and dramatizing of these songs by the devotees as they sit or dance around a small lighted ritual lamp symbolizing Krishna's presence, imagining themselves to be *gopīs.*

The invocation of Krishna's presence into the lamp takes place in two steps. First the lamp is decorated with a garland of flowers and lighted by a leading devotee of the group as it stands under lithographs of Krishna and Rādhā on the wall. A light-offering is then made to the deity in the lithograph, accompanied by a Vedic *mantra.* This symbolizes a transfer of power from the lithograph to the lamp. After the host has distributed flowers and scented sandalwood paste to the active male devotees, the leader takes the lighted lamp in his hand; while he holds the lamp and dances clockwise around the floor with it, four songs, two in Sanskrit and two in Kannada, are sung. The lamp is then placed on a small wooden pedestal in the center of the floor, which is decorated at that spot with geometric drawings of rice powder. As long as the lamp is in the center of the floor, it is regarded as a spot made sacred by Krishna's presence. The action of the *bhajana* takes place as the devotees sit or dance in a circle around the lamp.

The themes of the *bhajana* are based mainly on incidents in Krishna's life as described in the *Bhāgavata Purāṇa,* but they are expressed and elaborated in songs from various regional saints: Vijayagopāla, Bhadrādri, Nārāyaṇa Tīrtha, Rāmdās, Mīrā, Āṇḍāḷ, and others. In one of the most dramatic parts of the *bhajana,* the devotees, after they have been dancing and singing of the *gopīs'* play with Krishna, suddenly sit down and sing the *Gopīḳā Gītā,* lamenting Krishna's disappearance from their (the *gopīs'*) midst and begging him to return.

To re-enact and celebrate Krishna's reappearance, the devotees stand, sing, and do a number of dances that are considered appropriate expressions of joy by the *gopīs* as they "sport" with Krishna again. These dances are based on South Indian folk dances usually performed by women. They include the circular dance (*rāsa krīḍā*), in which there is imagined a Krishna who has multiplied himself so that there is a Krishna between every two *gopīs;* a churning dance, in which the devotees pair off, cross hands, and embrace; a stick dance (*kōlāṭṭam*); and a Kummi dance (the last two being country folk dances).

The songs sung during and after these dances include folk songs and songs in Sanskrit and other regional languages. There is also a group of philosophical songs in Tamil, called *"siddha,"* composed by Tamil sages known as *siddhars, abhaṅgs* in Marathi by Tukaram and Ekanātha, songs on the ten manifestations of Viṣṇu, and songs on Śiva and other deities.

After these dances and songs, each devotee prostrates himself before the others and then rolls full-length clockwise around the lamp to take the dust from the feet of the other devotees. When he gets up he is embraced by the other devotees.

In a final circumambulation, the devotees go around the lamp singing a Sanskrit song on Krishna. A song is then sung in praise of Śiva, another in praise of Jagannāth, followed by a *nāmāvali* on Govinda and a stanza in praise of Āñjaneya. Women and children join in these songs for the religious benefit of the entire *bhajana.* A light offering is made to the lamp and then to the lithograph. The leading devotee now picks up the lamp and, singing the third *aṣṭāpadī* from the *Gītagovinda,* dances with it and returns it to its original place under the lithograph. The other devotees prostrate themselves toward the lithograph, indicating that Krishna's power has been transferred back to the picture. Another light-offering is made to the lithograph, and the *bhajana* closes with the same invocation of auspiciousness (*maṅgalam*) used at the end of weekly *bhajanas.*

This type of *bhajana* is also performed on the occasion of a festival, on Rāma's and Krishna's birthdays, and on days commemorating the birth and death days of the *gurus* Bodhendra, Ayyaval, and Sadgurusvāmī. It may also be performed on the birthday of some member of the family or when a noted Bhāgavatār comes to visit. Shorter forms of the *bhajana* may last from four to five hours.

3. The third type of *bhajana,* the Marriage of Rādhā and Krishna (*Rādhā-Kalyāṇam*), which is performed annually, has a special and pre-eminent status among *bhajanas,* because in the story of Krishna, his marriage to a favorite *gopī,* Rādhā, represents a consummation of Krishna's romance with the *gopīs,* and because on the allegorical plane the marriage symbolizes the human soul's union with the Absolute. The preparations and arrangements for this type of *bhajana* are far more elaborate than for the others. Hundreds of people come to it, requiring a very large house, a small hall, or, as is customary, a street pavilion (*pandal*) like those used in actual marriages. Professional musicians are frequently employed and also Vedic priests (*purohitas*), who know the ritual of an orthodox Hindu wedding, to chant Vedic *mantras.* The number of devotees who come to one of these *bhajanas* may be so large that it is necessary for them to form several concentric circles when they start to sing and dance, or for many to drop out from active participation. At one *Rādhā Kalyāṇam* I attended, the host thinned out the circle of devotees by arbitrarily tapping individuals on the back at random and asking them to withdraw.

The marriage part of the *Rādhā-Kalyāṇam bhajana* usually takes about six hours and is performed on a Sunday morning following a lamp-type *bhajana* the preceding night. However, it is now customary to have the marriage *bhajana* culminate a ten-day program of *bhajanas* that is becoming the great festival (*mahā-utsava*) of *bhajanas* for the year, echoing, perhaps, the traditional ten-day temple festival. During these ten days, *bhajanas* are performed, usually in the evenings, grouped according to special regions and composers. In 1961, one Madras festival included special *bhajanas* based on the *Gītagovinda* and the *Krishnalīlā Taraṅgiṇī,* on songs of the Tamil Śaivite saints (*Dēvāram*) and Vaiṣṇavite saints (*Tiruppāvai*), and on songs by Mīrābāī, Kabīr, and Purandaradās. Individual singers and *bhajana* parties from different regions were featured during the festival. Recitations with songs (*hari̤kathā*) on Krishna and other Purāṇic themes were also given, and comic relief was provided by mimicry and imitations.

On the Saturday night preceding the marriage *bhajana,* there is a discourse (*janavāsam*) to welcome the bridegroom (Krishna) to the bride's (Rādhā's) house for the marriage. This is followed by an all-night *bhajana* that combines features of the weekly and the monthly *bhajana* types, but uses more objects (fans, metal images, garlands, etc.) than are usually used when these are performed separately. Two to three hundred people may come to this all-night *bhajana* and remain there until it ends at about 4:00 the next morning. After the devotees and other guests have had a chance to get a few hours' sleep, either at the place where the *bhajana* is held or in their own homes, they gather again early in the morning. A small party is formed under the leadership of a distinguished devotee to go and beg for rice and other presents for the wedding. The leader wears the traditional costume of devotees on this occasion and carries a tamboura and begging bowl. Housewives come out to put their gifts in the bowl or are visited at their doors by members of the party. This custom is called *uñcha vṛtti*.

While the party is out, the *bhajana* proper begins with a brief *pūjā* and with invocations, stanzas, and *nāmāvalis* similar to those used at the beginning of the weekly *bhajana*. Songs from the monthly *bhajana* are also used. It is usual for each *bhajana* leader to sing songs from his own tradition. The marriage ceremony is obviously the most popular part of the *bhajana,* and by the time it is ready to begin, as many as five hundred people may have gathered in and around the pavilion. The ritual of the marriage ceremony follows that of an orthodox Hindu marriage of the South Indian type, with variations, especially in the use of songs that are peculiar to the Rādhā-Krishna *bhajana*. The most important song is the twenty-second *aṣṭāpadī* of the *Gītagovinda,* which expounds the union of Rādhā and Krishna. Telugu songs on the same theme are also used.

Much of the ritual is acted out by the male devotees. Rice mixed with turmeric powder and water is pounded in a mortar with a pestle, and groups of devotees take turns dancing with the pestle toward and away from images of Krishna and Rādhā, while singing a song of auspiciousness to Krishna. This dance is said to be a village dance common during the South Indian harvest festival (*Poṅgal*) and is interpreted by some devotees as a dance of the *gopīs*. A similar combination of rice and turmeric powder is used for marriages and domestic *pūjās* but the pounding is omitted. The bride and bridegroom, represented by lithographs and metal images, are anointed and adorned. Turmeric powder and limewater, and a red substance (red is an auspicious color) are applied to their feet to beautify them and as a good augury for them. Gifts of cloth are placed under the images, and Vedic *mantras* for marriage are recited by the Vedic priest. A thread moistened with turmeric and carrying a gold pendant at one end is hung around the neck of the bride. This is an emblem of marriage when tied by a bridegroom around the bride's neck and is called the *tāli*. As at a regular marriage, the lineage of the couple is recited for three generations on each side, giving the names of the father, the father's father, and the father's grandfather.

Some of the ritual resembles that of a Western marriage—for example, the throwing of rice and flowers at the couple—and seems to express the blessings and joy of the audience. Among the songs sung to convey this joyous mood, there is one by Nārāyaṇa Tīrtha saying: "I see Krishna here with His eight other wives—all in resplendent glory." Many of the Rādhā-Krishna songs are also used in Hindu marriages. At this point in the ceremony the day's priest is given a present of money and perhaps some other gift (*saṃbhāvana*). Further attentions are then bestowed on the couple: their feet are painted again, flower balls are exchanged, they are given a ride in a boat and a swing. Much of this is done only in song and symbolically, but some of it is acted out. If a small swing and metal images are available, the leader will swing these to and fro while singing two or three Sanskrit and Tamil songs about Rādhā and Krishna. The bride and bridegroom are also supposed to address satirical Telugu verses (*padyas*) to one another.

One of the most moving parts of the ceremony is that of putting Rādhā and Krishna to sleep. Sanskrit and Kannada lullabies are sung, a light-offering is made, and a curtain is drawn to give the bridal couple privacy and to symbolize their union. One of Jayadeva's songs is sung, asking Rādhā to go to Krishna (*Aṣṭāpadī* 21). A slightly humorous conversation between Rādhā and Krishna is sung in Sanskrit by one devotee. Their sleep is indicated by the singing of a lullaby and by a period of silence while the devotees close their eyes and meditate.

Distinguished devotees are selected to act as guards at each of the four gates of the palace. Their leader sings a song for each direction, asking the guards to see that all is well, and the devotees respond. After another brief silence, Sanskrit, Tamil, and Telugu songs are sung to Krishna in a *rāga* for waking.

With offerings of light and milk, the *bhajana* closes after a final *maṅgalam*. The presents are then distributed to the devotees, and food is also given to them, as well as to all the participants and to the poor. These large wedding *bhajanas* always involve a feeding of the poor. Sometimes a leading devotee will make a speech to close the ceremonies, although the festival may go on for another day, with additional discourses, street processions of Rādhā and Krishna around a temple and tank, and a special celebration in honor of Hanumān. On the last day of the festival *Aṣṭāpadīs* 23 and 24 are sung.

In the last few years a Sītā-Rāma marriage (*Sītā Kalyāṇam*) and a Vaḷḷi-Subrahmaṇya marriage (*Vaḷḷi Kalyāṇam*) have been added as annual *bhajanas,* but these have not yet become as popular as the Rādhā-Krishna marriage *bhajana.* One section of the city which celebrates all these marriages has changed its name to "Kalyāṇam Nāgar" —town of marriages.

The swing festival (*Dolotsava*) is sometimes included at the end of a monthly *bhajana,* in which case it comes in the early hours of the morning. At the marriage *bhajana* it usually comes, in abbreviated form, at about noon. It is also part of a Hindu wedding and was probably held in the past as a garden festival in spring and summer. The boat or floating festival is a regular temple festival at the large southern temples. On this occasion temple priests, staff, and invited guests accompany the images of the temple deities on a lighted platform that is pulled slowly around the temple tank several nights in succession. A bystander at one of these festivals explained that "just as anyone would like to take a boat ride on a warm night, so we think our gods enjoy it too."

4. The fourth type of *bhajana* is a street *bhajana* conducted very early in the morning, and occasionally at night, around the temple tank. These are especially popular in the holy month of Mārgaśīrṣī. Among Krishna devotees, the explanation of these *bhajanas* is that the

gopīs waked at 3:00 A.M. during this month, and sang and prayed to the goddess Kātyāyanī (Pārvatī) for Krishna's hand. A leading devotee will sometimes organize and train a band of children to sing these early morning *bhajanas.*

The devotees believe that the human year is a day for the gods. The twelve months of the human year represent the twenty-four hours of the divine day. The month of Mārgaśīrṣī is holy and auspicious for gods, since it represents the two-hour "interval" from 4:00 to 6:00 A.M. for them, the time when they wake from sleep and begin to be active. Each subsequent month represents another two hours. That is why the *gopīs* are said to have chosen this month for Kātyāyanī *pūjā,* or *ḳratan,* and why *bhāgavatārs* hold *bhajanas* in the morning.

The songs at the morning *bhajanas* are similar to those sung at other types of *bhajanas,* with *nāmāvalis* and Tamil songs, Śaivite as well as Vaiṣṇavite, more common than at other *bhajanas.*

The pattern of the morning *bhajanas* is also followed during festivals on full-moon nights and when the temple deities are taken in procession. On these occasions *bhajana* parties follow the deities, along with Vedic chanters and singers of *Dēvāram.*

5. The fifth *bhajana* type is not an independent kind of *bhajana* but a selection or combination of the preceding four types, for performance on some special occasion. The most common occasions are the visit of a dignitary, a wedding, Republic Day, and other holidays. *Bhajana* groups are invited to an individual's house to conduct these *bhajanas,* or some active group may organize a number of them on its own premises. Many of the *bhajanas* given during the *bhajana* festival are occasional *bhajanas* of this type.

6. A sixth type of *bhajana,* the daily *bhajana* or *Nitya Bhajana,* is no longer commonly observed, although it is reported to have been more common, at least among very sincere devotees, in the preceding generation. This type of *bhajana* is performed daily in one's house for an hour or two in the evening, with members of the family and perhaps a few neighbors and friends attending. About fifteen songs on different deities, *gurus,* and saints, in Sanskrit, Telugu, Tamil, Marathi, and Hindi, are sung each day, a different fifteen each day for the first twenty-four days, and then the cycle begins to repeat. It has

been reported that the Divine Life Society at Rishikesh conducts evening *bhajanas* the year around. In Madras only the well-known devotee Gopālakrishna Bhāgavatār is said to conduct daily *bhajanas.*

II. Social Organization of the Bhajanas

The basic unit of *bhajana* social organization is the social group which meets weekly to conduct an evening *bhajana.* This is usually a small neighborhood group consisting of the members of one or two households. The organizers and active participants are generally male adults, although in the last four or five years a few *bhajanas* have been organized by women. A weekly *bhajana* group will include father and sons, women and children of the household, several other relatives who may live in the same household or nearby, and friends and acquaintances from one or two other households in the immediate vicinity. These friends are not family relations, although they may belong to the same subcaste; the friendship is usually based on neighborhood acquaintance or on professional or occupational association. If some members of the *bhajana* group move away, the weekly *bhajana* meetings rotate from one household to another, unless the distances are too great, in which case a new *bhajana* group is formed in the new neighborhood. The formation of local *bhajana* groups is quite informal and spontaneous. New ones are organized constantly in different parts of the city, but not all survive with equal vigor and seriousness. Some of the groups are closely tied to a father, grandfather, or great-grandfather who was a distinguished devotee and who himself conducted *bhajanas.* Most of the local groups do not have a very long and continuous history, however.

The more successful a local *bhajana* group becomes, the more quickly its membership expands beyond the small neighborhood group. New members are attracted from outside, or by its own organizational activities the local group expands its membership. This is especially apt to be the case for the monthly and annual *bhajanas,* when large numbers of people participate. Several different local groups may combine on these occasions, but it is also likely that one of the more active groups may organize the larger *bhajanas* in its name.

This process can be illustrated by an example from Mylapore, one of the Madras suburbs, where one of the local *bhajana* groups, first formed in 1945, has sponsored annual as well as occasional *bhajanas.* This group elects officers, solicits donations, prints announcements and invitations, and issues an annual report with an audited account of its revenues and expenditures. During 1959 and 1960, this group, in addition to conducting its usual Saturday night *bhajanas,* organized daily morning *bhajanas* around the temple streets for about two weeks at the end of December (during Mārgaśīrṣi); was invited to conduct *bhajanas* in private homes and public institutions on fifteen occasions, in various parts of the city; held special *bhajanas* five times on its own premises, the home of one of its members, to honor distinguished visitors and to celebrate holidays; and organized marriage *bhajanas* for Rādhā and Krishna for ten days in January, for Rāma and Sītā one day in April and again for a day in November, when it also held a one-day marriage *bhajana* for Vaḷḷi and Subrahmaṇya. Each of the marriage *bhajanas* included feeding of the poor. The group also organizes *bhajana* pilgrimages to places of religious interest.

The organization of so many activities sometimes puts a strain on the resources and co-operativeness of the group. On one occasion, when it was invited out of town to conduct a *bhajana* at someone's home, the host expected the *bhajana* to go on through the night. One of the officers, however, decided that a three-hour *bhajana* was sufficient for the occasion. This so offended another officer that he resigned his post in protest.

The major activity of this group is the organization of the annual marriage *bhajana* for Rādhā and Krishna and the associated *bhajana* festival which goes on for ten days. Donations are solicited for this purpose by members all over the city in offices and homes. From 1959 to 1960, about 2,000 rupees were donated by more than 800 people. About 700 of these donations were of 2 rupees (about 50 cents) or less. The donors represent many different classes and occupations. Of the 322 that could be identified, about 55 per cent were Smārta Brahmans; 10 per cent Śrī Vaiṣṇava Brahmans, 10 per cent Mādhva Brahmans, 20 per cent non-Brahmans, and 5 per cent of the donations were made in the names of women. The occupational representation is definitely middle class and professional, and includes government, education, business and industry, law, medicine, religion, journalism, and the arts. The government group includes a retired high-court judge, a retired deputy collector, and a member of the state legislative assembly; the education group includes the principals of two colleges, a university professor, and several teachers; the business group includes a bank officer, the director of a steel factory, chartered accountants, shopkeepers, and merchants; the arts group includes actors, employees of a film studio, and musicians. Probably the most numerous groups are office assistants, Vedic *purohitas,* and medical people. Not all donors are necessarily active participants in the *bhajanas,* and not all participants make donations, but there is considerable overlap between the two groups.

The money collected for the 1959–1960 festival was spent approximately in the following manner: the pavilion, Rs. 119; orchestra, Rs. 261; *pūjā,* Rs. 78; food for the poor, Rs. 518; flowers, Rs. 62; procession, Rs. 35; camphor, Rs. 119; printing, Rs. 366; transportation, Rs. 154; carpet, Rs. 50; cloth for gifts, Rs. 225. A balance of about Rs. 255 was used for the expenses of weekly and occasional *bhajanas.* The group is also hoping to collect enough money to construct a permanent building of its own.

The organizational drive and leadership of this Mylapore *bhajana* group probably come from two of its officers, one an outstanding and highly respected Tamil writer and journalist, a Smārta Brahman; and the other a successful chartered accountant, a Śrī Vaiṣṇava Brahman. They live next door to one another in one of the newer sections of Mylapore. The accountant's house is now used for weekly and special *bhajanas,* and the street in front for the marriage *bhajanas.* The accountant is also a leading worker in the Congress Party of Madras, and he has organized the distribution of free CARE milk to poor children, using his house as a distribution center. The milk distribution cards carry the name of the *bhajana* group as well as his own name.

In 1958, through the initiative of these officers of the Mylapore *bhajana* group, a conference was called of all leading devotees in the city. As a result of this meeting an association of Madras devotees was organized under the title Madras Bhāgavata-Mahā-Sammelanam Samāj. Officers and a governing body of about fifty members were selected. This association is a federation of *bhajana* groups in the city and hopes eventually to include all *bhajana* groups in the state. About forty-five local Madras *bhajana* groups were affiliated with it in 1961 and paid dues of one or two rupees a year. The association now holds a conference once a year, when it elects officers, discusses its plans, and conducts special *bhajanas.*

The activities of the association are similar to those of the Mylapore local group but are carried on over a wider field. It undertakes to furnish *bhajana* leaders to any group in or out of the city that requests them. One of the secretaries estimated that there are now about five hundred requests a year, and said that he himself goes out about three times a month to lead *bhajanas.* When the association sends out a *bhajana* leader, he is usually given the cost of his transportation and a gift by his host. Other association services include regular notice of *bhajana* meetings all over the city and the organization of special *bhajanas* for visitors and on other occasions.

Not all the local *bhajana* groups in the city are affiliated with the association, nor are they all as highly organized as the Mylapore group. Some of them regard so much organization as uncongenial to the spirit of the *bhajana.* One of these groups, led by the son of the famous Madras devotee, S. V. Aiyer, claims not to have any fixed program of performances or even a regular meeting time. It sends out no invitations, requires no special arrangements, and makes no collections, because the son believes this kind of organization leads to quarrels and to expectations of privileged treatment that are contrary to the spontaneous feelings of love and equality that should prevail among devotees. This group does seem to follow a regular program in its weekly meetings, as established by the father. The program begins with a recitation of the divine name (*Nāma Saṃkīrtana*), songs in praise of the *guru* and father, of Rādhā and Krishna, and of the saints. It concludes with an *aṣṭāpadī* from the *Gītagovinda,* a song from the *Krishnalīlā Taraṅgiṇī,* and one of Mīrābāī's songs. A special feature of this group's *bhajanas* is the more active participation of the women, although they sit separately from the men. There is probably an influence here both of the Caitanya type of *bhajana* and of Mīrābāī.

The type of *bhajana* performance and the kind of social organization are clearly interrelated. Each type of *bhajana* calls for a somewhat different kind of social group and social organization. On the other hand, the composition of the social group and its organizational propensities definitely affect the type of *bhajana* performance. Each local group introduces some variations of its own into the program, and, as the groups get larger, the sources of these variations become more diversified. The variations are in turn codified into a fixed program that soon becomes traditional. Whatever the long-run outcome of this interaction may be, there is no doubt that the trend of the last fifty years in Madras *bhajanas* has been toward larger-scale organization and greater formality and fixity in the program. There is continuity with the earlier seventeenth-century codifications of the traditional program, but there are also many innovations of regional and national significance. An urban, centralized organization, the Madras Bhāgavata-Mahā-Sammelanam Samāj, has developed to take official charge of the movement, with practically all media of modern communication at its disposal and with good prospects for a permanent institutional center of its own. This organization sponsors a regular festival calendar that parallels and intersects the traditional calendars of temple and domestic worship. Professional musicians, Vedic priests, semiprofessional devotees, and expensive ceremonial arrangements are employed for the larger *bhajana* performances. Printed *bhajana* books have made it easier for a large number of people to follow a uniform program.[4] Affiliated groups have been formed by Tamils in Calcutta, Delhi, and other large cities in and out of India, and there is a plan to extend the movement into villages and towns of Madras State.

It is arguable whether these developments can be characterized as the formation of a new "cult" or of a "great tradition." Perhaps "modernization and urbanization" of an old cult and tradition is an apter characterization. They are in any case a significant growth in one cultural traditional of contemporary Hinduism. The nature of this tradition and the processes involved in its growth can be further clarified by a discussion of the leadership, transmission, support, and meaning of the *bhajanas*.

III. Leadership and Transmission of the Rādhā-Krishna Cult

Leaders of *bhajanas* are those who know the songs best or have a reputation for devotion. Sometimes these two criteria do not coincide: those with musical skill do not always have a reputation for devotion, nor are the devotees necessarily gifted musically. There are special roles in the performance of *bhajanas* that are usually reserved for elderly and distinguished devotees—the conduct of a *pūjā* and the carrying of the lamp in the lamp *bhajana.* These devotees may or may not be musical and familiar with the ritual. On the other hand, the role of priest in the Rādhā-Krishna marriage *bhajanas* is usually assigned to a professional Vedic priest, who is paid for his services. Some of these priests, who may come with no interest in *bhajanas,* eventually cultivate this interest and become members of regular Saturday-night *bhajanas.* They do not, however, forgo their fees for performing the marriage service.

The role that a devotee plays in a *bhajana* does not itself determine his leadership status. On the contrary, if a devotee has a reputation for devotion he is invited to conduct *bhajanas.* What then testifies to such a reputation? One answer to this question was framed by a leading Madras devotee in a speech he gave in 1960 to close the celebration of a Rādhā-Krishna marriage *bhajana.* His answer set severe standards for a true devotee; he who looks like a devotee only during *bhajanas* is not a true devotee. He is like a workman who does not think about his work after hours; he is only a "*bhajana* workman" who knows the sequence of songs and has the musical skill to sing them. To become a true devotee he must be a devotee throughout his life: pure in speech, thought, and action. He must be sincere and firm in his belief that all beings in the world are children of God and that everything—whether calamity or good fortune—happens by His grace. He must be rid of egoism, humble to all, and speak in a sweet manner. Although this speaker did not seem to think that singing *bhajana* songs would quickly transform the singers into true devotees, he nevertheless urged cultivation of friendship with groups of devotees and singing as the best means available in this age for meditating on God and asking His forgiveness and help.

This austere ethical interpretation of the requirements for a true devotee is not, I think, shared by average participants in *bhajanas.* They are more apt to agree with the same speaker's admission that the devotional path (*bhaktiyoga*), being available to all and not requiring any external aids, is a more accessible path to salvation in this age than the path of knowledge or of works. They may not disagree with the qualities stipulated for a true devotee, and they would certainly greatly respect anyone who possessed these qualities, but in choosing *bhajana* leaders they will settle for less: anyone who manifests sincerity and constancy in his devotion qualifies as a leader.

Bhajana leadership is formalized in two different ways—through the organization of *bhajana* societies and through the *guru*-disciple relation. When *bhajana* societies have adopted a formal organization, the election or appointment of officers is a way of designating leaders. Among the officers now serving in some *bhajana* societies, some are obviously distinguished for the quality of their devotion, and others rather for their organizing abilities, acquaintance with a wide range of people, and interest in seeing the Rādhā-Krishna movement become an organized movement. It is perhaps paradoxical that a cult that emphasizes spontaneous, personal devotion should become an organized social movement, but this transformation could not take place without the help of the organizing type of leader. It may even happen that the same individual provides both the spiritual and the organizational leadership (the devotee who made the speech on the qualities of a true devotee is an example). There is an institutional precedent for this in the heads of the South Indian monasteries, whose spiritual authority has been recognized by the Indian Supreme Court to depend on their secular property rights.[5] The most common situation in *bhajana* organizations, however, is more akin to the separation of secular and religious leadership, as in the temples.

Gurus and disciples.—The *guru*-disciple relationship is not generally considered a formalized relationship, since anyone is in principle free to choose his *guru,* and a *guru* is in principle free to accept or reject a disciple. What makes the relationship formal is the requirement of a formal initiation ceremony in which the *guru* imparts a secret *mantra* and a set of instructions to the disciple. When a *guru* or set of *gurus* is recognized by a series of disciples, a particular cultural tradition (*saṃpradāya*) is established, and its authentic transmission is traced through a chain of disciples, who in turn become *gurus* to the next generation. In this sense, every Indian sect or philosophical school forms a cultural tradition. Each traces itself through a historical or putative chain of disciples to a founding *guru* or *gurus*. The Vedas are traced through certain families to the original revelations of *Ṛṣis* or

Seers; Buddhists look to Buddha as the founding *guru,* Jains to Mahāvīra, Smārta Brahmans to Śaṃkara, Mādhvas to Madhva, Śrī Vaiṣṇavas to Rāmānuja, Liṅgayats to Bāsava, Sikhs to Guru Nānak, and the Rāmakrishna followers to Rāmakrishna and Vivekānanda. In the South Indian Rādhā-Krishna cult, three *gurus* are recognized as having given the Rādhā-Krishna *bhajana* its canonical form. These three are praised in stanzas recited at the very beginning of each *bhajana.* Other saints from other regions and periods whose songs are sung in the *bhajanas*—for example, Caitanya, Tukaram, Mīrābāī, Kabīr, and Purandaradās—have also been assimilated to the South Indian *bhajana* tradition, but these do not have the pre-eminent status of the three *gurus.*

There does not yet exist a generally recognized chain of disciples of the three *gurus,* although one occasionally hears attempts to trace such a chain. By reciting stanzas in praise of the three *gurus,* contemporary devotees make themselves disciples in unilateral fashion, so to speak. There are, however, devotees who have been initiated by an older generation of devotees, who in turn claim spiritual descent from the three *gurus.* One who has been thus initiated, a retired film actor, is also an officer in one of the *bhajana* societies and is frequently called upon to lead *bhajanas* in different parts of the city. He is usually asked to lead the *bhajanas* of his own society during the Rādhā-Krishna marriage ceremony. On this occasion he comes dressed in the traditional costume of a devotee, with a turban around his head and a tamboura under his arm. This is the same costume which the *guru* who initiated him wears when he visits the city. In his domestic shrine the retired film actor has pictures of the three *gurus,* of two Maharashtrian saints, of a family *guru* who is said to have reached the age of 161, of Gopālakrishna Bhāgavatār, who initiated him into the *bhajana* field, and of the initiation ceremony. He also keeps on display near the shrine a string of beads, called *sūtram,* that he received when he was initiated, with which he counts the names of the deities. This devotee's family comes from a town in South Arcot district. His grandfather, father, brother, he himself, and two of his sons have Śrī Veṅkaṭeśvara as their chosen deity. Two of his other sons, however, have chosen Durgā and Murugan as their favorite deities.

In addition to Gopālakrishna Bhāgavatār, who is a master among living *bhāgavatārs* and who has published a standard collection of *bhajana* songs in Tamil, there are other *gurus* frequently mentioned who are within living memory of the present generation of Madrassis. All are said to have conducted *bhajana* according to the program laid down by the founding three *gurus,* but each is also credited with some individual innovations.

One of these is Tillistana Narasiṃha Bhāgavatār, who is said to have been the first to print in Grantha script, at Kumbakōṇam in the early 1900's, a collection of *bhajana* songs, based on Sadgurusvāmī's codification. Narasiṃha Bhāgavatār, a Telugu Smārta Brahman, was invited to Madras City for *harikathā* recitals and for *bhajana* parties. These parties are remembered by T. V. Seetharama Aiyer, who came to Madras from Kumbakōṇam in 1904 to become the librarian of the Hindu High School in Triplicane. He describes the *bhajanas* of this period as emphasizing classical music and being restricted to Brahmans. Narasiṃha Bhāgavatār and other early *bhajana* leaders are also remembered by Sūlumaṅgalam Svāminātha Bhāgavatār.

Three of these leaders were contemporaries, and are frequently singled out for special mention. They are Rāmacandra Aiyer, S. V. Aiyer, and Kōthamarāma Aiyer. All three came to Madras from Tanjore district and were familiar with the *bhajana* tradition deriving from the three *gurus.* Through their personal experience and travels, each of them added to this tradition something from Bengal, Maharashtra, and North India.

Rāmacandra Aiyer, popularly known as "Hari," a retired elementary schoolteacher, came to Madras in about 1913 from Tanjore district to live with his younger brother, who had a government job in the city. "Hari" conducted *bhajanas* in his brother's house and wherever asked. He is said to have started the Rādhā Kalyāṇam and Sītā Kalyāṇam *bhajanas* and also to have added Sunday *bhajanas.* He died in 1953 at the age of 73.

Veṅkaṭarāmana Aiyer (or S. V. Aiyer) called himself "Mīrādāsī" because he believed Mīrābāī had possessed him. The incident is described in the following words by a contemporary:

> As this blessed devotee lay on his back one starlit night, on the top floor of his residence in Madras, a voice beckoned to him and bade him look at a meteor in the sky. There actually was a meteor then in the sky, and this

premī [lover] saw a blue figure descend therefrom and reach his side. As it approached him, he recognized it to be Mīrā enveloped in a dazzling cool blue light. From that time onwards, Mīrā possessed him and he felt he was a tool in the hands of Mīrā who was herself living in the blue boy of blessed Vṛndāvan.[6]

This incident changed S. V. Aiyer's life and behavior. From then on he imagined that he was a *gopī,* at least in his own house, and he lived in an esctatic condition. His gait, smile, and talk, became "naturally attractive and bewitching." He dressed daily in a cape, put on anklet bells, and went out with a begging bowl to beg for rice. On his deathbed, when he could not move his limbs or speak much, he asked his disciples to write "Rādhākrishna" on his tongue, and when this was done, he felt ecstatic.

S. V. Aiyer came from Tanjore district to Madras for his education. He studied Sanskrit, German, and Latin, among other subjects. In 1900 he was employed as a superintendent in the Accountant General's Office. This was probably the time of the Mīrābāī incident. In 1914 he was transferred to Calcutta for about two years, and after that to Delhi. While in Calcutta, he learned at first hand about the Caitanya movement and drew inspiration from Caitanya's life. Although S. V. Aiyer, too, followed the *bhajana* program of the three Tanjore *gurus,* he was probably responsible for innovations giving greater prominence to Mīrābāī songs and to Caitanya-type *bhajanas.* His son, who is one of his devoted disciples, believes his father took the *bhajana* out of the hands of the professional devotees who conducted it for fees in the homes of the well-to-do. He mixed with the poor, he stayed up late at night, and, above all, he taught that all formalities could be dispensed with in a *bhajana* if the devotees loved Krishna and believed that he was merciful. The son reports that when the father would say to the family, "Let us do some *bhajanas,*" the children would ask, "With what?" The father would then tell them not to depend on externals but to sing the Lord's praises. He would even permit them to keep their shoes on, since he believed that the Lord was so merciful that he would forgive any mistakes the devotees might make.

S. V. Aiyer probably also introduced the type of *bhajana* where men, women, and children all sit together, singing and developing the same ideas.

A third Madras *guru,* Kōthamarāma Aiyer, was a contemporary and "chum" of S. V. Aiyer. He, too, came from Tanjore district. He studied at Madras Christian College, where he received his B.A., and later studied law and took a B.L. degree. He was a lecturer in English at the Arts College of Madura and served as headmaster in several high schools before he was appointed to the post of manager in the Administrator General's Office in Madras city.[7]

Kōthamarāma Aiyer annually visited the Pandharpur shrine for Lord Viṭṭhala in Maharashtra. Once when his superior officer refused to give him leave, he resigned his job and made the pilgrimage anyway. He learned Marathi in order to study the works of the Maharashtrian saints and their songs. He sang these songs in the *bhajanas* that he conducted weekly and on special occasions. In 1921, he built a temple for Lord Viṭṭhala, in Triplicane, a Madras suburb, with a *Bhajana Mandir* (temple), and established a permanent endowment for daily worship in order to fulfill a vow he took when he resigned his position. Before he died in 1934 at the age of 73, this pioneer in the *bhajana* cult published, in Telugu script, the following books for the use of devotees:

1. *Bhajana—Paddhati*
2. Śrī Jayadeva's *Gītagovinda*
3. Śrī Nārāyaṇa Tīrtha's *Krishnalīlā Taraṅgiṇī*
4. Hindūstan *Kīrtana Mālā,* comprising the songs of Mīrābāī, Kabīr, Tulsī Dās, and others
5. *Bhajana—Utsava paddhati* (Rādhā, Rukmiṇī, and Sītā *Kalyāṇams*)
6. *Divyanāma Saṃkīrtana* (singing and dancing of devotees around a lamp)
7. A true translation in Tamil of the Marathi commentary on the *Bhagavad Gītā* (known popularly as *Gñāneśwarī*), by Śrī Gñānadeva.

Another complete collection of *bhajana* songs, also in Telugu script, was published by M. S. Subrahmaṇya Aiyer, a superintendent of the Madras Postal Audit Office, under the title *Nitya Bhajanāvali.* This collection, intended for daily *bhajanas,* contains fifteen sections of twenty-four songs each; one song may be taken from each section, so that there will be no repetition until the twenty-fifth day. M. S. Subrahmaṇya Aiyer knew all the songs by heart, and it was said that if all *bhajana* books were to become extinct, they could be brought out again with his help. He conducted daily *bhajanas* at his house, as well as other types of *bhajanas* wherever he was invited to conduct them. His wife and three daughters would join the chorus of the daily *bhajanas* at home, and they also conducted *bhajanas* when invited to other women's homes. He had two sons, both of whom died in youth.[8]

The *guru*-disciple relationship, according to some students of Hinduism, offers a pure personal and religious relationship that transcends Hindu society and culture. This interpretation seems to me an overstatment, in view of the many formalities, social and cultural, that surround the relationship in India. There is a definite etiquette governing the behavior of *guru* and disciple toward each other, and in the older *Gurukul* system of education this etiquette defined a kind of apprenticeship not only in religious matters but in secular and technical crafts as well. It may, however, be true that the characteristically Indian *guru*-disciple relationship, as a mutual, voluntary relationship between individuals, provides a channel for transmitting and changing cultural traditions that is independent of the channels defined by the hereditary social groupings of family, caste, sect, language, and region. This is in any case an interesting hypothesis to explore in connection with the transmission of the Rādhā-Krishna cult in South India.

The facts we have already adduced concerning this cult give great weight to transmission through chains of *gurus* and disciples. These same facts, however, also show that this mode of transmission is not wholly independent of the social structure, but sometimes follows the grain of that structure and sometimes cuts across the grain. Predominating among the leaders and followers of the cult is a subcaste of Brahmans, the Smārta Brahmans. On the basis of a preliminary estimate, about 55 per cent of *bhajana* participants in Madras city are Smārta Brahmans. Among *bhajana* leaders, the percentage is much higher. In South India, then, the Rādhā-Krishna cult is cultivated by particular social groups. But not all Smārtas are Krishna worshipers, and there are also other Brahman subcastes, the Mādhvas and Śrī Vaiṣṇavas, as well as some non-Brahmans, who belong to the cult. This suggests that in about 45 per cent of the cases the *guru*-disciple relationship may cross subcaste, caste, and sect lines.

If we look at family histories, we find that some families have cultivated the Rādhā-Krishna cult for four to five generations, while in others only one generation has practiced it. Since the father is normally the first *guru* for his children, it is not surprising that the sons should follow the traditions of their fathers. But this continuity is a result more of childhood upbringing and paternal example than it is of creed. Since every individual is free to choose his favorite personal deity (*iṣṭa devatā*), the sons may, and sometimes do, choose deities different from their fathers', as in the case of two sons of the retired actor who took Durgā and Murugan as their favorites. When this happens, the pictures or images of the sons' deities are simply added to the family shrine.

A crisis of choice.—We do not know enough details of the family histories of the three Tanjore *gurus* or of the Madras *gurus* to say in each case how far there was a departure from family traditions. It is likely that each of the individuals introduced innovations that are now publicly recognized. In the family history of one highly respected Krishna devotee whom I know in Madras, there is evidence of profound personal choice and, in theological language, of a "calling," although there does not appear to be any innovation in the family tradition. This devotee, now about sixty-nine, feels that he inherited his love for Krishna from his father, his grandfather, and his great-grandfather, all of whom were great devotees of Krishna, although he received his formal initiation and *sūtram* from an ardent devotee named Rādhā-krishna Bhāgavatār of Ammaṅgudi, who had retired from the railway service. He has passed this love on to his sons. As a child he was brought up by his father—his mother had died when he was four days old—in an atmosphere completely permeated by love of Krishna.[9]

> My father was the first person on whom my eyes were set. He is my spiritual *Guru,* and he has left me and my sons his legacy of extreme and inimitable love for Śrī Krishna.
>
> It is said in *Bhāgavata* that *bhakti,* or devotion to God, should be taught to men and women while they are young—when their minds are most receptive, impressionable, retentive, and fresh. My father believed in this and used it to great advantage while teaching his pupils.

The reality of Krishna was conveyed to the impressionable boy not so much by didactic instruction as by his father's whole-hearted devotion:

> When my father initiated me in my early devotion to Śrī Krishna, there were no formal rites or ceremonies whatever. My *bhakti* just grew as

informally as my early secular education did. My mere constant movement with my father (who was a veritable embodiment of *bhakti*) and his very company at all times inspired in me, without my knowledge, ardent *bhakti* even at my early age, or rather because of my early age. The very air of the house was saturated with love for Śrī Krishna. His divine name was ever in the mouth of my father. When he began to do some work or other, he said that Śrī Krishna would help him to do it. When he was confronted with some trouble or difficulty, he said that Śrī Krishna would help him out of it. Before he took his food, he would offer it to Śrī Krishna. If he was in need of something, he said that Śrī Krishna would enable him to get it. If he planned to do something, he would invoke Śrī Krishna's aid to do it successfully. "Śrī Krishna" was his father's and his grandfather's chosen god, and he got Him for himself by heredity or inheritance. I got Śrī Krishna as patrimony from my father. I inherited Him from my father as I inherited his landed property. When he was tired, he would say, "Śrī Krishna." He gave the name Krishnasvāmī to me so that as often as he called me by name he could remember Śrī Krishna, and he did call me very frequently.

This natural growth of Krishna love was challenged and recovered during a "religious upheaval" experienced in college:

While I was in Madras Christian College for the B.A. Hons. course, a professor taught us Christianity. He eulogized Hinduism for the first six months of the term, and during the remaining three months he undid his work practically, and eulogized Christianity. He made it appear that Hinduism was only a bundle of superstitions. As I was always very earnest about religion, I could not reconcile what he had taught us of Hinduism with what he taught us of Christianity. He had gained my heart and my ears in the first six months by saying things that my heart was after and endeared himself to me. He had gained my trust or confidence and I considered his words as Gospel Truth. He had worked upon my mind very successfully. I could not decide easily what attitude I should take toward the two religions presented to me. I was a youngster and a student. He was an elderly person and my professor. A mental conflict appeared in me. I was comparing the two religions for several days in the light of what the professor said of them in his very beautiful attractive English, fluent and impressive, gripping like that of a wizard. A great religious upheaval took possession of me now, which lasted for days. One day, however, I came across a book of Śrī Rāmakrishna's sayings compiled by Svāmī Abhedānanda that led me to read all the sayings of the saint available, and all the literature concerning Him. This was the first time that I knew of Śrī Rāmakrishna. I had not heard of him before. I read Svāmī Vivekānanda's "My Master" and his other works. I discussed questions with Svāmī Śarvānanda, then the head of Śrī Rāmakrishna Mutt in Madras. He was a man of realization, who was very useful to me at that time. In the Rāmakrishna literature I came across references to and accounts of Lord Gaurāṅga or Saint Śrī Krishna Caitanya of Bengal. I read two or three books on this saint. Śrī Rāmakrishna hailed from Bengal, too. I was given to know Śrī Rāmakrishna was an avatār of Śrī Krishnacaitanya, who was himself an avatār of Śrī Krishna. I picked up the Bengali script with a view to reading the original literature on and of these saints. I read two or three Sanskrit books of this category in the Bengali script. Many were the books that I read at this time. I used the Library of the Theosophical Society, Madras, as well. The result of all this was that I caught hold of Hinduism again and found myself completely deluged by the sweeping flood of Krishna Love which I had had at one time, and which I had lost sight of and grip of for a time. I do not know how this was effected, I mean this revival of Krishna Love in me. It is enough to say that I experienced it in some mysterious way without my knowledge. I was thereafter for some days alive with a new vigor or force of spirituality of the Devotion Type centering round Śrī Krishna and I was absolutely unconscious of everything around me. I muttered the word Śrī Krishna in season and out of season, spoke of Him and sang of Him likewise. I was not aware of sunset and sunrise for a few days and the time of the day. . . . A strong foundation was laid in the spiritual structure of my being and all doubts departed, never more to return in my lifetime. I found solutions now for all the problems of life, of human society in all the countries, of the whole universe, to be brief. I lead an easy life now and my heart and my mind are now carefree. I say to myself and with Śrī Rāmakrishna that the end and aim of life is to see God and I am praying when I can to Śrī Krishna for this. My hairs used to stand on end at the mere mention of the name "Śrī Krishna" and tears of joy would trickle down freely from my eyes. It was indeed the most happy period in my life. It is true that I did not care for the family at that time and I sometimes thought of adopting more severe measures for attaining God-realization forthwith. My father was naturally alarmed. But my fervor abated and I could again attend to the normal duties of life. My father always thought that I was safe in Śrī Krishna's protection and I thought and think so, too. I feel He is lending His helping hand to me at all times. He has helped me in life on several occasions, remaining invisible, of course, and if He becomes visible to me at any time I shall then have reached the goal. I find that *bhajanas* help me a lot in my spiritual aspirations and attend them whenever I can

It is to be regretted that this kind of detail is not available for the life-histories of other devotees, particularly those recognized as leaders of the Rādhā-Krishna cult. When it becomes available, we shall have a great deal more insight into the relative parts played by the *guru*-disciple relationship and by family, caste, and sect membership in the transmission of Krishna worship, and into the scope for individual choice. Several tentative conclusions, however, may be drawn from the fragmentary evidence presented. This evidence suggests that, far from being an independent mode of transmission that transcends the social structure and the culture, the *guru*-disciple relationship operates as the very lifeline of the culture and the social structure. In theory it is a voluntary relationship between two individuals, but these relationships are not found in a vacuum. Each brings to the relationship a background of group affiliations and culturally defined outlooks. When these are shared between *guru* and disciple, there is likely to be continuity in the transmission with the disciple's inherited traditions of family, caste, sect, and so on. When these are not shared, there is likely to be some discontinuity, at least from the individual disciple's point of view. This generalization cannot be made in an unqualified way, since there are different levels of the social structure and of the culture that may or may not be shared. A *guru* with no family relation to the disciple may help bring him back to his family tradition, as Svāmī Śarvānanda seems to have done with Krishnasvāmī. A father, on the other hand, acting as a *guru,* may not succeed in rearing all his children to follow the family cult, as in the case of the retired actor. Whenever discontinuities in the transmission emerge, there is the possibility of innovation and new cult formation. And in this sense the Rādhā-Krishna cult itself may be an innovation among Smārta Brahmans in South India, a possibility I shall discuss later.

The discontinuities and innovations need not create serious problems, since in principle every Hindu is free to choose a favored personal deity of his own. This holds even for Advaitins who do not find the qualityless monistic absolute as emotionally satisfying as a loving personal God with concrete attributes. The degree of deliberate choice exercised by an individual will, however, vary of course with his age and the accidents of his personal history. Children brought up in a family of Krishna worshipers are likely to imbibe the cult without being conscious that they have made a choice, unless their beliefs and practices are later challenged. Adults, on the other hand, may, for reasons not always clear to themselves, suddenly decide to worship a deity outside the usual choice of their family, caste, or region. One of the interesting features of the Rādhā-Krishna cult, perhaps characteristic of

Hinduism, is the latitude that it allows for both kinds of choices—the innovative choice as well as the choice of affirmation. In the *bhajanas* one frequently finds active participants whose personal deities are not only not Krishna but no aspect of Viṣṇu. The *bhajanas* are in this respect like the family shrines—capable of incorporating the diverse personal choices of their participants.

The role of Smārta Brahmans.—The Rādhā-Krishna cult in Madras draws its leadership and massive support from Smārta Brahmans. We have estimated on the basis of the Mylapore figures that about 55 per cent of the contributors and participants in the *bhajanas* are Smārtas. The next largest group are non-Brahmans, who probably account for about 20 per cent of the supporters. The other major Brahman groups in Madras, the Śrī Vaiṣṇavas and Mādhvas, account for about 10 per cent each of all supporters. The Smārta Brahmans' predominance among the leadership of the movement is even more striking. All of the three Tanjore *gurus* were Smārtas, as well as the Madras pioneers, and most of the contemporary leaders.[10] This emergence of a Rādhā-Krishna cult among Smārta Brahmans is perplexing, in view of their reputation and status in South India. As followers of Śaṃkara and Advaita Vedānta, Smārtas have traditionally accepted a monistic, nontheistic theology in which worship of personal deities is considered a sign of spiritual immaturity. Insofar as worship of a particular deity has been associated with Śaṃkara's name, it has been Śiva, and not Viṣṇu and his manifestations. In theory, Smārtas say they worship five (or six) deities impartially—Śiva, Viṣṇu, Devī, Gaṇeśa, Sūrya (and Subrahmaṇya). Smārtas also have a reputation for being orthodox in following the traditional (*smṛti*) rules of ritual observance and in cultivating Sanskrit learning in all its branches. Their approach to religion has been intellectual and scholastic, rather than the popular, emotional approach of Krishna *bhakti,* which some of them feel to be intended for Śūdras, women, poor people, and other groups excluded from the "high-church" approach. In Madras today, there are Smārtas who look upon the Rādhā-Krishna movement as "too emotional" and who may even refer to it as an "aberration," but there is no doubt that the movement is popular among a large segment of the Smārta Brahman group and draws its main support and leadership from them. This is not the case in other parts of India, where the Rādhā-Krishna cult is supported by Vaiṣṇavas and by non-Brahmans.

When I posed this problem to Madrassis, I received a variety of replies. Two of the most frequent were that Smārta Brahmans take the lead in organizing religious and cultural functions generally and that they worship the five deities. The former is a restatement of the fact needing explanation, and the latter states a permissive condition; it does not explain why they should cultivate a Vaiṣṇavite tradition. One Śrī Vaiṣṇava Brahman, who is himself a leading Rādhā-Krishna devotee, suggested that Smārtas have taken the active lead in Rādhā-Krishna *bhajanas* because they are new to them, whereas they are an old tradition among Śrī Vaiṣṇavas. This is an interesting suggestion; it does not, however, take account of the fact that Vaiṣṇava *bhajanas,* in Madras at least, are part of the temple service; they are not held in private houses, nor are they generally multilingual and attended by diverse sects. They are confined to the singing of songs, some about Rādhā and Krishna, from the canon of Tamil Vaiṣṇavite saints.

The special role of Smārta Brahmans in the development of a Rādhā-Krishna cult is probably to be explained by a number of other considerations. One might argue that, because Smārtas have been so closely identified with orthodox ritual observances and with Sanskrit learning, they have felt the need to develop Krishna *bhakti* as an "easier path to salvation," since their middle-class and professional occupations, their Westernized education, and their increasing secularism have made the older and more difficult paths less accessible to them. Advaita Vedānta would not stand in their way if they wished to embrace Krishna worship, since for an Advaitin such worship may be as good a steppingstone to self-realization in the Absolute as any other mode of worship. And there is also in Advaita a kind of built-in dialectic to transcend sectarianism of any kind, which disposes Advaitins to favor intersect, if not antisect, movements. The head of the Śaṃkara *maṭh* at Kāñcī, who is one of the leading spiritual authorities for Advaitins in South India and who personally does not regard Krishna worship as a very orthodox form of Hinduism, nevertheless supports the *bhajanas* and urges joint public performances of Śaivite and Vaiṣṇavite prayers and songs. He has also lent his support to the organization of an association of the heads of *maṭhs* of all sects in the South to represent the interests of the *maṭhs* against legislative restriction.

No doubt some of these interfaith activities are a common defensive measure against the trend of increasingly secular legislation and, particularly in Madras State, against the outspoken and sometimes violent anti-Brahman, anti-Hindu attacks sponsored by two regional political parties, the Dravidian Federation and the Dravidian Progressive Federation. It is the Smārta Brahmans, however, who have been the first to see these trends as a danger to Hinduism and to respond by joining and organizing movements that cross sect, and even caste, lines. Although the predominance of Smārta Brahmans in the Rādhā-Krishna cult associates that cult with one particular subcaste, the ideology and traditional theology of that subcaste predispose it to play an ecumenical and even cosmopolitan role in guiding the responses of contemporary Hinduism to the challenges of modernization and secularization, and to the divisiveness stemming from caste, sect, and regional differentiation.

This kind of role is not one which the Smārta Brahmans have just assumed in the last generation or so. In South India, the role is a historic one for them. When their leader and codifier Śaṃkara led a Hindu restoration against the Buddhists in the eighth and ninth centuries, he tried to build an all-India Hinduism that could rise above the doctrines and practices of any particular group or region. This founding pattern has been confirmed through the vicissitudes of later South Indian history. Although the Vijayanagar emperors, the Nayaks of Tanjore, and the Mahratta rājas of Tanjore were by personal religious persuasion Vaiṣṇavites, they generally adopted religious policies that extended toleration (and sometimes temples and village grants) to Śaivites, Smārtas, Jains, Muslims, and Christians. Histories of these dynasties suggest that outstanding Smārtas and Advaitin scholars influenced these policies: Madhvācārya under the Vijayanagar, Appayya Dīkṣita and Govind Dīkṣita under the Tanjore Nāyaks, and a large number of Advaita Ācāryas under the Mahratta rājas of Tanjore.[11] One of the three Tanjore *gurus* who codified the Rādhā-Krishna *bhajanas,* Śrīdhara Veṅkaṭeśa, came from a village in Tanjore that had been given to forty-six paṇḍits of his court by Shāhjī. This village became a seat for scholarly study of language, literature, philosophy, and medicine as well as religion.

Since these three dynasties that ruled over the Tamil country were all foreign to that region, they brought into the culture of the area languages and literature and religious, musical, and other forms that combined with the local forms to produce a cosmopolitan Tanjore culture, from which the multilingual Rādhā-Krishna *bhajanas* are one striking development. Smārta Brahmans, by virtue of their special traditions, were qualified to make a unique contribution to this culture. The uniqueness of the contribution consists not only in the many excellent literary, linguistic, philosophical, musical, and other works produced by Smārta Brahmans, but especially in the capacity to build ever new syntheses from the cultural currents flowing into the South. Some of these syntheses—the Rādhā-Krishna cult is undoubtedly one—have resulted in transformations of Smārta traditions, changing a preference for Śiva to devotion to Krishna, and perhaps, too, upgrading devotional Hinduism generally relative to intellectual and ritualistic Hinduism.

The critical role of the Smārta Brahmans in the transmission of the Rādhā-Krishna cult has thus involved them both as a group and as individuals in the making of innovative choices that have changed their own traditions in some respects. That they are also involved in making choices reaffirming other aspects of their tradition makes it easier for them to accept the changes.

IV. Meaning and Function of the Rādhā-Krishna Bhajanas

The preceding discussion of the role of the Smārta Brahmans in the leadership of the Rādhā-Krishna cult suggests that the *bhajanas* may be performing two kinds of functions: (1) providing an easier path to salvation in an age when the paths of strict ritual observances, religious knowledge, and ascetic withdrawal have become difficult or inaccessible, and (2) reducing the consciousness of caste, sect, and regional differences and the tensions generated by this consciousness. I should now like to examine the evidence for these interpretations of the *bhajanas*.

The range of relevant evidence is very broad and the varieties of it rather complex: There is the observed behavior at the *bhajana,* programed and unprogramed; the explanation of this behavior by participants; the speeches of leaders on the meaning and functions of *bhajanas;* observed behavior of participants outside the *bhajanas;* the life histories of participants; the *bhajana* songs; the history of the *bhajana* tradition and its relation to *bhakti* movements; the social organization and transmission of these movements; and the philosophy and theology of the *bhajanas* expounded by the texts and leaders recognized by the participants. In interpreting the function and meaning of the Rādhā-Krishna *bhajanas,* I shall try to take account of the full range of evidence.

From the point of view of the Smārta Brahmans, accentuation of differences between castes, sects, and linguistic regions is disruptive and generative of harmful tensions. Whatever reduces consciousness of these differences will therefore, in their opinion, have a socially integrative effect. The Rādhā-Krishna *bhajanas* are viewed by some of their leaders as moderating the tension-producing differences. Many features of the *bhajanas* contribute to this function. Linguistic regionalism, for example, is bypassed by the use of songs in various languages composed by saints from different regions of India or sung in praise of such saints. On special occasions *bhajana* groups from Maharashtra and other parts of India are invited to Madras to participate in the local *bhajana* programs. Caste differences are minimized by inviting non-Brahmans to *bhajanas,* by feeding the poor and even untouchables on the occasion of the marriage *bhajanas,* and by the salutations and prostrations of the devotees to one another irrespective of caste. Many participants say that "there is no caste in the world of devotion" and that they "forget their caste differences in the *bhajana.*" By holding the *bhajanas* in private homes or public halls rather than in temples, sectarian differences are also muted.

To those who know the history of the religious devotional (*bhakti*) movements of medieval India, the antiparochial, anticaste, and antisect features of the *bhajanas* will sound familiar. It would be an incomplete interpretation, however, to say that the Rādhā-Krishna *bhajanas* of Madras City are merely survivals of an old tradition. In contemporary Madras specific trends are at work that give the *bhajana* movement a special significance. There is, for example, an intense pro-

Tamil, pro-Dravidian agitation that is aggressively opposed to the use of Sanskrit and Telugu, two languages associated with Brahman cultural hegemony in Madras State. This agitation is also directed against the Brahmans as an alien Āryan priesthood from the North, which was supposed to have foisted "superstitious" religious practices and beliefs on the South for its own private gain. In this particular context, the multilingual, multicaste, and multisect *bhajana* may be seen as a defensive effort to unify those very groups that the pro-Dravidian movement tends to divide: Tamil and non-Tamil; Brahman and non-Brahman, Śaivite, Vaiṣṇavite, and all "believers" in Hinduism. In this respect, the integrative functions of the *bhajanas* are related to developments in Madras City and State that are only about fifty years old.

Consistent with the integrative function, but perhaps independent of it, the *bhajanas* may also be seen as providing forms of sociability and intimacy in an urban setting that transcend kin, caste, sect, and region. Although each local *bhajana* group usually begins with a family household, it quickly expands to include neighbors and friends from office and shop who are not kin and who may even come from a different caste, sect, or linguistic region. Newcomers to *bhajana* groups are usually brought into them by neighbors or by professional colleagues. The weekly *bhajana* remains essentially a neighborhood group, the monthly *bhajana* overflows neighborhood lines, and the annual *bhajana* festival draws crowds from all parts of the city. Thus, *bhajanas* in a large city may perform functions quite different from those they may have performed in villages and small towns. For an urban population that is still village-conscious and many of whose members return to their natal villages for family ceremonies about once a year, the pastoral themes and activities of the Rādhā-Krishna stories must add a village flavor to city life. This flavor is not, of course, otherwise missing from the city, for many city people keep cows and buffaloes, and there are streets of houses in parts of the city that might have been directly transplanted from nearby villages.

An American observer of the Rādhā-Krishna *bhajana* is apt to interpret the informal sociability and friendly atmosphere, the mixing of castes and sects, the mutual embracing and prostrations, as expressing a democratic spirit of equality. He may even find some *bhajana* participants, especially among the younger members, who will so interpret these features of the *bhajana* to foreigners. As he talks with more participants and learns more about the *bhajanas* and their history and philosophy, however, he will soon discover that to interpret the *bhajana* in terms of democratic ideology can be very misleading. One *bhajana* leader and respected devotee, for example, emphatically disclaims any political implications of the *bhajana.* He is opposed to the Congress government and particularly to its democratic egalitarian tendencies. The best form of government, in his opinion, is a benevolent monarchy based on an aristocracy of talent and wisdom, as were the monarchies of Aśoka and the British Rāj. Another leader of the same *bhajana* group is an active Congress worker, and he sees democratizing effects in the *bhajana.* These effects consist, for him, in the improvements of non-Brahman speech, attitudes, and behavior that come from association with Brahmans. The sociability of *bhajanas* may appear to be more "democratic" than meetings segregated by caste or sect; yet a full analysis of this sociability points to sources that have little to do with democratic ideology and more to do with *noblesse oblige,* the need for friends in a big city, the need to find a substitute for strict ritual observances, the prestige of opening one's house for religious meetings, and so on. Similar observations apply to other apparently "democratic" features of the *bhajanas,* such as feeding the poor, mutual prostration, the use of songs from different regions, and so forth. When one looks at them closely, they do not turn out to be very "democratic," or at least they are not so interpreted by the participants. The feeding of the devotees and of the poor is regarded by many participants as a ritual requirement of a *bhajana,* without which it would be incomplete and inefficacious. The mutual prostrations are commonly interpreted by participants as expressions of humility and of respect to the element of divinity present in other devotees. "They do not prostrate to one another but to the Lord Krishna who is between them."

These problems of conflicting interpretations of the *bhajanas*—which include conflicting opinions among participants, as well as differences of interpretation between participants and nonparticipants—can be resolved, I believe, by widening the range of evidence and the frame of interpretation. The problem will not be solved so long as we restrict ourselves to individual items of observed behavior at the *bhajanas* and to explanation of these items offered by this or that participant. We must in addition view the *bhajanas* as cultural performances designed to bring religious merit to the participants in them. From this point of view, the activities of the *bhajana* are rites that find their sanctions in scriptural texts and their interpretations in a theology and philosophy based on these texts. To interpret the meaning of the observed behavior at the *bhajanas* and to assess the opinions of participants about this behavior, it becomes necessary to relate behavior and opinion to rite and text and to the philosophy expressed in them. Some of this philosophy is contained in the *bhajana* songs—those, for example, that tell the devotee not to be ashamed to sing names of the Lord with other devotees as a means of acquiring merit. Such songs are themselves taken as scriptural texts sanctioning *bhajana* recitation and singing. Most of the songs, however, are ritual texts, which happen also to express invocations, supplications, and many other forms of devotion to Krishna, Rāma, and other deities. The more comprehensive philosophy and theology of the Rādhā-Krishna *bhajana* is formulated in other scriptural texts, in commentaries on these, and in the writings and sayings of leading devotees. T. K. Veṅkaṭeśwaran has made a preliminary study of these texts from the point of view of nondualist theology (Advaita Vedānta) and Krishna devotion (*bhakti*).[12] It is clear from his study that such observed features of the *bhajana* as informal sociability, mutual prostration, singing, dancing, eating together, the use of songs in different languages all have specific scriptural sources and sanctions and may be interpreted in terms of theological doctrines of "calling," "surrender," the presence of divinity in all things, and so on.

According to his account, the behavior of the devotees in embracing each other, taking the dust from one another's feet, and making mutual prostrations is sanctioned by references to instances of similar behavior in the *Bhāgavata Purāṇa* and in other Purāṇas cited in a treatise on *bhajanas* by the devotee Sadgurusvāmī. A stanza from the *Bhāgavata* is quoted in this treatise: "By ignoring those who belong to oneself, those that mock at oneself, by giving up the sense of bodily conceit and shame, one [the devotee] should offer prostrations [even] to the horse, the outcaste, the cow, and the donkey."

The theological implication here is that the devotee should recognize and see God in all things, although "the presence of God in men has a clearer [and] more significant dimension."

Following Sadgurusvāmī, Veṅkaṭeśwaran also points out that these salutations are a reversal of the Vedic observance, at least for Brahmans, in which such salutations are offered only to an older person by a younger person with an appropriate formalized recitation of one's *pravara, gotra, sūtra,* and *veda.*

This reversal in salutation has not led, however, to a reversal in other behavior. The new salutation has itself become formalized and restricted to the appropriate phase of a *bhajana* performance. One elderly and distinguished devotee explained that although it would not be becoming for him to prostrate himself before a younger devotee, he does prostrate himself before the devotees as a group. On one occasion this devotee met a *bhajana* group coming toward him and prostrated himself before it. This group turned out to include his own son.

While the behavior at the *bhajana* tends to become formalized and ritualized, it is not without significance for behavior and social relations outside the *bhajana* context. A lucid and penetrating explanation of what this significance may be was given by devotee K.:

> The relation between devotees as one of complete equality is only their *ideal.* They wish to make it a matter of fact and a reality. But, at the same time, it does not replace the traditional respect of sons for fathers, of young for old, of the less devout for the more devout, of the lower castes for the higher castes, and so forth. Devotees fall at each other's feet and take the dust of the feet of each other and place it on their heads, embrace each other, and do other such things. It needs *constant* practice of these things so that they may become perfect equals. In actual life, the equality has not yet been achieved or realized. It is only the *ideal* and devotees wish to reach this ideal sooner or later. It has not yet come, as I have said before. Fathers do think that they are superior to their sons, the elders do think that they are superior to youngsters, the more devout do think that they are superior to the less devout, the high-caste devotee thinks that he is superior to the low-caste devotee, and so forth. Thus they *think* one way and *do* another way when they exhibit equality or express democratic sentiments. There is no correlation between their *mind* and *body.* They do not act alike. They think one thing and do another thing. When by constant practice, their minds imbibe equality as their bodies express it, the ideal is reached by the harmony between the mind and the body. The two then act alike and there is correlation between them. Till then there is no talk of complete equality as the

body expresses equality and the mind does not. What the body expresses is thus only a gesture of the ideal to be attained and *constant* gesture of this kind will bring about the ideal in its own good time. The body expressing equality and the mind expressing inequality produce insincerity in a person, a great sin in a devotee.

This explanation is particularly valuable for its suggestion that the *bhajana* is a kind of acting out in dramatic form and bodily gestures of an ideal, for the purpose of evoking in men's minds the sentiments and attitudes that may eventually bring their behavior closer to the ideal.

There are indeed *bhajana* participants who report that the *bhajana* evokes such sentiments in them. Even non-Brahman participants testified that at the moment of the *bhajana* they felt that "all are equal in the midst of God." They also added, a little sadly, that this feeling did not last. A few reported more continuity in their states of mind and seemed to have acquired reputations for being "true devotees throughout life." Such reputations do not require complete withdrawal from the world, for most devotees are "householders" who carry on their mundane responsibilities. I found this to be true even of the most withdrawn and mystical of the Krishna devotees. One of these said he was aware of the power of *bhajanas* to reduce caste differences and bring about other social effects, just as he was aware of the power of a candle flame to burn one's finger, but he was "not enamored of this power." Yet this same devotee insisted that Rādhā-Krishna devotees were especially conscientious and efficient in their daily work, since they did not want to give critics any grounds for saying that *bhajanas* distracted people from work. There is also evidence of direct carry-over of behavior and attitude from *bhajanas* in the reports of devotees who appeal to and are helped by other devotees in matters of jobs, loans, and other needs.

The salutations and prostrations as items of observed behavior at *bhajanas* are thus related to an ideal of equality but not in a direct and obvious way. The relationship has been discovered by tracing the links between the behavior and the scriptural texts whose sanctions convert the behavior into symbolic and ritual acts. The meaning of these acts in the ritual context is explained by the theological and philosophical doctrines associated with the particular cult. The meaning of the acts for the non-ritual everyday context will be found through analysis of the testimony of observant and thoughtful participants who are also familiar with the theological meaning. This method of determining the "meaning" of *bhajanas* can be applied to other items of observed *bhajana* behavior. I propose now to apply it to determine the meaning of the behavior that is so central to the monthly type of *bhajana,* namely, the singing and dancing of the devotees about the lamp. This behavior is more complex than the salutations and prostrations, since it consists not of discrete single acts but of a connected sequence of acts that tell a story, the story of the milkmaids' (*gopīs'*) infatuation with Krishna, of Krishna's "sporting" with them in the woods, of his separation from them, and of their final reunion. This story provides a kind of "script" and "choreography" for the singing, dancing, and dramatization of this type of *bhajana.* The general principle of interpretation, nevertheless, remains valid.

Just as the Western observer is apt to interpret equalitarian features of a *bhajana* directly in terms of democratic ideology, so he tends to interpret the singing and dancing in terms of the emotional and orgiastic tendencies of Western religious cults. The devotional *bhakti* movements in Hinduism are in a sense more "emotional" than the paths of ritual and knowledge, and occasionally lead to ecstatic behavior. But they are not governed by uncontrolled and irrational emotions. The path of devotion is also a discipline, a *yoga,* subject to well-understood rules and based on a "rational" philosophy. This philosophy assumes that the emotions expressive of certain human relations—for example, servant to master, child to parent, friend to friend, lover to beloved—are appropriate ways to express a devotee's attitude of devotion to a deity. A devotee is free to choose the kind of relationship he will assume toward a deity, being guided by the example of famous devotees who have gone before him. Once he has chosen a particular relationship, the devotee will discipline his emotions and actions to accord with the requirements of the relationship. He will act out the role as sincerely and as well as he can in the hope of evoking a reciprocal response from the deity.

An additional aspect of this philosophy prescribes the singing of divine names and devotional songs, the reciting of scriptures, and the joining with other devotees in song and dance as the best means of expressing devotion and gaining salvation.

Much of what happens at the Rādhā-Krishna *bhajana* can be explained by reference to this philosophy of devotion.

The story of Krishna and the *gopīs,* or at least major episodes from it, is well known to the participants, from the *Bhāgavata Purāṇa* and other scriptural texts. Many of the songs they sing are based on these texts and provide the built-in scriptural sanction for the action at the *bhajanas*. Some of these songs, as well as the Purāṇic texts, also attribute a theological meaning to the story, that is, the *gopīs* represent the human soul in search of salvation; because their love for Krishna is so constant and intense, it is transformed into a spiritual and blissful devotion to a transcendent deity; the circular dance in which Krishna has multiplied himself to dance between every two *gopīs* symbolizes how devotees are related to one another through their relation to God, and so on.[13]

If some of the *bhajana* actions are a ritual dramatizing of episodes from the Krishna story that have a transcendental theological meaning, it remains to be explained why groups of male devotees in Madras City should choose this medium to express their devotion. The answer to this question requires testimony from individual devotees and information about their individual and family histories, as well as reference to the philosophy of devotion. Since the *gopīs* represent any human soul, any devotee is free to identify with them. In Vaiṣṇavite doctrine, at least, there is also the belief that all souls are female and that Viṣṇu is the only male. Then there is the psychological tendency of devotees to look for concrete and successful models of devotion to imitate. In Vaiṣṇavite theology such models may even be necessary as intermediaries.[14]

Beyond these general considerations, the *gopīs'* love for Krishna occupies a unique position as a model of devotion because of its extraordinary intensity and constancy. Through this intensity and constancy what begins as carnal love becomes transmuted into a "holy" and "spotless" love because it is bestowed on a god. Indeed, according to the philosophy of devotion, any emotion—hate, anger, fear—if directed *constantly* toward a god will lead to salvation, although love is the most "fruitful" emotion. This would not be true if love or the other emotions were directed to mortals, because these relations are not permanent and because unpleasant emotions would provoke unpleasant reactions. But God, being eternal, is quite indifferent to the kind of emotion shown. The *gopīs'* love for Krishna is so intense, the most intense possible kind of love and devotion, because it is a kind of lawless love, the love of married women for their lovers. The conclusion of this line of reasoning is logical enough: If the devotees persist in their imitation of the *gopīs'* love for Krishna and that of his favorite, Rādhā, their own devotion too will become as intense and effective as that of the milkmaids, and they will be rewarded by the physical presence of Krishna and by the blessedness that the *gopīs* achieved. This is not an easy attainment, especially for male devotees, but it can, with constant practice and discipline, be achieved, at least so the devotees believe.

This explanation for identifying with the *gopīs* applies to devotees whose personal deity is already Krishna as well as to those who have chosen other deities. The following statement from devotee K., already devoted to Krishna, restates the general theory and makes the application to *bhajana* behavior:

> The love of a woman for her husband or for her lover is very much more intense than any other sort of love in the world, and I mentioned the *gopīs,* Rādhā, Rukmiṇī, Satyabhāmā, and so forth, as instances in point. Their love was indeed transcendent. Even when the husband or the lover is a man, the woman's love for him is of a very high order and when the Lord Supreme is the husband or the lover of a woman, you can find no other love excelling or surpassing this love. The ladies mentioned above can therefore be said to be the most blessed in the world. If we concede this, we can ourselves aspire for this kind of supreme love for God. We can imagine ourselves to be these women or at any rate ordinary women, imagine that the Lord is our husband or lover and bestow the maximum love on Him. *Whatever we think intensely, we become that soon.* Mind makes the man. Think constantly that you are a sinner and you are that. Think that you are virtuous and you are virtuous. Think constantly that you are a woman and that God is your husband or lover, then you will be a woman and God will be your husband or lover. It is for this purpose that in *bhajanas* a lamp is lit up and placed in a central place and that spiritual aspirants go round and round it singing the Lord's glories. The Lord is invoked to be present in the lamp and the spiritual aspirants imagine themselves to be *gopīs* playing with Śrī Krishna. You know the philosophy here that all men and women in the world are spiritually women, and the Lord alone is male—the Puruṣa. The love of the *gopīs,* Rādhā, Rukmiṇī and Satyabhāmā explains the principle of the human soul being drawn to the Supreme Soul and getting merged in It. Likewise Sītā represents the human soul, and Rāma the Su-

preme Soul; Pārvatī the human soul and Śiva the Supreme Soul; Vaḷḷi or Deva-senā the human soul and Subrahmaṇya the Supreme Soul

In the opinion of this devotee, an awareness of the theological meaning of the *gopī* story or an imitation of the *gopīs'* external behavior will not automatically lead to attainment of the blessed state. What are required are a love for Krishna as deep and constant as theirs, a renunciation as great as theirs, and, perhaps, Krishna's grace. *Bhajanas* may stimulate a sense of these, but they do not assure them; they dramatize the ideal to be attained in gesture and behavior.

The great intensity of the *gopīs'* love for Krishna, according to devotee K., comes from its being the love of a woman for her lover. This kind of love is even more intense than the love of a woman for her husband, because it is not subject to the discipline, respect, and obedience of wifely love. It is a love among equals which is

bound to be more intense and more sweeping than love between a superior and an inferior. Fear, respect, sense of inequality, absence of liberty, . . . are all distracting factors in the intensity of love.

The *gopīs* had their own husbands, but they chose to transfer their love to Śrī Krishna, who they thought was their lover. They were captivated and charmed by His entrancing and fascinating beauty of form and by his bewitching personality. Their love was infinitely more intense than the love of Rukmiṇī, Satyabhāmā and the other wives of Śrī Krishna for Him. The love of the *gopīs* for Śrī Krishna was wild and dashing like the storm or the gale and it swept everything before it. It was like the "wild west wind" described by poets and it knew no check or restraint. The *gopīs* forgot themselves absolutely. They forgot their own bodies, their dress, their homes, their people (husbands, sons and daughters, parents-in-law, and so forth), and forgot the time when they met Śrī Krishna. They were not aware how the time was gliding and were quite unconscious of their surroundings and of what happened to themselves. They had given up everything for Him. In this respect, they were like the holy saṃnyāsīs, or ascetics; like Buddha, for example, who had given up his kingdom, wife, son, father, mother, friends and so forth for the sake of Truth. They were like the great, ancient Ṛṣis of India who had sacrificed all their earthly pleasures and possessions for seeing God and remaining with Him for all time. The love of the *gopīs* for Śrī Krishna was carnal. It was lust. But Śrī Krishna transmuted it completely into holy and spotless love for God, for He was God and they were mortals and His grace enabled them to rise to immortality in the least possible time or interval. The *gopīs* thus cast off their mortal nature and become Divine in nature by mixing with the Divine Śrī Krishna.

For men to identify themselves with the *gopīs* and their "wild love" is "rather difficult." But "if a man can do it, by dint of constant practice of his thoughts, infinite gain is the result, in his spiritual aspiration and practice." "Persistence is the most vital thing needed—constancy of emotion or attitude toward God. If this is present, the quality and content of the emotional feeling do not matter if you want slow realization of God and do matter if you want quick realization, easy, pleasant and so forth."

Although the quality of emotions expressed by a devotee may not matter, the object does matter: "A male devotee should on no account pose himself as a lover or husband of a female manifestation of the Lord, for example, Durgā or Lakṣmī or Sarasvatī or Rādhā. Such love is completely ruled out. It is prohibited and is considered as the worst sin in life." A male devotee

> imagining the Goddess to be his Consort and loving and worshiping Her as such is certainly ruled out. He may worship Her and love Her in any other relationship and praise Her. This is not ruled out. A devotee must never imagine a Goddess to be his Consort, spouse, wife or lady-love. He may imagine Her to be anything else for him. . . . So, it follows that the praise of Pārvatī, Durgā, Lakṣmī, Rādhā and so forth is *not at all* ruled out in Bhajana. . . . A goddess can be imagined to be his mother, sister, child, or friend but should never be imagined to be his wife or consort. . . . A devotee may also imagine himself to be a servant of a goddess

Female devotees find it easier to identify with the *gopīs,* although in contemporary Madras women are not generally active in Rādhā-Krishna *bhajanas.* There are, however, famous women devotees who imagined themselves lovers of Krishna. Two of these are Mīrābāī, from the province of Rajasthan, and Āṇḍāḷ, from Tamilnad. Each literally believed she was Rādhā and the consort of Krishna, and wrote many moving hymns expressing her devotion. Some of these are sung in the Rādhā-Krishna *bhajanas.* There is a Tamil collection of Āṇḍāḷ's hymns known as *Tiruppāvai.*

There were also a man and wife, Harnāth and Kusuma-Kumārī, both of whom imagined themselves to be Rādhā and worshiped Krishna. They are now themselves worshiped as saints.

Famous male saints who imagined themselves female lovers of Krishna are also numerous. In addition to Caitanya and Rāmakrishna, there is the great Vaiṣṇava teacher Vedānta Deśika in the South, who described his experiences in a drama, *Acyuta Śataka*. In the South there is a festival every year for this saint. On the fifth day of the festival his image is dressed as a woman (*mohinī*) and taken in procession facing the idol of Krishna, and both are worshiped that day by devotees who are husband and wife. In the Tamil Śaivite tradition, the saint Māṇikka Vāssagar imagined himself and other devotees as women, with Śiva as their lover. His devotional songs are still well known—in a collection called *Tiruvembāvai*.

The most detailed description we have of the use of *gopī* love as a means of reaching Krishna is that given in the biography of the modern Bengali saint, Śrī Rāmakrishna, compiled by one of his disciples.[15] Even as a child Rāmakrishna liked to act the parts of women characters—such as Rādhā and her companions. Putting on a woman's dress and ornaments, he would take on the gestures, voice, and movements of a woman. "The village women would say that nobody could recognize him then. . . . With his love of fun, he would often pass in that disguise in front of men, with a pitcher under his arm, to fetch water from the Haldar-pukur; and no one would ever suspect that he was not a woman!" (p. 63).

In his adolescence, "knowing that the *gopīs* of Vraja had Krishna, the embodiment of pure Existence-Knowledge-Bliss, as their spirtual husband through love, because they were born as women, he used to think that he too would have been blessed to love and have Krishna as husband, had he been born in a female form" (p. 239). On these occasions he imagined he had become a child-widow with long hair, living simply on coarse food, spinning yarn, singing songs about Krishna, and weeping for him to come (p. 239).

As an adult, Rāmakrishna undertook a systematic discipline of devotion as a woman to Krishna. In Bengali Vaiṣṇavism this is classified as "the Sweet Mood" (*Madhura Bhāva*), one of the several devotional moods which a devotee may assume toward a deity. For about six months Rāmakrishna wore women's clothes and ornaments (sari, gauze scarf, bodice, artificial hair) and mimicked the movements, speech, smile, glance, and gestures of women. Some of the women he knew "were so much charmed by his womanly deportment and by his genuine care and affection for them that they regarded him as one of themselves and could not at all maintain their bearing of bashfulness, hesitation, etc., in his presence" (p. 234). He prayed, longed, and wept for Krishna, and under the sense of separation from Krishna "drops of blood oozed out then . . . from every pore of his body." "All the joints of the body seemed slackened or almost dislocated, the senses completely desisted from functioning and the body lay motionless and unconscious sometimes like that of a dead man—all because of the extreme anguish of the heart" (p. 235). Believing that he could not attain the vision of Krishna without Rādhā's grace, Rāmakrishna identified with her. "He was very soon blessed with the vision of the holy form of Rādhā, devoid of the slightest tinge of lust. He now saw that this form also disappeared into his own body like the forms of other deities when he had had their visions" (p. 237). Through his constant feeling of identification with Rādhā, he believed his love for Krishna became as profound as hers. "He became so much absorbed in the constant thought of himself as a woman that he could not look upon himself as one of the other sex even in a dream" (p. 238). In this way he attained a vision of Krishna, and the form of the vision united with his own person. "We have heard from the Master himself that at that time he lost himself completely in the thought of Krishna and sometimes regarded himself as Krishna and all beings, from Brahmā down to a blade of grass, as forms of Krishna. When we were frequenting Dakshineswar and were in his company, one day he plucked a flower of grass, came to us with his face beaming with delight and said, 'The complexion of Śrī Krishna I used to see then (at the time of practising the Madhura Bhāva) was like this'" (p. 239).

None of the devotees participating in the Madras Rādhā-Krishna *bhajanas* has reported attaining similar visions of Rādhā or of Krishna as a result of *bhajana* participation, although many have been influenced by Rāmakrishna and his movement. Devotee K., however, reports that as a youth he did see Krishna once, but has since lost sight of him. He hopes to recover this vision as the *gopīs* did after Krishna disappeared from their midst. In the meantime his participation in *bhajanas* gives him a sense of "infinite joy" and a "seeming" presence of Krishna. What he aims at is an ascetic's life, but he will probably remain a householder and be content with its small gains.

Commenting on his desire to see Krishna in the concrete form in which he stood before the *gopīs* as described in the *Bhāgavata Purāṇa,* this devotee says he does not see Krishna now, although he has "a very vivid sense of His presence." He "longs to see Him again as the *gopīs* did." And he compares his loss with that of the *gopīs:*

> Even the *gopīs* lost sight of Him for a *short* while, but He appeared before them again very soon and they felt blessed. It occurred on a bright new-moon night in autumn in the most pleasant groves of Vṛndāvan on the banks of the holy Jumnā, near the town of Muttrā and the village of Gokul, at some distance from Delhi.

There is no doubt that at least for this devotee the enactment of the *gopī* episode in the *bhajana* has a deep personal meaning:

> It is a long, *long* while, a very long while indeed since I lost sight of Him in 1918. It is now 1960. He has not yet appeared before me again, because I am not able to think of Him and of His sweet attributes constantly, even without a moment's break. The *gopīs* actually shed tears of grief at His separation and cried out aloud with extreme love for Him. This pleased Him to give them again His company. I am not able to do so. They had renounced everything in the world for Him. I am not able to do so. One can see Him if one loves Him in the extreme, i.e., if one loves Him only and none other and nothing else. I am not able to do so. The renunciation of the *gopīs* is greater than that of any other person in the past, present, and future. It is an *ideal* to be reached by men and women.
>
> I long to reach this ideal and I long to have their deep love for Śrī Krishna. I should love Him as *well* as they did. I am not able to do so. Till I do so actually, therefore, I cannot *see* Him and the moment I do so I can *see* Him.

During the *bhajanas,* this devotee says his mind is "deeply engrossed with the attributes of Krishna" and that he "seems to see Him . . . and to enjoy His company." But when the *bhajana* is over, his mind is centered on other things "like money straits at home, duties to the family members, things that I should do for them and which I have not yet done, and so on, which may cast a gloom over my mind. . . . I feel infinite joy while attending a *bhajana,* and there is this joy in me all the time that I sense continuously a great happiness." This kind of vision, he admits, is not the same kind as that which the *gopīs* had or that which Rāmakrishna had. That vision lasts forever, "without a second's break," when the devotee sees the deity "as vividly and as actually or truly as I see you or as you see me or as you and I see others in the world today." However, Krishna appears to him in dreams sometimes, "but it is not often enough." He also believes that Krishna sometimes shows his favor to one unasked, and that he may do so in his case, "but one cannot count on it for a certainty in one's life." Meanwhile he feels that he has to make himself fit to receive His grace. "This is my life at present. There is the desire in me now for God realization. It should grow from strength to strength. My love for Him must increase to a very, very great extent for me to attain the goal in life and I feel His hand in it."

This ideal toward which he aims is the life of an ascetic and not of a householder, he believes, but he wishes to practice as much of it as he can as a householder.

> Whatever is gained is a gain, however small it may be. I am now 66 years old and it is now time for me to achieve the maximum I could, of spiritual attainment. One must accomplish something at least in one's life before he dies, and death may overtake one at any moment. I think of Dr. Johnson's bewailing in the church on his birthday. He said, "One more year of my life is gone to-day, O Lord! and I have not done anything worth my while in learning to love You." I feel like him and wish to do something worth while spiritually, at least as much as is possible.

It is clear from this Krishna devotee's life history that the story of Krishna and the *gopīs* is taken as a parable of the individual's spiritual odyssey. What happens to the *gopīs* happens to any individual in search of salvation. The *gopīs'* love explains "the principle of the human soul being drawn to the Supreme soul." So deeply ingrained is this identification with the *gopīs* in the minds of some devotees that when I asked devotee K. in a private conversation how the devotees' love for Krishna leads to mutual love among the devotees in the *bhajana,* he replied by spontaneously describing three different incidents from the *Bhāgavata Purāṇa* in which the *gopīs* discover each other's love for Krishna, come to share that love with one another, and so develop a mutual love. He did not think it necessary to mention that something similar takes place with contemporary devotees as they imitate the *gopīs*. But the identification of Krishna devotees with the *gopīs* and Krishna worship is not fanatical or exclusive. In the *bhajanas,* they sing the praises of, and identify with, other devotees of Krishna as well as with devotees of Rāma, Śiva, Subrahmaṇya, Gaṇeśa, and other deities. Outside the *bhajanas,* too, many of the devotees are explicit about this flexibility and, if they are Advaitins, relegate Krishna devotion to the sphere of individual choice and personal preference, a choice, however, that may be the ladder to the impersonal absolute without qualities.

The one God appears in many forms or manifestations—as Viṣṇu or Nārāyaṇa, Śiva, Rāma, Krishna, Vināyaka, Subrahmaṇya, Durgā and so forth—to please the different kinds of devotees in the world, of different temperaments and inclinations and of different outfits of intellect and heart. It is like the same person appearing in cinemas or picture shows as different persons at one and the same time. It is thus silly or stupid for Vaiṣṇavas to hate Śiva, for Śaivites to hate Viṣṇu, and so forth. To me, the Lord is Śrī Krishna, to you He is God the Father, to the Muslim He is Allah, to one He is Rāma, to another Śiva and so on. There should therefore be the most perfect catholicity in the world in the matter of religion. If this exists, equality will establish itself between different individuals and different groups of men and women, and legislation for social evils, which is no remedy at all, is quite unnecessary. So, *bhakti* brings all the hearts in the world together in their common vibrations of yearning for God and is attained in the easiest way possible. If sugar and sugar-candy are given, it is possible that one person prefers to have the candy and another the sugar. A person may have greater relish for a particular victual than for another. He may not hate the latter. Thus, preferences will always exist in the world and it is good that they exist.

The interpretation of the Rādhā-Krishna *bhajanas* as ritual dramatizations of the ideals of social equality and of supreme devotion to God seems to me to accord with observed behavior, with the statements of participants, and with the religious texts. This interpretation does not imply that all participants share these ideals to the same degree or with the same self-consciousness. It implies only that the *bhajanas* are dramatic cultural performances in which these ideals are symbolically acted out. In this respect the *bhajanas* belong with a large class of other cultural performances that have become media for the expression of devotion (*bhakti*)—devotional plays and films, dramatic recitations of stories from the epics and Purāṇas, dances based on these epic and Purāṇic themes, devotional songs, etc. Many different kinds of people participate in these performances for many different kinds of individual reasons. The meaning and function of the performances will of course vary with different individuals and their psychological needs. We have tried to pick out several clusterings of meanings and functions for the Rādhā-Krishna *bhajanas* that are linked to the changing role and status of the Smārta Brahmans in Madras, to contemporary conditions and ideologies, and to the perennial Indian quest for individual salvation.

These clusterings of meanings and functions have different psychological and historical sources and motives and, perhaps, different destinies. But in the Rādhā-Krishna *bhajana* movement of Madras City there seems to be a temporary convergence and interpenetration of the different meanings and functions. Confronted by the increasingly secular and impersonal social life of a large urban center, orthodox Hindus find it increasingly difficult to cultivate their highly intellectualized, scholastic traditions or to follow the numerous rituals prescribed for their caste, sect, or family. At the same time, the Dravidian movement for linguistic regionalism, with its championing of Tamil against Sanskrit, Telugu, Hindi, and other Indian languages; of non-Brahmans against Brahmans; and of "rationalism" against "superstition," drives the orthodox Hindu, and particularly the Smārta Brahman, to a defense of his religion, his culture, and his caste. Under these circumstances, many find appealing such a devotional cult as the Rādhā-Krishna *bhajanas,* which permits them to pursue an easier path to individual salvation while simultaneously countering the political trends of the times. For the love that leads Krishna devotees to yearn for Krishna also brings them into intimate social contact with their urban neighbors of different caste, sect, or language, and to a sharing as devotees in the mutual affection which inspires their faith. Whether these Rādhā-Krishna *bhajanas* will develop into a casteless, sectless, ecumenical form of Hinduism is difficult to say. Already tendencies have appeared toward new forms of ritualization, intellectualization, and sectarianism that make such an outcome unlikely. There is no doubt in the minds of devotees, however, that the Rādhā-Krishna *bhajanas* of Madras City have, like Krishna's descent to rectify specific evils on earth, become the timely instrument of an integrative and unifying religious movement.

VI. RĀDHĀ-KRISHNA *BHAJANAS* OF SOUTH INDIA: A PHENOMENOLOGICAL, THEOLOGICAL, AND PHILOSOPHICAL STUDY *

by T. K. Venkateswaran

The theology of Krishna worship and the theology and philosophy of Krishna incarnation are in themselves a vast subject. In the following pages, treatment is limited to the understanding of Krishna, the worship and the love of the Hindu devotees, and other aspects of the Krishna story in relation to the Rādhā-Krishna *bhajana* of South India. This study will be brief and preliminary in character. We do not seek here to take into consideration such aspects of Krishna and Krishnalogy as Krishna the warrior, the statesman with a vision, the poet, the teacher, the philosopher, and the savior.[1] The theme that has been taken from the *Bhāgavata Purāṇa* and centralized in the Rādhā-Krishna *bhajana* in South India is that of the great mystery of the *rāsa-krīḍā* dance of Krishna with the *gopīs,* the unlearned, innocent cowherd damsels, although the other *līlās,* the mysterious sports, of Krishna, also find a place and meaning. It should be remembered that there has not been a development of "pure" theology in Hinduism. On the one hand, there have been profound developments in the area of the philosophy of religion; on the other hand, the theology must be discerned from its relation to the hard facts of life situations, religious

* This study has been made possible by the time and opportunity kindly provided by Professor Milton Singer and the Committee on Southern Asian Studies at the University of Chicago. I am very grateful for this. I am particularly indebted to Professor Singer for the clarifications and suggestions as a result of my long discussions with him on several aspects of the subject.

The earlier phases of this study began in a germinal form several years ago and I received great help from my father, T. S. Krishnaswami Iyer and from my Vedānta-guru, the late Sastra Ratnakara Thethiyur Subramanya Sastriar of Madura and Madras. I am also grateful to Professor V. Raghavan of Madras University.

My participation in Harvard University's Center for the Study of World Religions as a Resident Scholar has been of considerable assistance and stimulation. My thanks are due to Professor R. H. L. Slater for this participation.

experiences, and fields connected with the psychology of religion. There has been a marked absence of "pure" Hindu doctrine, for Hinduism has always sought to encompass every aspect of human life.

The Birth and Growth of the Southern Bhajana Tradition

The history and development of present-day expressions of the *bhajana* can be traced through more than ten centuries in the Smārta Brahman tradition of Krishna worship and in the fostering of study and exposition of *Bhāgavata Purāṇa* by the Smārtas in South India. This tradition can be seen even today in a city like Madras, in the nature of the groups that arrange for exposition of the work and in those persons who acquire a liking, mastery, and skill, and expound the work to large audiences by recitation, narration, storytelling, and philosophical discourses.[2] Reference will be made in greater detail to the history and the tradition of the Smārta Brahmans after a discussion of the immediate scene of the *bhajana,* the importance of three *gurus,* the textual sources, and some of the important songs and stanzas.

The Three Gurus of the Southern Tradition

In the beginning of the *bhajana,* prostrations are offered and songs are sung in praise of three important *gurus* of the southern *bhajana* tradition, Bodhendra, Śrīdhara Veṅkaṭeśa, and Sadgurusvāmī. Prostrations are then made to all the other teachers who were devotee-composers, in various languages, and their songs are sung. But this honoring of the three teachers with special preference in the beginning is a distinctive feature of the *bhajana.*

These three *gurus* were responsible to a great extent for the revival movement during the latter half of the eighteenth century, from which the present *bhajana* has developed. There were other movements in the fields of music, drama, and dance in South India. Some of the composer-devotees, such as Tyāgarāja, combined all the refinements of music with devotion in an effort to harmonize *nāda* (pure music) and *bhakti* (devotion) into one path to God. The three *gurus* played a role in the interaction of these various movements by linking together the various trends thus contributing to the revival of *bhakti.*

Nārāyaṇa Tīrtha and Upaniṣadbrahma-yogin also strengthened the revival by linking and generalizing the separate movements.[3] One result of their mediating efforts was the birth of simple *nāmāvalis,* strings of sweet names of Krishna (also of Rāma and others), some in two or four feet, some in only one line, with simpler, less-sophisticated musical forms and melodies. These were easily sung by those who had had no elaborate training in classical music. The history of this and other movements in music, dance, and drama, and the mutual influences between devotion and these arts deserve a separate and detailed treatment. Some of the lay devotees in the *bhajana* find a place in their personal devotions for these three teachers, who provide spiritual mediation, inspiration, and guidance. A few devotees stand in direct relationship to one of the three teachers through initiation by a disciple in a line of succession that extends back over four or five generations. Many of the devotees, by singing the *gurus'* praise, acknowledge their sense of indebtedness to these tradition builders, preservers, innovators, and leader-teachers.

Textual Sources of the Bhajana

The theology of the southern *bhajana* is mainly based on the *Bhāgavata Purāṇa,* especially on those portions dealing with the love of the *gopīs* for Krishna. This theology, combined with the philosophy and theology of the divine Word (Name) as found in the works of the three teachers, forms the basis of the *bhajana.* Bhagavan-nāma Bodhendra is the author of several works, including such significant ones as *Nāmāmṛta rasodaya, Nāmāmṛta sūryodaya,* and *Bhagavan-nāmāmṛtārṇava. Bhagavan-nāmabhūṣaṇa* of Śrīdhara Veṅkaṭeśa (otherwise reverently known as "Ayyaval") and the *Bhakti-saṃdeha-dhvānta-bhāskara,* attributed to Sadgurusvāmī of Marundanallūr (also known as Veṅkaṭarāmadeśika), are also among the important contributions to be taken into consideration here. Other stanzas, songs, and *nāmāvalis* that are sung are the compositions of Jayadeva, Nārāyaṇa Tīrtha, Sadāśiva Brahmendra, and a host of others, including Līlāśuka (Bilvamaṅgala).[4]

Before a detailed discussion of some of the ideas from these works, including the *Bhāgavata Purāṇa*—ideas of central importance in the theology of the *bhajana*—it is important to note a group of nearly twenty stanzas, from the *Viṣṇu Purāṇa,* the *Bhāgavata Purāṇa,* and the *Garuḍa Purāṇa.* These stanzas, some of which have a long tradition, are sung at the beginning of the *bhajana,* whatever its type; they set the theological tone and act as a flexible, unformulated creed for the group of devotees. The leader of the *bhajana* recites these stanzas, and the others either recite them with the leader in very low voices or silently listen and meditate on their meaning. These stanzas are translated here.

(On Lord Gaṇeśa; this stanza also finds a place in domestic Vedic rituals and in temple worship)

The Lord who wears white cloth and is all-pervasive,
He is four-armed, of complexion brown;
His face is pleasing.
One should meditate on him for the removal of all impediments.

(Also on Gaṇeśa)

Viṣṇu, the loving lord of Śrī, is his uncle;
The woman who is the giver of all auspiciousness is his mother;
Deva Śaṃkara is his father.
I offer my salutations to him, the elephant-faced Lord.

Guru is Brahmā, and *Guru* is Viṣṇu;
Guru is also Lord Śiva;
Guru is the supreme Brahman;
To that *guru* [who is all manifestations] our prostrations.

(In praise of the teacher Bodhendra)

He is the embodiment of the richness in the form of the kingdom of God's name.
Let us resort to and revere him, the best among teachers and *yogins,* Śrī Bodhendra.

(In praise of Śrīdhara Veṅkaṭeśa [Ayyaval])

He has a deep-rooted and clear knowledge of God and His Name.
He has also great love toward Him, Īśa [same as Īśvara], and toward those who are dedicated to Him, and he is indifferent to others.
His vision of the world as permeated by God and His compassion is well established.

My homage to him, the teacher Veṅkaṭeśa, who is the enemy of death, in human form.

(In praise of Śrī Veṅkaṭarāma Deśika, otherwise known as Sadgurusvāmī)

He is a [combined] embodiment of Bhagavan-nāma Bodhendra and Śrīdhara in one.
We pay our homage to him, the teacher, Śrī Veṅkaṭarāmadeśika.

Our prostrations also to those who offer salutations to Bodhendra and Śrīdhara;
They are the Divine Name in embodiment [on earth].

Prahlāda, Nārada, Parāśara, Puṇḍarīka, Vyāsa, Ambarīṣa, Śuka, Śaunaka, Rukmāṅgada, Bhīṣma, Arjuna, Vasiṣṭha, and Vibhīṣaṇa
These holy and great *bhāgavatas* [devotees] we [now] remember.

Hari's Name, Hari's Name, and Hari's Name alone is my vocation.
In the Kali age there is no other, no other, indeed no other course (for *mokṣa*).[5]

Bhagavān says:
Who studies and chants [6] My Name incessantly without feeling shame,
He along with a crore of generations [in his family] obtains My abode.

O Brahmā, the singing, dancing, and gesturing of Viṣṇu [Krishna]
Should be performed by the Brahmans as their obligatory rites.

One should not delay and throw away time.
Life's every moment is waning.
Yama, the god of death, has no mercy.
Hari's *kīrtan* [singing] should be performed.

Bhagavān says:
I do not live in Vaikuṇṭha [the world and heaven of Viṣṇu].
Nor do I live in the heart of the *yogī* [performing penance] or in the sun.
Where my devotees [are gathered] and sing [My Name]
There do I stand, O Nārada! [7]

By meditation in the Kṛta Age,
By sacrifices [*yājña*] in the Tretā Age,
By worshipping [through the help of an image having God's presence] in the Dvāpara Age

What one attains thus, that he reaches in the Kali Age by having sung
about Krishna [Keśava].[8]

O king Parikṣit: in the Kali Age
There is a great and unique quality:
By the mere devout singing of Krishna,
One released from the bondage [of *saṃsāra*] can reach the highest.[9]

To those whose minds are rendered turbid [dirty, sinful] in the Kali
Age,
To those who have to live by the materials that are sinful,
To those who have fallen away from actions prescribed by Vedic
injunctions—
The refuge is singing of Govinda [and His Name].

Having pondered over and read through all the *śāstras,*
Having also analyzed them again and again,
This is one [thing] clearly discerned:
Nārāyaṇa is to be meditated upon [and sung].

The following two stanzas are also sung before performing the *divya-nāma-bhajana,* singing and dancing around the lamp. The circle around the lamp represents symbolically the complete world and its activities. The stanzas are from the *Garuḍa Purāṇa.*

Bhagavān says:
Devotees, coming together and mutually sharing [the devotion],
Placing the lamp in their midst [by forming a circle],
Meditating on Me in the light
And singing my powers and qualities,

Moving and dancing around [the lamp],
Attain the results of covering the complete earth.
There is no doubt indeed—
O Garuḍa, delighter of Vinatā [your mother].

The basic messages in the above stanzas are self-explanatory.

Smārta Brahmans and Krishna Worship: Saṃnyāsins in the Advaita Tradition

We have already referred very briefly to the long history of Krishna worship among the Smārtas of South India. In order better to understand the significance of this history, we should say a little more about the origin and development of the Smārtas themselves. Also connected with the history is the work of a large number of *Saṃnyāsins* in various centuries who promoted the study and exposition of the *Bhāgavata Purāṇa* among the Hindu laity. These *Saṃnyāsins* appeared in the Advaita tradition of Śaṃkara and were Smārtas in the earlier stages of their lives, either during *brahmacarya* or during the period of the householder. Here we may mention the names of Śuka, Madhusūdana Sarasvatī, Sadāśiva Brahmendra, Nārāyaṇa Tīrtha, Āśramasvāmī, Nirañjana Yati, Raghunāthendra Yati, Upaniṣadbrahma Yogin, and Bhagavannāma Bodhendra, to select only a few.[10] Such endings as "Yati," "Tīrtha," and "Sarasvatī" in the above names show that these men were *saṃnyāsins*. Theologically, there are two important developments to be noticed here. The first is the interaction between the way of Vedic rites and the path of *bhakti* to Krishna. The second is that the path of *jñāna* interacted with that of *bhakti* to Krishna. The importance of these interactions is derived from the figure of Krishna himself.

One cannot definitely say when the Smārta sect originated and was crystallized. However, we can say that the sect's religious orientation as it was formed was connected with the way of life prescribed in the *kalpa sūtras* (a name applied in common to three different types of writings: the *śrauta sūtras,* the *gṛhya sūtras,* and the *dharma sūtras*). The word *"smṛti"* is usually understood to mean that branch of literature called *dharma śāstra,* made up both of aphorisms and of elaborate commentaries, digests, and manuals which deal with the development of Hindu socioreligious practices and institutions, and with individual and social duties. But, actually, *"smṛti"* and *"smṛti* literature" refer to all three types of writings included in the term *"kalpa sūtras."* As such, it includes Vedic rituals (individual and community); domestic rituals, including *pūjā* (a subsequent development); and the institutional duties dealt with in the *dharma śāstra* works. *Smṛti,* meaning "what is remembered," therefore properly includes all three *sūtra* literatures and the whole tradition that was developing around them. But there were varying developments in the *smṛti* literature as it grew; there were creative innovations, as well as rigidities, and deviations and differences from *śruti* literature.[11]

Smārtas were originally those who sought to adhere strictly to the ways of the *smṛti* or *kalpa* literature. They had already developed within themselves the seeds of both conservatism and expansion, that is, tendencies both to freeze tradition and to alter it creatively. In addition to practicing Vedic rites, they worshiped God by offering *pūjā* and through material substances, such as the *śālagrāma* in devotions to Vedic Viṣṇu or the *bāṇa liṅga* in the worship of Vedic Rudra or Śiva. These practices were in force by the time such works as the *Āśvalāyana-gṛhya-sūtra-pariśiṣṭa* and Āpastamba's *Śrauta Sūtras* and *Gṛhya Sūtras* were written, that is, sometime between 600 and 300 B.C.[12] But the *pūjā* seems to have been offered to *eka mūrti* (one deity) only, either Viṣṇu or Śiva. Several centuries later, a new line of development was initiated when Śaṃkara, the great theologian-philosopher, appeared and gave his Advaita exegesis on the Upaniṣads. The scene changed to one of emphasis on *mokṣa,* or experience through the realization of Brahman.

Śaṃkara brought a new dimension to the religious thinking of the Smārtas, most of whom accepted his Advaita theology. Believing that the One Brahman has several manifestations and maintaining the principle of the uniqueness of each individual human being and his mental equipment, Śaṃkara, after a long process of reorganization, reformation, and unification, established six schools or cults: the Śaiva, the Vaiṣṇava, the Śākta (worship of God as She), the Saura (worship of Brahman in the sun), the Gāṇapatya (worship of the elephant-faced Gaṇapati as the supreme God), and Kaumāra (worship of the son of Śiva, Skanda, as the ultimate God). In the household worship of the Smārta sect, the practice of worshiping *five* of the above deities in a formation known as *pañcāyatana pūjā*—worshiping God in five forms or residing places—came to be established.[13] There could be different formulations and arrangements of these forms or material substances; the particular manifestation to which the householder was most drawn was central, and the other forms were at the sides during *pūjā.* This innovation permitted new arrangements and led to such developments in later times as *Krishna pañcāyatana* and *Rāma pañcāyatana,* in which Krishna and Rāma were worshiped as the supreme Brahman. In such instances, Krishna or Rāma occupied the center, and other forms or images were grouped around. This trend of worshiping different deities as manifestations of One had started even during the time of Bodhāyana himself. While discussing the rules for *pūjā,* Bodhāyana suggests that, in the same *liṅga,* various deities should be invoked—Brahmā and Viṣṇu in the front, Pārvatī and Nandi to the north, Skanda and Gaṇapati in the south, and Śūla and Mahā Kāla at the back of the *liṅga.*

With the development of Advaita theology, which affirmed the oneness and ultimate reality of God, this trend grew into the flowering of *pañcāyatana pūjā.* Soon it was thought that the householder should always worship in this way and not with only one *mūrti,* or form, since the latter form of worship was deemed appropriate solely for those who had renounced society and were full of the spirit of detachment. *Pañcāyatana pūjā* was for those who took to the life of *pravṛtti,* engagement and involvement. The complex structure of the family, with the various capacities, equipment, and needs of the members, called for symbolic recognition in the complex structuring of God's manifestations and the utilization of these for worship in the family.

Until the impact of Krishna and his incarnation was felt, most of the Smārtas were Vedic-Śaivites, and some were Vedic-Śākta followers. Either Śiva or Devī was central in their *pūjās,* and they adhered to the *smṛti* rules in their individual and social practices. But with greater delineation of the Person of Krishna and of the meaning of God incarnated as Krishna, through such works as the *Bhāgavata Purāṇa,* great changes were begun in the religious experiences and thinking of the Smārtas. There followed further interactions between the *smṛtis* and the *purāṇas* in the Smārta tradition and history.

Before we move into that interesting subject, it is important to deal with the theological meaning that the Advaita-Smārta tradition saw in Krishna. Related to this meaning is the experience of *saṃnyāsa,* the culmination of the dedicated, lifetime pursuit of a study of the philosophy and theology of Brahman. *Saṃnyāsa* is the fourth *āśrama,* or stage in life, voluntarily accepted. It is a life of complete freedom to pursue the study of Brahman, a life of renunciation, sacrifice, and service. *Saṃnyāsins* must always live in participation and involvement in God, study Vedānta, meditate on and contemplate the relationship between man and God, live by *bhikṣā* food offered by the householders, and serve society by spiritual guidance, pastoral counseling, and in other ways. Some may enter into this stage even from the first stage of *brah-*

macarya; such *saṃnyāsins,* who do not pass through the stages of *gṛhastha* and *vānaprastha,* are called *naiṣṭhika brahmacārīs.* The young sage Śuka who expounded the *Bhāgavata Purāṇa* to King Parikṣit was a great *naiṣṭhika brahmacārī.* There are several types of *saṃnyāsins* and different orders among them. We have already referred to several devotees of Krishna found among *saṃnyāsins* who were Smārtas in their earlier stages of life. If we are to understand this interesting phenomenon, and study the nature of their religious experiences, we must turn to at least one or two case studies. This will also help us to understand the theology of, and the approach to, Krishna in their individual lives.

Madhusūdana Sarasvatī and His Religious Experience

The life of Madhusūdana Sarasvatī can be discussed here as a typical instance. He lived during the sixteenth century and wrote several works, including probably a commentary on the *Bhāgavata Purāṇa.* He was a *saṃnyāsin* and a great upholder of the Advaita theology of Śaṃkara. One of his most important writings is the highly polemical work *Advaitasiddhi,* which is couched in the trenchant and terse language of Sanskrit Neo-Logic (*Navya-nyāya*); it is considered a high-water mark in logical and philosophical sophistication and scholarship in Hinduism. The name of the work literally means the achievement and establishment of Advaita, the oneness of the transcendental Brahman and the relative unreality of the world. The work is divided into a large number of *vādas,* or arguments. Against this background, in the midst of the work, something unique, something that should interest everyone who wishes to study a religious experience, took place. Madhusūdana Sarasvatī had accomplished the writing of one of the most important *vādas,* the *nirākāra vāda,* and had successfully, logically, and philosophically, established the case of the ultimate absence of any *ākāra,* or form, to Brahman. He was to proceed to the next *vāda,* to demonstrate that Brahman does not possess *jñāna,* or knowledge, such as human beings possess, that Brahman is *Cit* or *Jñāna.* But before he proceeded to work on this next chapter, at the end of the *nirākāra vāda,* he underwent a religious experience, which he described in the form of a stanza at the end of the *nirākāra vāda*.[14] The stanza, which is highly paradoxical in several ways, is as follows:

I do not know any other ultimate and supreme Truth [*tattva*] than Krishna.
His palm is adorned by the flute. He is [all bluish-dark] like a fresh cloud.
He wears the golden *pītāmbara* silk. His upper and lower lips are reddish like the *bimba* fruit.
His face is charming and sweet like the full disc of the moon.
His eyes are verily lotuses.

There are several elements to be noted here. Such experiences, in which various aspects of the phenomenology of religion and the "logic of the heart" are involved, deserve separate treatment and study. Here, in our study of the meaning of Krishna, we shall refer to only some of these elements. First of all, it is very interesting that there are no other stanzas, no other such statements in the body of the whole work, which is cast in the terse prose style of logical language. This stanza is a singular occurrence and stands in a highly significant place. Madhusūdana Sarasvatī considers Krishna as the ultimate *Tattva* and expresses his experience with the philosophical word in a phenomenological way and context. This *tattva* to him is highly concrete, so vivid that the color scheme of that truth or thing is felt and expressed fully by him.

Another stanza from Madhusūdana, from another work, may also be included here. This one was written, perhaps, after he had had the previously described experience while working on *Advaitasiddhi*. He says:

There are those who have controlled their *minds* by constant and intense meditation. By such *minds* they see the unique supreme Light. Let such *yogins* do so. As for *me*, let that Thing alone be for the delight of my eyes, That which is somewhat dark-bluish in Effulgence, and which runs and plays on the banks of the river Yamunā.[15]

Such experiential utterances show the complicated nature of the move towards *bhakti* and point out that it is not a mere question of naïve reduction or division into "philosophical" Hindus and "popular" Hindus. They also set aside the usual understanding of *bhakti* and such a picture of a *bhāgavata*, or devotee of Bhagavān Krishna, as that given in the following stanza, a traditional verse.

Those who have no capacities in the field of *śāstras* become poets. Failing in poetry also, they take to exposition of the *Purāṇas.* If they are not successful therein, they turn to agriculture. Finally, if they lag behind in agriculture also, they become *bhāgavatas,* devotees of God.[16]

Madhusūdana's experience, which occurred on a very "high level" and after lifelong scholarship and sophistication, shows how such simple reductions are based upon either a sense of *hubris* in scholarship or a lack of comprehension of the complexity and the paradoxical nature of the issue. His experience reveals the dialectical and paradoxical tension in which his mind lived, between the qualityless, transcendent impersonal Brahman, on the one hand, and the particular, concrete, quality-flooded Person Krishna, on the other. The philosophical paradox that could not be resolved on paper was understood, and the conflict was removed by the existential living of an individual life. The "call" aspect of such experiences will be dealt with later. What we have to note here, however, is that there is a move, a return, to *bhakti,* but at a "high level." It is from *"bhakti* to *jñāna* and *back."* Such a *bhakti* becomes *ahaitukī,* or an end in itself, without any ulterior purpose to serve. A stanza in the *Bhāgavata Purāṇa* says that "even sages who revel and feel blissful in the experience of Ātman in themselves, though they have attained complete release from all shackles, still consciously engage in devotion to Hari without any ulterior purpose to be achieved. Such is the nature of the qualities of God Hari."[17] *"Bhakti* has a double place in the scheme of spiritual life. It leads the *mumukṣu* to *mukti,* and the *mukta* (released person) wishes to revert to it, to dwell in its region, laying aside for a while the inarticulate bliss of *Advaitānubhava* (Advaita experience)."[18] All this emphasizes the "return" or the "move" to *bhakti.* This return or opposite movement can also, sometimes, be seen as the generating of self-criticism and the maintaining of balance, synthesis and integration.

The move to *bhakti* also involves a return to society by the *saṃnyāsin.* It is a return to the study and exposition of the *Bhāgavata Purāṇa* with lay disciples, devotees, and the public. It is also marked by a withdrawal on the part of the *saṃnyāsin* only to return more effectively, a return in which there will not be the same earlier type of binding involvement, but a new involvement, a new *pravṛtti,* which will not bind him but will keep him a unique and spiritually free individual. The spiritual withdrawal is like the mechanism of physical withdrawal employed in ancient warfare to gain perspective and distance for shooting the arrow more effectively and precisely. It is a sort of withdrawal for perfection and rearmament, for a re-entry into the world and practical affairs. It is a plunge, after great transcendence; or a rising to the surface, after a reaching to the depths. We can use several images to express the *pravṛtti,* or involvement, that follows the *nivṛtti,* or withdrawal.[19] This return characterizes the activities of many *jīvanmuktas,* persons who are liberated and have had *mokṣa* experience and yet continue to live and serve society. We shall say more about this later.

Now, what one is in the habit of calling Indian Thought is for the very great part the thought of the *saṃnyāsī,* that is to say of someone who has denied society, who is dead to society and has transcended his caste and castes in general. Knowledge of the absolute presupposes not only the renunication of the world but the rejection of social forms. In fact things are more complicated, for the *saṃnyāsī,* although dead to society, not merely has the right to speak but also is a sought-after spiritual teacher; his thought, which is a negation of caste, in this way filters back into the caste. The two kinds of thought, or thought on one side and worldly wisdom on the other, blend; one can live in the world and still make the philosophy of the *saṃnyāsī* one's own. It is here, around the dialogue of the *saṃnyāsī* and the man of the world, that religio-philosophical speculation revolves, concealing a contradiction, a dichotomy.[20]

Krishna and Brahman Are One

There are numerous other *saṃnyāsins* like Madhusūdana Sarasvatī. Many devotee-composers whose songs are sung in the *bhajanas* were such *saṃnyāsins.* Sadāśiva Brahmendra, for example, sings in one of his songs as follows:

All is One Brahman. Lo, All is One Brahman!
What is there to be said? What is there not to be said?
What is there to do? What is there not to do?

What is there to be learned? What is there not to be learned?
What is there to be worshiped? What is there not to be worshiped? [21]

In another song he sings of experiencing the bliss that is Krishna:

Krishna wearing the garland *vanamālā* is playing in the cattle yard [in Gokula].
Krishna is playing.

He is the savior of Prahlāda and Parāśara, Hanumān and Jāmbavān;
He is playing.

He in whom the noble *saṃnyāsins,* Paramahaṃsas are strung like flowers in a garland and who is hidden inside the lotus of Praṇava,
He is playing.[22]

In some other instances, Krishna is the crowning climax of all the findings of the Upaniṣads, even of the *nirguṇa* Brahman (qualityless, transcendental Supreme God). A verse in the beginning of the *Bhāgavata Purāṇa* says:

The fruit that has slipped from the tree of the Vedas and Upaniṣads,
To which has been added the juice of *amṛta* [nectar, immortality] by contact
With the beak [mouth] of the parrot [Śuka, the sage who narrated the *Purāṇa*].

Another verse speaks of the *sūris,* the sages and the learned *saṃnyāsins,* swooning from the enchantment and the "call" of Krishna in the *Bhāgavata* story and the *Krishnalīlā.* The experiences of men like Madhusūdana and Sadāśiva Brahmendra show how they struggled to resolve the contradiction between the otherworldly transcendentalism and the realism and the deep humanity of Krishna and his love, between the particularity and the universality of God as Krishna, between the naturalness and the supernatural mysteries centered around Krishna.

The lay devotees in the Rādhā-Krishna *bhajana* also understand Brahman and Krishna as identical. "The other manifestations, such as Rāma, Paraśurāma and Narasiṃha are partial ones of Bhagavān. Krishna is Bhagavān Himself."[23] And yet, he is man too. Nārāyaṇa Tīrtha, another *saṃnyāsin*-composer whose songs, from his *Krishnalīlā Taraṅgiṇī,* are sung in the *bhajanas,* says in a song that is never omitted during any *bhajana:*

I think [and feel convinced] that you are verily God Mādhava [Viṣṇu];
Also that you have accepted of your own accord
The human form and nature by your *māyā* [*līlā,* divine power] [to save human beings].

Your nature and conduct, the Mystery and Truth of the same, is understood by the fortunate.

Krishna as Brahman of the Upaniṣads is *sat* (existence), *cit* (consciousness) and *ānanda* (love). He is also the *rasa* of the Upaniṣads, the relish or the sentiment that is ultimate. It is the *rasa* aspect, coupled with that of *ānanda,* that shines forth in the total surrender and love of the hearts of the *gopī*-maidens, the love that has become the model of the southern *bhajana*. The *gopīs* concentrated upon the "feeling" and "love" of their hearts directed to Krishna. They spoke of a distinctive "logic of the heart." This is set down and revealed in a highly dramatic episode in the *Bhāgavata Purāṇa*. Krishna had left the village of Gokula, had gone to Mathurā, had suppressed and killed the evil King Kaṃsa, and had retired to Dvārakā to rule. He wanted to provide a unique experience for his friend Uddhava, the wise and bold scholar seeking to realize Krishna and to have release through his Vedāntic knowledge. He sent Uddhava with a comforting message to the *gopīs* whom he had left behind. Uddhava arrived and tried to convince them and instruct them in the *yoga* of knowledge. However, he discovered the deep reality of their love and experience and realized the glory of the path of love to God. In one of his songs, the poet Sūrdās recaptures some of the aspects of this drama and says that Uddhava learned from the cowherd maidens that the heart finds its guidance by making a radical choice. The *gopīs* told him that the choice was like that of an insect that grows on poison, ignoring sweet fruits and tasting only poisonous plants, that it was also like that of an insect that in his habit of boring through a hard tree courts death rather than make an effort for lotus petals. In such a feeling of the heart, "content and consciousness, subject and object form an indistinguishable whole; the separation of the one from the other would mean abstraction or hollowness and consequent loss of the feeling tone. As no empirical emotion comes up to this ideal, the demand would be to realise a state of perfect amplitude or fullness (*paripūrṇatā-ānanda*)."[24] Yet the *gopīs* found that human love, the love of the beloved for the lover, was the way to human love of Krishna and they expanded this into a greater transcendental love for Krishna. The *Bhāgavata Purāṇa* records the praise of these *gopīs* and their sacrifice and love:

Blessed are the *gopīs* who have fixed their hearts on Krishna, who while attending to their various household duties, such as milking the cows, threshing the paddy, churning the curds, brushing the courtyard and smearing it with cowdung, rocking crying babies in cradles and lulling them to sleep, or sprinkling and sweeping the floor, sing songs in praise of Krishna, with a heart full of Love, with eyes wet with tears, and in a voice shaking with emotion.[25]

This, however, does not rule out the possibility that a devotee may sometimes follow the example of certain other devotees who have shown devotion to Krishna by listening, singing, meditating, feet-worshiping, performing *pūjā,* prostrating themselves, serving, befriending, and in other ways. There are numerous illustrations of these forms of *bhakti* in stories about Hanumān, Prahlāda, Draupadī, Vibhīṣaṇa, Kuntī, the elephant-king, and others who are described in the *Bhāgavata.*

The Relation of the Devotee to the Other Devotees of Krishna

The devotees of Krishna invoke his presence in an auspicious lamp, and they sing and dance around this lamp, identifying themselves with the *gopīs,* who danced around Krishna. Again, the central theme is the *rāsa* dance of Krishna in the company of the *gopīs.* The enactment of the various sports of the *gopīs* and Krishna and the dramatization of the *rāsa* dance form the central part of the southern *divyanāma bhajana.*[26] It is necessary, here, to understand the symbolism of the *rāsa-maṇḍala.* This is described in great detail in the tenth *skandha* of the *Bhāgavata.* The five chapters therein, known as *"Rāsapañcādhyāyī,"* have been discussed with an eye to their symbolism and mysticism both by Śrīdhara Svāmī, who has commented on the whole of the *purāṇa,* and by Dhanapatisūri. Some of the deepest insights into love mysticism are to be found here. On hearing the call from Krishna through the music of his flute, the *gopīs* hurried to Krishna, each one seeking him and his love secretly and individually.[27] "The women whose souls were conquered by Krishna, did not have any more attachments to the world. In spite of the impediments caused by their husbands, relatives, parents, and others, they hurried towards

Krishna."[28] When they all converged, they found themselves sharing Krishna's love, and themselves loving Krishna together. They all met in Krishna and through Krishna discovered the mutual relations between themselves. Thus they illustrated the independent pursuit of individual souls in search of God and their discovery that there is a fundamental fellowship and relationship between those various *jīvas* who try to meet and reach God through love.[29] Also shown through the *gopīs* were the pride and selfishness that may develop in an individual who searches alone for God. The idea of *sarva-mukti,* liberation of all through Krishna, was also clearly conveyed.

When the *gopīs* reached Krishna and sported with him, they soon grew proud of having won Krishna by their love. Krishna disappeared from their midst to punish their sense of pride. Soon they realized their folly and lamented the disappearance of their beloved Lord. Krishna reappeared and performed the *rāsa* dance—a dance full of *rasa* (relish, sentiment)—with them. The *gopīs* formed a circle; in the center stood Krishna, playing on his flute while the *gopīs* danced around him. Between every two *gopīs* in the circle was to be seen a Krishna, and there was a *gopī* between every two Krishnas. This dance against the background of the Yamunā, the river of life, on a beautiful moonlit night, has been a source of inspiration for many composers, poets, and painters, and has enriched their works. The presence of a Krishna between two *gopīs* is symbolic of the relatedness of two devotees or two human beings through God.[30] And the presence of a Krishna on either side of a *gopī* indicates the constant protection provided by God to the devotee in the various vicissitudes of his life. The *gopīs* themselves referred with love and gratitude to the constant protection that Krishna gave them during the calamities that had visited them in their village: "You have protected us again and again from the poisonous waters of the lake [in which the serpent Kāliya lived], from the demon Agha, from torrential downpours, from the fire of storm and thunder [caused by Indra], from the demon in the form of a ferocious bull and one in the form of a gale, and from other numerous disasters."[31]

The human world of devotees on the "periphery" has Krishna or God as its only "center," and since Krishna is the greatest value of the devotees, they do not have any desire to obtain *mokṣa,* nor do they value *mokṣa* itself.

The *gopīs* also speak of Krishna as the "in-dweller in the hearts of all embodied living creatures." He is "not only the son of a cowherd woman Yaśodā"; he has taken his birth in the Yādava clan in order to protect the world.[32]

The Lord and his group of *gopī* devotees also symbolize the ideal of a primary society in which interpersonal relationship and intimacy of love and knowledge between the members would be possible, with a common bond and value binding them together. This ideal is the same as the *sat-saṅga* ideal of the *Bhāgavata,* which corresponds to some extent to the *koinonia* of the early Christian church and to the elected group of Yahweh in early Judaism. The ideal occurs in Tamil devotional Śaivism as *aḍiyār-kūṭṭam*. This leads us to the nature of the divine "call" and its development in certain important areas of Hinduism. Aspects of the "call" have already been seen in the discussion of the religious experiences of devotees like Madhusūdana.

The Idea of Iṣṭa Devatā in Hinduism: the "Call" and Its Several Expressions

In the *Bhagavad Gītā* there are at least two clear indications of the nature of the "call." One takes the form of a doctrine and philosophy of works. Krishna calls Arjuna back to his duty. He also reveals to him the way of acting, and indicates for all human beings a general way of acting without being bound or obsessed by a desire for the fruit of the actions. Krishna speaks of the paradox of "seeing action in inaction and inaction in action" by men in the world. He stresses the dignity and purity of any vocation that is performed without a selfish desire for the results and that is offered to himself (Krishna) as a worship offering. "Neither let your motive be the fruit of action, nor let your attachment be to non-action." [33] The arts, the branches of learning, the various types of work, all have their place in the world in relation to God, as various forms of worship. He is behind every activity: "Worshiping by the performance of one's duties Him from whom is the endeavor of men, by whom all this is pervaded, man attains perfection." [34] This concept of vocation in Hinduism, symbolically powerful, has had an influence in shaping men's interests and activities, especially during recent centuries. This doctrine of vocation and "calling" comes very close to the Calvinistic doctrine of "calling" in Protestant Christianity.[35]

Another approach to divine "calling" found in the *Gītā* and further developed in the *Bhāgavata Purāṇa* seems not so much concerned with any particular doctrine of works but, rather, takes the form of a demand from the devotee for complete surrender and a highly emotional involvement through love and *bhakti.*

> Be with thy mind fixed in Me, be My devotee, be My worshiper, bow down to Me, and thou shalt come even to Me; this I verily swear unto thee; thou art beloved of Me. Abandoning all acts, take sanctuary with Me alone. I shall liberate thee from all sins; do thou not grieve.[36]

These stanzas so emphatically spoken by Krishna to Arjuna have also held the minds of devoted Hindus and have given rise to considerable exegesis and application.

The Doctrine of Prapatti, Surrender to God in Vaiṣṇava Tradition

To digress for a moment, and take leave of the Smārta tradition of the understanding of Krishna worship and love, it will be of great interest to see how differences in exegesis on the above stanzas dealing with surrender have been a primary source of the twofold division among Vaiṣṇavas and in Vaiṣṇava theology. The issue is as follows. A *prapanna,* one who has surrendered himself totally in *bhakti* to God, is faced with the question of performing the *nitya* and *naimittika* religious duties and rites, i.e., the daily and the seasonal. According to Lokācārya, a prominent religious teacher and leader of the Teṅkalai school of Vaiṣṇavism, "abandoning" or "having abandoned" would mean a sequence in the steps in the act of *prapatti,* i.e., surrender to the Lord. It would be like "having bathed, one should eat." So the performance of Vedic rites is to be abandoned as a prerequisite qualification for a surrender to the grace of God. Vedāntadeśika, the great *ācārya,* leader and teacher for the Vaḍakalai Vaiṣṇavas would have it a different way. To him, "having abandoned" would rather indicate a situation over which man does not have control. It corresponds to Karl Jaspers' "boundary situation" into which man finds himself thrown. If one says, "having come into this world of suffering, it is one's duty to seek some means of deliverance from it," in this instance "having come" would not indicate a free act on the part of man or a sequence but the situation of either a fall or an inability on the part of man to perform Vedic rites. According to Vedāntadeśika, only one's own inability or situation over which one has no control entails such a surrender; otherwise, the performance of ordained Vedic *karma* should be carried on by all men.[37] This theme is developed at great length and discussed and argued in his theological treatise *Rahasyatrayasāra*. He stood for theistic *mīmāṃsā* (philosophy of Vedic rites).

This difference in emphasis is very marked within Vaiṣṇava theology, and gives rise to the two radically different schools. It is also interesting to note that, with all the charismatic trends that emphasized *bhakti* in the origin and development of Viṣṇu worship, there have been constant movements in Vaiṣṇavism towards a return to the performance of Vedic rites and attempts at a "bureaucratization," somewhat similar to a "routinization" of the "charisma."[38] In his commentary on the first *sūtra* of the *Brahma-sūtras,* Rāmānuja definitely establishes a sequence between the study of the earlier portion of *śruti* literature (known as *karma kāṇḍa*) and the practice of the Vedic *dharmas,* and the beginning of the study of Brahman for the realization of *mokṣa*.[39] He establishes this sequence when he comments on the meaning of the word *atha,* meaning "after." Śaṃkara, on the other hand, explains that the word refers to four necessary antecedent conditions, that is, the possession of four qualities prior to one's understanding of Brahman and the quest for *mokṣa*. They are: (1) discrimination between *nitya vastu* and *anitya vastu,* i.e., the essential and the accidental, the Being and beings, the eternal and the noneternal; (2) complete nonattachment to the enjoyment of the fruits of action both in this world and hereafter; (3) practice of the sixfold virtues, *śama* (mental tranquillity), *dama* (control of senses), *titikṣā* (being unaffected by the dual condition of pleasure and pain, heat and cold, etc.), *uparati* (withdrawal from acts for a time), *samādhāna* (concentrated attention), and *śraddhā* (faith); and (4) an "ultimate concern" and burning desire for *mokṣa,* or release.[40] According to Śaṃkara, the study of the earlier portions of the Vedas and the performance of Vedic rites, while they may help by creating *cittaśuddhi*—a certain purity and discipline for the mind—are not causally and organically related to the study and knowledge of Brahman leading to liberation; there is no sequential relation between the former and the latter. The two are totally different, in aim, result, method, and scope. The moment one develops the above-mentioned qualities, whether he has studied and performed the Vedic rites or not, he can proceed to the study of Brahman, leading toward *mokṣa*.

The "Call" in Individual Lives

The *iṣṭa devatā* (personal deity) phenomenon in Hinduism requires a careful understanding. The idea of choosing one's own deity, the particular manifestation of God, either as Śiva, Viṣṇu, Rāma, Krishna, or Devī, might seem to stress more the importance of man and less the field of God's activity and influence. If not correctly understood, the personal deity might become falsely equated with the small choices of the world that man makes, for example, in deciding upon a type of automobile or a television set. But the choice of man in *iṣṭa devatā* is a radical, ultimate choice, an act of faith involving his total person and life. It also has the aspect of a "voluntary association," and he enjoys a "freedom" to make his choice in worshiping a deity, regardless of group, family, caste, and other ties, including the *kula devatā*.[41] Sometimes one member of a family may have a "call" and a "conversion" experience through the same deity that is worshiped in the family—a separate, independent rebirth as it were. This happened in the case of Tyāgarāja, the devotee-composer, though Rāma was his "family treasure." One's religious studies, the influence of one's religious and spiritual *guru* with his own *iṣṭa devatā* and devotion, one's family, one's fundamental mental make-up, aptitude, and potentialities, one's environmental influences, and, finally, one's sense of "religious freedom of choice" are the various factors that are to be taken into consideration in studying the *iṣṭa devatā* phenomena. But the picture is never complete unless one describes the cases in which it is not a matter of a man choosing Rāma, Krishna, or Śiva, but, rather, of the Supreme Being encountering and overpowering or "calling" the devotee in the aspect of Śiva or Rāma or Krishna. It is Krishna as the "caller" or the "elector," who chooses the devotee. To understand adequately the religious experiences of these devotees, an experience that is very intimate between them and the deity, to know how they feel the deity operating in their lives, to probe into that which cannot be objectively communicated to another, one has to turn to the biographical statements of the devotees themselves, describing their own personal experiences. Earlier, we referred to such an "event" in Madhusūdana's life.

Līlāśuka, in his *Kṛṣṇa-karṇāmṛta,* has narrated several such experiences in a vivid and ingenuous way. He has a vision of Krishna and he had been roaming in the pastures of Vṛndāvan. He says:

> Is this Manmatha himself [god of love and beauty]? Is this a charming sphere of radiance? Loveliness incarnate is it? Eternal delight for my heart and sight? My beloved Lord returned after long absence, the desired of my soul, I think. My own Krishna and no one else distinctly manifest to my eyes.

In another stanza he describes how his family were Śaivas and how Krishna called him out as His devotee.

> We are indeed Śaivites [by family]. There is nothing to question about that. We are also initiated into the technique of the special worship through the *mantra* of Śiva, of five syllables (*Oṃ Namaḥ Śivāya*). Still my mind yearns constantly to remember and reflect on the beautiful darling of the *gopī* damsels, his face radiant with smiles, shining like the white *atasī* blossom.

We are reminded here of the Upaniṣadic text: "The Ātman cannot be known and experienced by mere study and exposition of the Vedas, nor by intellect, nor by learning. He, whom the Ātman chooses, by that man alone can Ātman be known and realized." [42] Or to take the experience of another, we have this statement of Appayya Dīkṣita: "I have no differential understanding between Lord Śiva, the overlord of the universe, and Lord Nārāyaṇa, the inner pervading Ātman of the world. But still, my love and devotion spring and proceed in the direction of that Person, adorned on his head with the young crescent of the moon [Lord Śiva]." It appears that in many instances there is a harmony between the "voluntary choice" and the "call," and that the two combine and coincide.

Let us proceed to another recent record, the life of the devotee-composer Tyāgarāja of South India. It was Rāma who discovered and fired Tyāgarāja with a sense of mission to spread His name and *bhakti* in South India. In one of his songs, Tyāgarāja refers clearly to the "spell" of *Rāma bandhu,* i.e., a Rāma bond (covenant) which the god had cast on Tyāgarāja and by which he was bound. He says in the same song that he knew definitely that the faith he was to follow was not predetermined by Brahmā, the creator-god; he thereby suggests a choice on his part as well as a forcible "call" from Rāma.[43] In another song, he sings:

> I have *today* found Śrī Rāma, the Lord of Sītā Devī, the gem of the solar race, with Bharata, Lakṣmaṇa and Śatrughna doing service to him, with Āñjaneya holding his feet, with heroes like Sugrīva singing his praise.[44]

In this song, Tyāgarāja clearly refers to his vision of Rāma. He sings elsewhere of a different experience:

> O Redeemer, adored by Brahmā, cheer me by fulfilling your oft-repeated assurance of protection. . . . O Lord, cheer me, to remove the mental agony [caused by your sudden disappearance] after having come to my house.[45]

The Interaction Between the Smṛti and the Purāṇa Traditions

To continue with an earlier theme, that of the rising Smārta interest in the study of the *Bhāgavata Purāṇa* and Krishna worship, and to resume the discussion of the interaction between the path of Vedic rites and that of *bhakti*—which again is connected with the meeting of the *smṛti* and the Purāṇa traditions—we should bear in mind the forcible thrust and the basic message of the Purāṇas in general, and that of the *Bhāgavata* in particular. In addition to their many secular elements, such as history, the Purāṇas emphasized passionate love and worship of God. The *Bhāgavata* taught its message of devotion to Krishna as the way to reach Him and the oneness of all human beings in and through *bhakti*. Some of the *smṛtis,* on the other hand, tried to change and sharpen the domestic Vedic rites, the *ācāras* (customs, conduct), and other individual and social behavioral patterns governing different castes. The Purāṇas had attained at least a semicanonical state during the early centuries of the Christian era. It had been accepted that the *itihāsas* (the two great narratives, *Rāmāyaṇa* and *Mahābhārata*) and the Purāṇas were necessary to complete and understand the central meaning of the Vedas. The Āgama literature had also developed, and had attained canonical status by this time. The Āgamas, the Śaiva,

Vaiṣṇava, and Śākta texts, dealt with the theology and philosophy of temple building and temple worship, and with the individual's practices in the fields of conduct, *yoga* and *jñāna.* These different types of sacred literature interacted in influencing the minds of men and guiding them in their religious and spiritual pursuits. This interaction has developed and spread during nearly fifteen centuries, and it has been operating in several directions. A detailed study of its various stages of development and different lines of activity is worth while.

For example, in the symbolism and services of several temples, both Śaiva and Vaiṣṇava, this problem of the Vedic way of conducting *pūjā* versus the Āgamic way was taken up and wrestled with in all seriousness. The *vaikhānasa* Āgamas stressed the Vedic elements for Viṣṇu worship. On the other hand, the *pañcarātra* Āgamas stressed an Āgamic way to be followed in the installation of the images, worship, and services. In other fields, such as nontemple community worship, like the *sat-saṅgas* (the gathering of God's people), *aḍiyār-kūṭṭams* (the gathering of the devotees), and the *bhajanas,* the interaction between the social behavior according to *smṛtis* and that stressed by the Purāṇas may be clearly seen.

The detailed study of this field would, by providing the historical background, help to clarify the conceptual studies of interactions between the "Little" and the "Great" traditions of India that have been explored and studied in great detail by social scientists in recent years. There are ample and penetrating studies on Sanskritization, popularization, universalization, parochialization, popular Hinduism, Sanskritic Hinduism, and Westernization.[46] For example, it has been shown that the term "Sanskritization" develops certain conceptual and practical inadequacies. If we envisage a situation, in the near future, in which the Sanskrit language, the language of "gods," would be used as a medium for expressing secular ideas on democracy, economics of growth, and atoms for peace, and so on, could this process be called Sanskritization or Westernization? It would be an instance of secular "contents" in a "sacred container" having a sacred association and prestige. Such works could be read and assimilated by pundits and religious teachers who are great scholars in Sanskrit and have a keen love for "analysis." The Government of India Sanskrit Commission has in fact recommended the creation of conditions that would foster

Sanskrit as a vehicle for all secular and scientific expression. This reminds us of the situation in ancient India, which continued through the eighth and ninth centuries, when Sanskrit was taken up and used freely to express ideas in Buddhism and Buddhist philosophy. This created a free flow of ideas in both directions between Hinduism and Buddhism, with great mutual influences in spite of the fact that Buddhism was fundamentally heterodox and opposed to acceptance of the Vedas as scriptures. Buddha was soon regarded as one of the *avatārs* of Viṣṇu and, to Jayadeva, he was a manifestation of Brahman, who is Krishna himself. Professor Daniel H. H. Ingalls feels that, if there had been a few more centuries of contact between Muslim rule and the culture of India, works would have appeared in Sanskrit that both elucidated the principles of Islam and attempted a synthesis of the ideas in the two worlds, Hindu and Muslim.[47] Similarly, there are several works in Prakrit and also in Indian languages—and there will be more in the future—that have for their theme Sanskritic ideas of Hinduism. In such instances, the process cannot be properly termed either Sanskritic or Prakritic.

In studying the meeting of the *smṛtis* and the Purāṇas, the movement opposed to Sanskritization is of greater interest. One expression of this has been described and discussed as "parochialization" by McKim Marriott.[48] This opposite movement can be studied in the behavior patterns of the higher castes or the Brahmans, who for several reasons have accepted and adopted the ways of the lower castes or the "little traditions," respectively. This movement, very apparent in the field of music, can also be seen in such areas as legal structures, literature, philosophy, and theology.

The interaction between the *smṛtis* and the Purāṇas seems to have accelerated, and perhaps had even become a crucial issue, by the time of Lakṣmīdhara in the fifteenth century. Lakṣmīdhara was the author of a highly erudite work, called *Bhagavannāma Kaumudī,* on the theology and philosophy of the Divine Name. He was a scholar of great repute in the Pūrva Mīmāṃsā philosophy (the philosophy of *dharma* and Vedic works). This Smārta Brahman, having undergone religious experiences, seems to have grappled with the problem of priority between the *smṛtis* and the Purāṇas in his own life. He sought to give expression to his feelings, findings, and experiences in his work; he states that "if the *smṛtis* should differ from the Purāṇas in regard to any vital matter, we would be justified in preferring the Purāṇas."[49] He has had a great influence in the Smārta tradition in the further development of this approach. Bodhendra, one of the three teachers in the South Indian *bhajana* tradition, is credited by legend with having met Lakṣmīdhara and having received from him a deep influence in the direction of *Nāma Siddhānta* (the philosophy of the Divine Name and its singing) and *Bhāgavata* studies.[50] Whether this tradition is historically accurate or not, there is no doubt that Bodhendra was influenced by Lakṣmīdhara, at least indirectly.

Another characteristic of parochialization seen in the southern *bhajana* is the incorporation into the dancing that is performed around the lamp of such folk dances as the *kummi,* the *kōlāṭṭam* of South India, and other folk dance movements like the milk-churning dance, and the pestle-and-mortar dance. These blend with the classical *abhinayas* (gestures with the help of symbolic *mudrās*) that are sometimes performed by certain Bhāgavatas (devotees) who are well versed in the art of gesture and dancing (*bharata śāstra*) at certain intervals during the performance of the *divya-nāma-bhajana* (lamp *bhajana*). These talented Bhāgavatas portray some of the events and episodes in Krishna's life by classical gestures, while the particular stanza or song describing the event is sung by other Bhāgavatas. Some of the folk dances mentioned above have, perhaps, been received from the "little traditions" in the North. Some of the Tamil songs of the *siddhars* (Tamil mystics) have a very long and ancient tradition, and folk tunes like the *kāvaḍi-sindu, nonḍi-sindu, kiḻikkaṇṇi,* and boat songs (*ōḍams*) have also been incorporated into the *bhajana.* The more sophisticated *paṇs* of Tamil music, the Tamil compositions in different *sandams* (rhythms), the songs of the Āḻvārs and Nāyanmārs, were and are freely included and utilized in the *bhajana* singing. Many of these folk melodies, perhaps, had become an integral part of the *bhajana* even during the time of Sadgurusvāmī, who lived in the latter half of the eighteenth century. Although we are here primarily concerned with the theology and philosophy of the *bhajana,* we are also interested in the movements and adoptions that result from the unifying depth experiences or "visions" of individuals.

Even at other levels of social activity, we notice that in the southern *bhajana* there are features that mark this parochialization. An important one is the spontaneous acceptance of songs describing the glories and episodes in Krishna's life from different composers in the different languages of India. Songs are sung from many different languages: Sanskrit, Telugu, Kannada, Hindi, Marathi, Tamil and even, sometimes, Bengali. Sanskrit, the language of the Vedas, does not have any special merit or halo around it in the field of the *bhajanas.*

Bhajana Songs in Non-Sanskritic Languages

A discussion of this point in a theological work, *Bhakti-saṃdeha-dhvānta-bhāskara* (a work in Sanskrit!), attributed to Sadgurusvāmī (the third *ācārya* for the *bhajana* tradition in the South), will clarify this further. The work is in the form of a lively and penetrating discussion between one of the disciples, presumably an active Bhāgavata (as we can see clearly from the nature of the questions raised), and Sadgurusvāmī of Marudanallūr.

Disciple: Svāmin, by the *śruti* "One should not [speak] a Mleccha language [either a non-Sanskritic or a foreign language];" there is no entry or qualification for Brahmans in other languages. My mind questions the reason why they sing songs in languages like Telugu, Maharastra, Hindustani, Tamil, and Kannada.

Guru: Dear, do not have any doubts. In the *Bhāgavata Purāṇa,* in the eleventh chapter, is the following statement [of the Lord]: "One should prostrate oneself to the Lord [falling at His feet] like a stick after having praised and sung to Him with hymns and songs, smaller and bigger [important and unimportant], with praises that are found in the Purāṇas and Prakrit languages." By this statement [we know] that the Lord is to be praised in any language and even in Prakrit words [grammatically unrefined]. . . . The import of the *śruti* text is to negate and criticize that language unadorned with the [descriptions of the] qualities of the Lord and not to criticize a language that describes the glories of the Lord.[51]

Change in Grace Recitations and Invocations over Food Among the Bhāgavatas

Another innovation is that of abandoning the recital of certain Vedic *mantras* like *brahmametu mām* while the Bhāgavatas congregate and eat after the *bhajanas* and reciting, instead, stanzas like *gandharva-rāja-pratimam* . . . that describe the glories of Bhagavān. This is alluded to in the same theological work. The *guru* replies to remove the doubt of the disciple:

It is only those who follow the way of Vedic *karma,* who chant Vedic hymns like the *annasūkta* [during their meal]. *Jñānīs* [who follow the path of knowledge] recite the stanza *brahmārpaṇam* . . . [i.e., this is an offering to Brahman]. *Bhaktas* [devotees] according to their *adhikāra* [distinctive propriety] sing the above-mentioned stanzas. . . . "In each mouthful [while eating] by reciting the name of Govinda, one should be understood as eternally fasting [as it is the Lord in him who actually eats]. He is indeed a *jīvan-mukta.* There is no doubt." On a consideration of the above stanza and the fruit of eternal fasting, [devotees] perform the singing of the qualities of Bhagavān Krishna while eating. Also from the statement [from the *Gītā*] "while eating, walking, sleeping, breathing."[52]

The Unique Joy of the Bhajana: the Jīvan-muktas, Mukta-jīvas Continue to Sing and Help Fellow Human Beings

In another place in the famous dialogue, discussing the way of *bhakti* and singing the Lord's names, the teacher, after quoting in great detail from several scriptural texts and the *Bhāgavata Purāṇa,* sums up with a firm conclusion:

"By reciting which Name, man gets released from *saṃsāra* immediately; That name creates fear of [the great] Fear [of *saṃsāra* residing in man]." This is also a statement from the *Bhāgavata.* By many such categorical statements, it has been ascertained and ordained that for all men, the way to *mokṣa* lies in the singing [and meditating upon] the names of the Lord, whether they belong to the different *varṇas* like the Brahman, the Kṣatriya, Vaiśya or Śūdra, whether they belong to different *āśramas* such as *brahmacārī, gṛhastha, vānaprastha,* or *saṃnyāsī,* or whether they are *caṇḍālas* [outcastes].[53]

He goes on to stress constancy in singing and meditating on the Divine Name, i.e., *āvṛitti* of the name. "By *āvṛitti,* the *vāsanas* [evil impressions and associations imprinted on the mind through the previous bad actions] are destroyed." In this way, Name singing and Name meditating also function as an effective *saṃskāra,* substituting for the Smārta *saṃskāras* (the Vedic rites of purification and embellishment for the mind and soul). The great joy of the *bhajana* even exceeds the joy of *mokṣa* experience. The bliss of the *bhajana* congregation can be shared with fellow human beings and can help them to obtain release from *saṃsāra,* here in the world. Sadgurusvāmī quotes from the *Bhāgavata* in this connection:

It has been said in the *Bhāgavata* that even sages, *jīvan-muktas* who delight in the bliss of Ātman, who have no further ends to achieve, who have destroyed all their sins, show spontaneous reasonless devotion to Hari incessantly, and that Hari's qualities are such. Hence we find even released persons like Nārada constantly singing the names and stories of Viṣṇu on their *vīṇās* [musical instruments] adorned with Brahman, the supreme God in the form of *svaras* [pure musical notes constituting *nāda-Brahman*].[54]

Many liberated persons have not cared for the bliss of *mukti* (release) but have continued to sing and meditate upon God and have lingered to help other devotees reach God. In some other instances, as in some *Āḻvārs* and *Nāyanmārs* (Tamil Vaiṣṇava and Śaiva devotee-singers), we find a further step in this direction. Although on the verge of release, they did not strive further for their release, but continued to show devotion and to serve God and His devotees, and preferred by a conscious choice to live continuously on earth in such capacities. We find such categorial preferences in the deliberate statements made in their songs. The sharp criticism from the mouth of Prahlāda, a great devotee, found in the *Bhāgavata Purāṇa,* is aimed at the lone and silent penance performers who retire to the forest to meditate and achieve their own individual salvation, but are indifferent to the sufferings of other people on earth. He says that until the most lowly and despised has reached salvation, until everyone has had *mukti,* he will not himself seek *mokṣa.*[55]

These phenomena are intimately connected with a study of one of the greatest and most central issues in Hinduism, that of *jīvan-mukti* (liberation while living) and the lives of many *jīvan-muktas* or *mukta-jīvas* (liberated persons, living and continuing to function in a *new* way in society). This is a field that unfortunately has not received adequate historical, theological, phenomenological, and social study from scholars.[56] The great phenomenon of liberated persons who continue to live and help society, and uphold the ideal of *lokasaṃgraha* (helping and serving the people), and of persons on the verge of liberation who do not care to proceed further but continue to work for the *mokṣa* of others, has always been taken for granted in Hinduism. As such, it has neither received any systematic study and exposition, nor has it attracted any ideological glamor to be held aloft and pointed out. It has always remained something that is to be lived, a thing that is to be practiced. The *Brahma-sūtras* refer to several stories of the lives of such great men, and in one of the *sūtras* (III.3.32) there is a discussion of the continued existence of certain persons, although they had obtained release. In an elaborate discussion, the various commentators refer to the lives of sages like Apāntaratama, Sanatkumāra, Vasiṣṭha and Nārada. Some of them were reborn intentionally, though they had reached *mokṣa* experience. They continued to live, or even chose successive rebirths, in order to fulfill their missions, either to carry out certain offices bestowed upon them by God to help people and the world, or voluntarily to stay and help others achieve *mukti*. Such instances, Śaṃkara says, are analogous to the self-assumed mission and responsibilities of a *jīvan-mukta*.[57] Related to this is the belief in Hinduism that *ciram-jīvī* devotees (ever living without being concerned about their release), like Mārkaṇḍeya, Nārada, Vibhīṣaṇa, Hanumān, and others, live and work for the salvation of all human beings. Some of these stories are to be found in the Upaniṣads, and others in the epic narratives and the Purāṇas. Some of the names of such eternally living devotees are invoked in the beginning of a Rādhā-Krishna *bhajana*, and their guidance and help are sought by the devotees.

Theology and Philosophy of the Divine Name (Word)

Commenting on the congregational singing in the *bhajana*, Sadgurusvāmī refers to the fact that the devotee not only delights in singing the songs and names of the Lord but also causes others to delight. Moreover, men may obtain the same results even by hearing the name chanted, and there is a cumulative effect, as well, in the efficacy of congregational singing. This topic leads to the various ways in which the efficacy of the Name is understood in the theology and philosophy of the *bhajana*. We will make only a brief reference to the various approaches. At one end is the belief that the Name, by itself, as Word, is efficacious, and that by the very uttering of the sounds comprising the Name one obtains the results. The Name has even greater power and efficacy than the person who possesses the Name (i.e., Bhagavān, or God). There lies in the background of this approach to the Name the whole philosophy of *sphoṭa,* the Word-Absolute, with its development through centuries. That which is broken by utterance, the sound, is *sphoṭa.* The believers in the *varṇa-sphoṭa* view see the letter-sound as the ultimate. Those who so believe would correspond and have relevance to the modern linguists interested in the importance of the "phonic element." Linguists who stress the "semantic element" also have their counterparts among the ancient grammarians and philosophers of other schools in India. *Śabda-sphoṭa* philosophers, differing from philosophers of the *varṇa-sphoṭa* persuasion, contend that the Word is the final Absolute. The followers of *vākya-sphoṭa* emphasize that *vākya,* or the sentence, is the ultimate unit. Some profound insights into the philosophy or psychology of the Word-Absolute are to be found in the writings of Bhartṛhari, Vacaspati Miśra, Maṇḍana and others.[58]

At the other end lies the philosophy of idea or meaning as the ultimate. According to this approach, the one meaning of all names, i.e., God, the Person who possesses the Name, is the source of efficacy, the granter of the results. By singing the Name, God's grace is invoked by the devotees. Between these poles is the belief, widely prevalent, that each Name is marked by one distinctive quality or one act of God and, as such, calls for meditation on that particular glory, act, or gift when the Name is recited or sung.[59] The name "Govinda," for instance, recalls Krishna's birth in the family of a cowherd and his tending and protecting of his herd of cows. The Name also has an immediate religious and mystical undertone. The belief that the utterance of the Divine Name delivers its result and saves men from all sins and its basis can be understood more clearly through a knowledge of *sphoṭa*-philosophy and its ramifications. Bodhendra says in his *Nāmāmṛtarāsayana:*

This is the concluding view that is shown. In whatever way, under any circumstances by the performance of the chanting and singing of the Name, all sins get destroyed and release does happen, whether the Name is recited by woman or man. It may be by any man [of any caste or position], or by one insane, by one having faith or without faith. It may even be by one for the sake of the removal of the distress created by thieves, [wild animals like] a tiger, or any disease. It may be for obtaining non-eternal results in the form of *dharma, artha* or *kāma* or for the sake of other gifts.[60]

A Different Sūtra (Holy Thread) for Name-Meditation

Another interesting step in the interaction of *smṛtis* and Purāṇas is the practice of some Brahman devotees in the southern *bhajana,* who wear and use a different *sūtra* (a holy thread, like the Vedic sacred thread worn and used in Smārta rites) in addition to the Vedic *sūtra* while performing *bhajana* or individual Name-meditation. Commenting on this development Sadgurusvāmī says that this new *sūtra* was used even by the sage Śuka; he relates that according to the *Skandopapurāṇa,* Lord Subrahmaṇya revealed this new *sūtra* to Śuka. The *sūtra* also helps the devotee to count the number of turns while he is meditating on the Name. "As the *yajñopavīta* (Vedic sacred thread) is necessary for performing the *śrauta* and Smārta rites, in the same way this *sūtra* is essential for singing the Name and this is the conclusion." [61]

Mutual Salutations Among the Devotees

Toward the end of the Rādhā-Krishna *bhajana,* the devotees embrace one another, take the dust from each other's feet and offer prostrations mutually to each other, irrespective of differences in age, caste, learning, position, and so on. Commenting on this to his disciple, Sadgurusvāmī refers to instances in the Purāṇas and in the *Bhāgavata,* particularly where elderly persons have prostrated and humbled themselves before younger ones. This is in opposition to the Vedic observance, in which one offers salutations only to one older, and only by a formalized Smārta form of introducing oneself by referring to one's *pravara, gotra, sūtra* (lineage, one's Vedic *sūtra,* such as Āpastamba, Bodhāyana, etc.), and the branch of the Vedas to which one belongs (e.g., Ṛgveda). This can be performed only to those who know how to respond with a formalized reply and blessing, in which the name of the person saluting must be lengthened to the *pluta* accent (one step beyond the long accent) and then the appropriate blessings offered.

In contrast to this one-way prostration, the relationships undergo a reversal, as it were, in the *bhajana.* The story that Mārkaṇḍeya, who had lived through a life of seven *kalpas,* prostrated himself and honored sage Parāśara, aged seven years, is recounted by Sadgurusvāmī. In this account, quoted from the *Nāradīya Haribhakti Sudhodaya,* there is an interesting new mathematics for the calculating of the actual age of a person. Only those moments count for real age and living that are spent in constant meditation and thought on Hari (Viṣṇu). This points to a different approach to time and stresses "lived time" as opposed to "clock time." By this count, the seven-year-old Parāśara was richer in age than the grand veteran Mārkaṇḍeya. Other examples are also quoted. Finally, Sadgurusvāmī quotes a stanza from the *Bhāgavata:*

> By ignoring those who belong to oneself, those that mock at him, by giving up the sense of bodily conceit and shame, one [the devotee] should offer prostrations to [even] the horse, *caṇḍāla* [outcaste], the cow, and the donkey.[62]

The devotee should recognize and see God in all living things, though the presence of God as the indweller in men has a clearer, more significant dimension.

The Meaning of Rādhā in the Rādhā-Krishna Bhajana of South India

Before concluding this chapter, a brief reference should be made to the meaning of the person of Rādhā, the particular female cowherd who has been singled out among the *gopīs* by Krishna, by the other *gopīs,* and by the devotees for her supreme sacrifice and love for Krishna. Symbolically, she is understood to represent the human soul in love with God. There is no direct mention of Rādhā by name in the *Bhāgavata,* although there is reference to one *gopī* whose unparalleled love won her the love and favors of Krishna. Sadgurusvāmī refers to the details of the life of Rādhā in the *Brahmāṇḍa Purāṇa,* and to the stories of devotions and austerities in the *Āgneyapurāṇa Saṃgraha,* the *Brahmavaivarta Purāṇa,* and the *Garga Saṃhitā.*[63] Nārāyaṇa Tīrtha, the *saṃnyāsin*-composer, develops the theme of Rādhā's love for Krishna in one of his songs in the *Kṛṣṇalīlā Taraṅgiṇī.* We need not, of course, remind the reader of the elaborate treatment of the theme in Jayadeva's *Gītagovinda,* a highly lyrical religious drama set in the charming language and idiom of the physical love of man and woman. These songs of Jayadeva and Nārāyaṇa Tīrtha are sung and danced in the Rādhā-Krishna *bhajana.*

When religion and philosophy had degenerated into barren academic games, completely divorced from living, when trends toward over-intellectualization had set in, when music, too, had developed forms full of virtuoso techniques without devotional depth, and when other branches of learning had also developed incrustations of intellectual systems and customs, the message of the devotees and their compositions came as a great liberating and elevating force. In many of the songs of the devotee-composers one can discern these sentiments. In the southern *bhajana,* in spite of the emphasis on the love of the *gopīs* and that of Rādhā, which symbolizes the burning embodiment of a powerful passion for God, the mood is of a "pentacostal" type. It is restrained; it is colored by the Advaita theology and philosophy that lies in the far background, the influence of which can be seen in the attitude of the devotees in the Krishna-*bhajana* toward such other manifestations of God as Śiva, Rāma, Subrahmaṇya, and Devī. These devotees, full of love, service, and devotion for God and their fellow men, make places sacred or more sacred, bring glory to actions, and provide their own distinct authority to the sacred writings, according to the *Bhāgavata.* In the speech to Uddhava, Krishna clearly states his own attitude toward such devotees:

> O Uddhava, neither Brahmā [the creator-god], who is my own creation, nor Śiva, nor Balarāma, nor Lakṣmī, nor even My own Self is so dear to me as are devotees like you. . . . To sanctify Myself with the dust of his feet, I constantly follow the footsteps of a devotee who has no worldly cravings, who is tranquil at heart, who has no enmity with anyone, who beholds Me equally in all living beings, and who is constantly absorbed in thoughts of Me.[64]

VII. SŪRDĀS AND HIS KRISHNA-*BHAKTI*

by S. M. Pandey and Norman Zide

Sūrdās: Life and Works

In the history of Hindi literature Sūrdās occupies an important place. He became famous in his lifetime for his deep personal devotion, the quality of his poetry, and his considerable musical gifts. Next to Tulsīdās, Sūrdās is perhaps the most popular poet in northern India, particularly in the Hindi-speaking region. Unfortunately, we know very little about his life. In some anthologies of the *bhaktas* of the medieval period and in the writings of the Vallabha sect, of which he was a member, mention has been made of him, but there is so much legendary material that it is difficult to separate fact from fiction. Nor do his own works throw much light on his life.

From the *Caurāsī Vārtā* ("Stories of the Eighty-four Vaiṣṇavas") of Gokulnāth, which was probably composed sometime before A.D. 1650, we can draw the following conclusions:

(1) Sūrdās was a great singer and had composed poems of salutation before he met Vallabhācārya at Gaughāṭ.

(2) Vallabhācārya inspired him to write *padas* on the *līlā* of Krishna. After meeting Vallabha, Sūrdās wrote thousands of poems; the standard collection of about five thousand of these is commonly known as the *Sūrsāgar,* i.e., the Sāgar (ocean) of Sūr.

(3) His fame reached the great Mughal emperor, Akbar, who came to visit him.

(4) He was blind.

(5) He died at Pārsaulī, a place near Mathurā.

There is another sectarian work, *Bhāvaprakāśa* by Hari Rāi, from which we obtain the following information about the poet.

(1) Sūrdās was born to a Sārasvata Brahman family at Sīhī, four miles from Delhi. He was blind from birth and was a musician with a very sweet voice.

(2) At the age of eighteen he left Sīhī and came to Gaughāṭ, and there met Vallabhācārya, who was traveling to Braj from Arail

(Allahabad). Vallabhācārya made him his disciple and introduced him to the tenth chapter of the *Bhāgavata Purāṇa* and explained the contents of his own *Subodhinī,* a commentary on the *Bhāgavata Purāṇa.*

The other works that refer in some way to Sūrdās are: (1) *Vallabhadigvijaya* by Goswāmi Yadunāth; (2) *Bhaktmāl* by Nābhādās; (3) *Bhaktvinod* by Miyāṃ Singh; (4) *Rāmrasikāvalī* by Mahārāj Raghurāj Singh; (5) *Bhaktnāmāvalī* by Dhruvdās; (6) *Nāgarsamuccay* by Nāgarīdās; (7) *Vyāsvāṇi* by Harirām Vyās (8) *Muntakhāb-ut-Tawārīkh* by Abdul Qādir Badāyūnī; (9) *'Ain-i-Akbarī* by Abul Fazl; and (10) Mūlgosāīṃcarit. In these works we get some information about Sūrdās, but it is not always possible to substantiate the statements that have been made. Sūrdās is a very popular name in India, and even today many of the blind people who live by singing are called Sūrdās. It is probable that many Sūrdās legends have been combined and associated with the name of the famous poet. Therefore, it is difficult to come to any definite conclusions on the basis of these stories and the references in them.

In the Vallabha sect, Sūrdās is believed to have been born ten days after Vallabhācārya. Gokulnāth has given the following information about Sūrdās's date of birth: "Sūrdās was born after Vallabhācārya, and he was ten days younger than he (Vallabhācārya)."[1] Vallabhācārya was born in A.D. 1478, so the date of Sūrdās's birth can be fixed in the same year. *Sūrsārāvalī,* which is attributed to Sūrdās, also supports this statement. This work was probably completed in Saṃvat 1602 (A.D. 1545) when he was sixty-seven years old. It also indicates that Sūrdās was born in Saṃvat 1535 (A.D. 1478).

According to sectarian evidence, Sūrdās died in the presence of Viṭṭhalnāth, Vallabha's son, who himself died in Saṃvat 1642 (A.D. 1585). Prabhudayāl Mītal has shown that Sūrdās was definitely alive in Saṃvat 1638 (A.D. 1581).[2] Therefore it can be assumed that Sūrdās died sometime between 1638 and 1642 (Saṃvat).

There is a great deal of controversy as to whether or not Sūrdās was blind from birth. There is no explicit indication that Sūrdās became blind later in his life. The scholars who believe that he became blind later say that no sightless person could have given such picturesque descriptions of the beauty of nature, and such detailed descriptions of children's activities as Sūrdās has given. This is the only proof that they adduce in support of their view.

The following works are attributed to Sūrdās: (1) *Sūrsārāvalī,* (2) *Sāhityalaharī,* (3) *Sūrsāgar,* (4) *Sūrsāṭhī,* (5) *Sūrpaccīsī,* and (6) *Sevāphal.* The *Sūrsāgar* is a collection of his *padas.* Sūrdās's fame rests on these poems from the *Sūrsāgar,* about which more will be said in the following pages. In the *Sūrsārāvalī,* we find a short description of the various *avatāras* of Krishna. In the *Sāhityalaharī,* the *līlā* of Krishna with various heroines (*nāyikās*) is elaborately described. Vrajeśwar Varmā, in his thesis on Sūrdās,[3] claims that these two works are not genuine, but no other scholar supports his view.

The last, *Sevāphal,* was composed on the model of Vallabhācārya's *Sevāphalavivaraṇa.*

Sūrsāgar and the Bhāgavata Purāṇa

According to the Vallabha sect, Vallabhācārya explained to Sūrdās the *līlās* of Krishna as described in the *Bhāgavata Purāṇa.* Then Sūrdās composed his twelve chapters of the *Sūrsāgar* according to the *Bhāgavata* and included also the *dānalīlā* and *mānalīlā.* After that, Ācārya (Vallabha) had him listen to the *Puruṣottamasahasranāma.* Then the *līlās* of Bhagavān Krishna awakened in his heart. After this, Sūrdās described them just as they are referred to in the *Bhāgavata Purāṇa* from the first to the twelfth chapter, and he included also a description of various *mānalīlās* and *dānalīlās,* and so on.[4]

Sūrdās himself confirms this statement and indicates that he has told the story of the *Bhāgavata Purāṇa* in the language of the common people:

> Vyāsa composed the twelve chapters of the *Bhāgavata* and recited them to Śukadeva. Sūrdās describes and sings the same ones in the popular language and in *padas.*
>
> Sūrdās says I tell this story in conformity with the *Bhāgavata Purāṇa.* You listen to it carefully.[5]

From these statements it is clear that Sūrdās followed the *Bhāgavata Purāṇa* in his *Sūrsāgar.* But it would not be true to say that Sūrdās followed the *Bhāgavata Purāṇa* chapter by chapter. Of course, he used the stories, but he adapted them in his own way, according to his faith and temperament. In this respect his poems of salutation, his poems on the child Krishna, and his bee songs are quite original. Similarly, many of the *padas* of separation are also in large part the original creation of the poet.

We will examine briefly how much Sūrdās has taken from the *Bhāgavata Purāṇa.* The first chapter of the *Sūrsāgar* consists mostly of poems of salutation. In about two hundred poems Sūrdās has depicted his position as a *bhakta.* He speaks of himself as a great sinner, of the way of devotion, and of the transitoriness of life. These poems are quite free of influences from the *Bhāgavata Purāṇa.* Actually the stories from the *Bhāgavata Purāṇa* begin after these poems. In this connection, Sūrdās does follow the first chapter of *Bhāgavata Purāṇa,* but the story of the birth of Śukadeva and the story of Vidura and of Draupadī in this chapter of the *Sūrsāgar* are not from the *Bhāgavata.*

The second chapter of the *Sūrsāgar* consists of only thirty-eight *padas,* in which the importance of *bhakti* and the importance of the repetition of the names of Lord Krishna, and the benefits of association with saints and pious persons is affirmed. As in the *Bhāgavata,* descriptions of the greatness of Krishna and of his all-encompassing and omnipresent nature have not been given by Sūrdās in detail. Sūrdās uses these themes in only one poem.

Sūrdās very briefly tells other stories from the *Bhāgavata Purāṇa* in the third and subsequent chapters. The third and the fourth chapters are very short and in narrative style. Sūrdās leaves out many stories from the *Bhāgavata Purāṇa* and includes such new stories as that of the birth of Vidura in his third chapter, and the story of Śiva and Pārvatī in his fourth chapter. In the *Bhāgavata Purāṇa* the fourth chapter is very important because of the descriptions of various dynasties of kings, social conditions of the age, and the low estate of Brahmans and because of the proclamation of the decline of Śaivite influence. In the *Sūrsāgar,* all these things have been ignored.

In the fifth chapter, the stories of Jarābharata and Ṛṣabhadeva are told in narrative style. Other descriptions of the several islands, worlds, and the various families of gods that are included in the *Bhāgavata Purāṇa* are not to be found in the *Sūrsāgar.*

In the sixth chapter, the stories of Ajāmila, Nahuṣa and Ahilyā are presented in narrative style.

Sūrdās describes very briefly the importance of the *guru* in this chapter, which the *Bhāgavata* does not. In the seventh and eighth chapters, Sūrdās describes the various incarnations of Viṣṇu, including those as Nṛsiṃha, Vāmana, and Matsya, and emphasizes the importance of repeating the name of Rāma.

The ninth chapter of the *Sūrsāgar* is longer than the previous chapters and contains the five stories of Purūravas, the sage Cyavana, Ambarīṣa, Saubhari, and Haladhara. Here the poet has followed the *Bhāgavata Purāṇa,* but he does not include the famous story of Hariś-candra. In this chapter Sūrdās also gives the full story of Rāma and a summary of the whole *Rāmāyaṇa,* from the childhood of Rāma to the end of his life. The story of Rāma has been given only briefly in the *Bhāgavata Purāṇa:* Sūrdās presents the story in greater detail. His attitude of reconciliation, one of the main features of the *bhakti* movement of the medieval period in India, is reflected in his depiction of Rāma's life.

The Tenth Chapter of Sūrsāgar

The fame of Sūrdās depends mainly on his descriptions of the activities of Krishna as a child and on his *līlā* with Rādhā and the milkmaids; these descriptions are found in the tenth chapter of the *Sūrsāgar*. This chapter is more than twice as long as the other chapters combined. Vallabhācārya's *Subodhinī* commentary on the *Bhāgavata Purāṇa* also treats the tenth chapter in detail. Sūrdās probably followed his teacher in this elaboration.

The tenth chapter of the *Sūrsāgar* can be divided into two parts. The first part comprises the activities of the child Krishna from his birth to his youth. Krishna was born in Gokula to Vāsudeva and Devakī, but his parents, filled with terror at Kaṃsa's killing of the innocents, took him to Nanda and Yaśodā in Vraja (Braj). In his childhood Krishna destroyed Pūtanā and many other demons—Tṛṇavarta, Vatsāsura, Vakāsura, Aghāsura, and others. Sūrdās tells these stories from the *Bhāgavata* as well as the story of Srīdhara, which does not appear in the *Bhāgavata Purāṇa.* Sūrdās's purpose in using these stories is similar to that of the *Bhāgavata,* i.e., to reveal the supreme power of the divine Krishna.

The originality of Sūrdās lies in such poems as those describing Krishna's *saṃskāras* (ceremonies)—celebration of his birth, the ceremony of his first feeding, and the ceremony of piercing his ears, and other activities of Krishna, such as his sleeping, kneeling, playing, grazing cows, and stealing butter. These poems present dramatically the psychology of an Indian childhood, in the context of vividly presented scenes of village life, and depict the various rituals, festivals, customs, and manners of common people of medieval India in Braj. Most of these customs survive today in the villages in northern India. In the descriptions of the activities of the child Krishna, Sūrdās is usually waiting to reveal the supreme power, divinity, and godhead of Krishna.

In the second part of the tenth chapter, Krishna's *līlā,* the circular dance (*rāsa*) with the milkmaids and Rādhā, begins. Rādhā, who is so prominent in the Vaiṣṇava literature of northern India was not mentioned in the *Bhāgavata.* The Rādhā of Sūrdās occupies a very significant position in the theology of *bhakti;* one important reason for this is that the status of Rādhā as *svakīyā* (wife) is different in many ways from the *parakīyā* Rādhā of the medieval Vaiṣṇavism of Bengal. Here, too, are found the flute (*mūralī*) poems. The single-minded response of the *gopīs* to the sound of Krishna's symbolic flute is recorded in them. Finally in the tenth chapter we have the bee songs (*bhramargīts*). Uddhava, a friend and a messenger of Krishna, and a follower of the qualityless and formless (*nirguṇa*) brahman, goes to the milkmaids to teach them *jñāna yoga* and meets with strong criticism from the women and girls of Braj who are faithful devotees of Krishna. The satire and irony in the statements of the milkmaids are notable, and extend the range of tone and subject that Sūr commands.

In the eleventh chapter of the *Sūrsāgar* there are only four poems, and in these the Nārāyaṇa and Kalki *avatāras* are described. From the philosophical point of view the eleventh chapter of the *Bhāgavata Purāṇa* is very important, for *bhakti, jñāna,* and *karma* are elaborately explained, and the superiority of *bhakti* is established. Otherwise, the eleventh chapter of the *Sūrsāgar* is rather weak and is quite short.

The twelfth chapter of the *Sūrsāgar* is also very short, consisting of only five *padas*. The Buddha and the Kalki incarnations are mentioned there. At the end of this chapter Sūrdās tells of several *bhaktas* and their freedom from worldly bondage.

Although the *Sūrsāgar* follows the *Bhāgavata Purāṇa* in many ways, the differences between these two works are equally significant. Sūrdās emphasises the *līlā* of Krishna, which is described mainly in the tenth chapter of his *Sūrsāgar*, whereas the *Bhāgavata Purāṇa* deals in detail with other more or less philosophical and theological problems. The social and the cultural background of the *Bhāgavata Purāṇa* is also rather different from that of the *Sūrsāgar*, the latter clearly reflecting the cultural and social background of the medieval period of India.

Sūrdās and the Child Krishna

The poems of Sūrdās about the child Krishna are important not only for their devotional feeling, but also for their literary beauty and psychological perception. In the Vallabha sect the worship of the child Krishna is prominent. All the poets of this sect have written poems on this subject, and among these the poems of Sūrdās and of Paramānanddās are the most important. Sūrdās, in nearly eight hundred poems, depicts the various activities of the child Krishna; the subjects of these poems can be classified broadly into the following categories: (1) the birth of Krishna and the poems on his various activities as a very young child; (2) stealing butter; (3) grazing the cows; (4) stealing the clothes of the girls of Braj.

There is tremendous rejoicing and happiness throughout Braj during the celebrations of the birth of Krishna. Yaśodā, Krishna's mother, is very happy. She calls the girls of Braj and they sing birthday songs. People flock to Nanda's door to share in his happiness. The bards come to sing congratulatory songs. Sūrdās has given a very picturesque description of all these happenings in some twenty poems.[6]

Yaśodā rocks Krishna's cradle and sings a lullaby "O sleep, come, and put my son to sleep." Krishna shuts his eyes for a while as if he were asleep, but as soon as Yaśodā stops singing, he opens them again; then Yaśodā repeats her lullaby.

As she nurses Krishna, she thinks about how fast he is growing, and how he will soon have his baby teeth. In such poems Sūrdās expresses the feelings and hopes a mother has for her child.

The child grows day by day. He plays near Yaśodā and Nanda. They celebrate his first-feeding ceremony, and after that the ceremony of piercing the ears. As Krishna gets bigger, he starts to crawl. He moves around the courtyard of the house but finds it difficult to cross the threshold. Soon he can stand on his feet. Yaśodā teaches him to walk. Krishna sets his feet on the floor and tries to move them, but soon he stumbles; Yaśodā picks him up.

When Krishna is five years old, he starts stealing butter from the houses of the *gopīs*. In many poems Sūrdās has depicted the child as a butter thief. He goes with his friends into a milkmaid's house. He steals butter and when he is caught—sometimes red-handed—he makes various excuses. In one poem, he talks to his own reflected image and feeds it butter.

Krishna grows older. He and his friends take the cows to graze. All day he is busy rounding up the cows. His friends do not work themselves; they put him to work instead. In the evening he comes home exhausted. He complains to his mother about his idle friends and she becomes angry with them.

Finally, we come to the poems in which Krishna steals the garments of the girls of Braj. Sixteen thousand girls were bathing in the Yamunā River and had left their clothes on the banks. Krishna took their clothes away and sat in a *kadamba* tree, watching. When the girls came out of the water they found that their clothes were gone. They ran to Krishna, whom they saw in the tree, and demanded that he return their saris. Krishna gave them their saris and revealed his divinity to them.

In the *Bhāgavata Purāṇa* episode in which Krishna steals the garments of the milkmaids, the *gopīs* worship Kātyāyanī and Bhadrakālī, to obtain Krishna as their husband; however, in the *Sūrsāgar,* they worship Śiva and the sun. In the *Bhāgavata Purāṇa,* Krishna explains to the milkmaids why he stole their clothes. "You are all engaged in the observance of a vow, and by bathing in the water with your persons naked, you have disregarded the divinities. For this reason sin rests on your heads." In the *Sūrsāgar,* Krishna makes no such statement, but, instead says that he has come to fulfill the desires of the girls, who wanted to have him as their husband. Sūrdās never loses sight of the divinity of Krishna. In his play as a child Krishna manifests continually his supreme power. Yaśodā once had doubts about the divinity of the child; then he showed her the three worlds and all the universe in his mouth.

In his childhood he killed many demons, and by doing so revealed his divine power. Sūrdās constantly emphasizes that Krishna was not a child, or not only a child, but God himself incarnated and accomplishing various deeds on earth.

In the love of Yaśodā and Nanda for Krishna, parental affection (*vātsalya bhāva*) is displayed. This parental love is considered to be the prototype of true and selfless love. This selfless love is central in *bhakti*. Yaśodā and Nanda are true devotees of Krishna because their love is free of all selfish desires. Moreover, when Krishna is away from them for a moment they suffer severe pangs because of their separation from him. In these poems of the child Krishna, the spirit of *bhakti* finds clear expression.

It is difficult to discover how the worship of the child Krishna became popular in India. There are references to the child Krishna in the songs of the Āḻvār saints of South India, particularly in the songs of Periyāḻvār and Āṇḍāḷ (before A.D. 900). Before them, the Sanskrit poet Bhāsa (A.D. 200–300) had also described the activities of the child Krishna. In the thirteenth century, the Marathi saint Jñānadeva wrote poems on Viṭhobā that described him as the child Krishna. In South India there are a number of child gods, including Bālasubrahmaṇya. The worship of these child gods is supposed to be very ancient.

The Purāṇas, *Harivaṃśa,* and the *Bhāgavata Purāṇa* describe the various activities of the child Krishna, so that we can say that before Vallabhācārya the worship of the child Krishna was popular in India. Apart from the *Bhāgavata Purāṇa,* it is likely that Vallabhācārya may have been influenced by the songs of the Āḻvārs. Vallabha, though he was born in northern India and was brought up in Banaras, was a Telugu Brahman and had spent many years in the south. Sūrdās, in his Bālakṛṣṇa poems and in other ways, owes much to Vallabhācārya and his thought and practice.

Rādhā in Indian Literature and in the Works of Sūrdās

Rādhā, who became so important in the medieval period of Hindi literature, is not mentioned at all in the *Bhāgavata Purāṇa.* There is, however, one *gopī* in the *Bhāgavata Purāṇa* whom Krishna favors most. In the literature of the Āḻvārs of the south, Nappinnai, a favorite milkmaid of Krishna, is mentioned as participating with him in the circular dance (*rāsa*). Charlotte Vaudeville believes that the author of the *Bhāgavata Purāṇa* was acquainted with Nappinnai as a partner of Krishna Māyon in the cowherd dances, and she concludes that this favorite *gopī* was probably Rādhā.[7]

The first explicit reference to Rādhā is found in the Prakrit work *Gāhāsattasaī,* which is attributed to Hāla:

> O Krishna, by the puff of breath from your mouth as you blow the dust from Rādhā's face, you take away the glories of the other milkmaids.[8]

Bāṇabhaṭṭa alludes to Hāla Sātavāhana and the Sattasaī in his *Harṣacarita* (seventh century); so it can be said that the *Gāhāsattasaī* was compiled before the seventh century. In the Pahārpur temple of Bengal there is an image of Krishna with his consort, but it is not certain whether this consort is Rādhā. Svayambhū, an Apabhraṃśa poet (probably eighth century), refers to Rādhā. In one couplet he says:

> The breasts of Rādhā made Krishna dance in the courtyard, and people were amazed.
> Now it no longer can matter what happens to these lovely breasts.[9]

The Sanskrit poet Bhaṭṭanārāyaṇa (eighth century) mentions Rādhā in one verse of his *Veṇīsaṃhāra.* Ānandavardhana in his *Dhvanyāloka* also alludes to Rādhā. In the work of an unknown Sanskrit poet of the tenth century, the *Kavīndravacanasamuccaya,* Rādhā is mentioned in four verses. Other poets who in one way or another have mentioned Rādhā before the twelfth century are Vikramabhaṭṭa, the author of *Nalacampū,* Somadeva Sūri, the author of *Yaśastilaka,* and Kṣemendra of Kashmir. In the twelfth century, Jayadeva in his *Gītagovinda* depicts the love of Rādhā and Krishna in a very lyrical style. The subject of the poem is the amorous *līlā* of Krishna with Rādhā and the other *gopīs*. Rādhā is the favorite of Krishna, but it is not clear from the text whether or not Rādhā is the wife (*svakīyā*) of Krishna, although this seems to be implied.

Jayadeva's influence on Bengali Vaiṣṇavism was great and it also extended to the Hindi poets of the Vallabha sect, but there is an important difference between Bengali Vaiṣṇavism and the Krishna poets of Hindi insofar as Rādhā is concerned. Rādhā is always described by the poets of the Hindi group as the wife of Krishna, but the Bengal Vaiṣṇava poets usually describe her as someone else's wife. Vidyāpati, who wrote in Maithili and is considered to be both a Hindi poet and a Bengali poet, drew inspiration from Jayadeva. Vidyāpati's Rādhā impresses the reader with her single-minded love for Krishna and with her deep sorrow when separated from him. Caṇḍīdās, a Bengali poet, who was probably a contemporary of Vidyāpati, also wrote love poems about Rādhā and Krishna that are very popular in Bengal. Vidyāpati and Caṇḍīdās both describe Rādhā as a *parakīyā* of Krishna. Another Hindi poet who wrote on the Rādhā-Krishna theme was Umāpati Upādhyāya of the fourteenth century. Some scholars confuse him with the Umāpati who was a contemporary of Jayadeva and served at the court of Lakṣmaṇa Sena. Umāpati Upādhyāya wrote several poems about Satyabhāmā and Krishna.[10]

In this chapter we shall discuss the position of Rādhā in Aṣṭchāp literature, and especially in the poems of Sūrdās. Sūrdās's Rādhā and Krishna grow up together and become friends when they are quite young. In the poems of Sūrdās, the affection of childhood turns into the deeper love of youth, and this bond of love becomes still stronger after they are married. In the poems of Caṇḍīdās and Vidyāpati, Rādhā is not a childhood friend of Krishna, nor do these poets describe the marriage of Rādhā and Krishna. In fact, these poets portray Rādhā and Krishna always in the fullness of youth; their sport is youthfully lively. Here Rādhā never becomes the wife of Krishna. Unlike the Rādhā of Sūrdās, in the poems of Caṇḍīdās Rādhā is always fearful of separation from Krishna. She is afraid that Krishna will leave her, and she is always worried and afraid that people will blame her for ruining her family's reputation if her secret meetings with him are discovered.

Sūrdās describes the marriage ceremony of Rādhā and Krishna in many poems. Thus, in one poem he says:

Śyām and his beloved Rādhā are a beautiful pair.
Gladly her friend tied Rādhā and Krishna's
marriage knot and with a sweet smile turned her face away.
He is the bee and she the lotus bud; one is clever, the other
not unwise.
Loving each other they experience joy and their conversation is
eloquent.
He is the young *tamāl* tree of Vṛndāvan and the fair one is the
golden creeper.
Sūrdās says: he is beautiful and wise and so is the young girl
Rādhā.[11]

Paramānanddās and Nanddās of the Aṣṭchāp group have also described the wedding of Rādhā and Krishna.

O friend, sing the auspicious songs. May the daughter of Vṛṣabhānu
and the bridegroom Krishna have a long life.[12]
The beautiful Giridhar (Krishna) is the bridegroom
And Rādhikā (Rādhā) is the bride.
Whoever saw them was abashed,
So beautiful was the couple Rādhā and Krishna.[13]

It should be pointed out that although the Hindi Aṣṭchāp poets—and Sūrdās is the most famous of these—follow Vallabha in making a point of Rādhā's married (*svakīyā*) status (they do this most memorably by describing her wedding), there is no suggestion that Rādhā and Krishna ever intend to, or will, settle down to conjugal life in Braj. They, of course, do not do so. After the wedding (no clear relative chronology of these events is given in Sūr) Krishna leaves for Mathurā to perform the task he was incarnated for, and Rādhā is left behind as a *virahiṇī* (a woman separated from her lover), indeed, as the *virahiṇī* par excellence for most of the Krishna devotees.[14] In making considerable devotional and poetic use of *viraha,* the *virahiṇī,* and of Rādhā as a notable *virahiṇī,* the Hindi poets are much like the Vaiṣṇava poets of medieval Bengal and elsewhere in India, Sūrdās and his associates of the Aṣṭchāp wrote a great many poems of *viraha* (love in separation) and many of these are moving and striking poems, but on the whole the Aṣṭchāp poets tend to be milder, more homely and conventional, and less addicted to the depiction of the extremes of physical passion than are some of the Bengali poets.

The implications which Rādhā's position as *svakīyā* have come to have in her *viraha* have not been examined in detail. Probably, they are few and tenuous. There is little evidence to suggest, for instance, that, because she is a *svakīyā,* she suffers more or less intensely the pangs of separation from Krishna. There are many poems describing the anguish felt by Rādhā, but there are also many poems in which an unspecified *gopī* (or unspecified *gopīs*) is described in the same way and as being equally anguished. The lines found elsewhere in the *Sūrsāgar* in which the *gopīs* praise Rādhā as the true consort of Krishna are not found or paralleled in the *viraha* poems. The marriage of Rādhā and Krishna seems to have been a marriage of theological convenience for the Vallabha sectarians. It makes their relationship more proper, and it gives such poets as Sūr a chance to continue to describe in his devotional, homely, and vivid way, additional scenes of village life, and of the life of Lord Krishna.[15] Whatever theological capital may have been made of Rādhā's position as *svakīyā* (of course, not by Sūr, who was no theologian), it did not filter down to Sūr's poems.

Rādhā is not portrayed as a wife in Sūr, and certainly never exhibits—never gets a chance to exhibit, if you like—the wifely virtues of Sītā or Sāvitrī. The few reconciliatory poems in the very brief group in the *Sāgar* on Krishna in Dwārikā conflate Rādhā and Rukmiṇī in an interesting, if largely perfunctory, manner. In Sūr's characteristically peaceful world, there is no competition, derogation, or jealousy when Rādhā and Rukmiṇī meet. They are assimilated in rather pat metaphors, and, he says, are simply two aspects of the same thing.

Rukmiṇī and Rādhā met as two daughters of the same father meet after long separation. They are alike in temperament, both are of the same age, and both are beloved of Krishna. Both have one [i.e., the same] heart, and one mind, and their bodies are beautiful to look at. Rukmiṇī took Rādhā to her house and arranged various receptions. Sūrdās says that he set his feet there where two goddesses (*ṭhākurānī*) were present.[16]

But this reconciliation or assimilation is described in only a few poems, whereas there are hundreds of poems of *viraha* in which Rādhā and the *gopīs* suffer in separation from Krishna, and where Rukmiṇī is quite properly completely out of the picture. For the *gopīs* in Sūr (and almost everywhere else in this literature) what is important is not where Krishna is or what he is doing, but that he is not in Braj with them and that, conceivably, he may come back. Mathurā is nearby but not a place to which they can go looking for him. Dwārikā is part of another world and of another story and has nothing to do with them or with Braj except in the charming but very peripheral rapprochements in the few poems of this sort by Sūr and others.

Sūrdās personalizes Rādhā and gives her more prominence than she is given by earlier writers using the same themes, or by Krishnaite poets in other languages and traditions. There are several obvious motives for his doing so, and there are a number of areas in which Rādhā is singled out for special notice. One reason for distinguishing Rādhā from the other *gopīs,* is to provide Krishna with a proper consort.[17] With the tendency to remodel Krishna into a full-scale major god like Viṣṇu and Śiva and the Rāma of many medieval texts, the need for an appropriate consort is increasingly felt. The likeliest candidate for this position for Krishna in his Braj days is Rādhā. This development seems to be unrelated to Rādhā's *svakīyā* status, or to the wedding descriptions that do not parallel or model themselves on those descriptions in classical literature of the weddings of Śiva and Pārvatī and of Rāma and Sītā. What Sūr does bring out in talking of Rādhā as a fit consort for Krishna is that she is a far more worthy object or vessel of Krishna's love than are the other *gopīs.* The *gopīs* themselves commend her greater virtue, saying that they themselves are turned away (*bimukh*) and that she is the real beloved of Krishna. Sūr follows up these statements in the poems with the more or less commonplace conceits that Rādhā and Krishna are really one, that their love is eternal and has always been in all of their previous lives, that Rādhā is *prakṛti* and Krishna is *puruṣa,* and that they are really one and the same and that Krishna distinguished the Rādhā aspect of himself solely for the purposes of joy and *līlā.*

Thus in one poem (*SS* 3434), he says, "You should not think that this love is new. Listen Rādhā, your love for Mādhava is eternal." In the same poem Krishna tells Rādhā that "whenever you sulk at Mohan he becomes more upset. The fire of separation from you then consumes the whole world. . . . He is the *puruṣa* of *prakṛti,* the husband of Śrī and the spouse of Sītā." He thus aligns her with these divine consorts. In another poem (*SS* 2305), "Krishna said to Rādhā: 'Living in Braj you have forgotten yourself [i.e., who you really are]. Know that *prakṛti* and *puruṣa* are the same; there is a difference only in word.

. . . We have two bodies but the soul is identical. I created you for the sake of joy [*sukha*].' "

The other *gopīs* praise Rādhā, telling her that she is a virtuous and pious woman, and the true beloved of Krishna (*SS* 2461). "Rādhā, you are a very pure woman. I tell you this with soul and mind having no doubts in my heart. Only you have known Śyām; the others are inconstant (*durācāriṇī*) women; you move like a full vessel; the others splash noisily like half-empty ones." In another poem Sūrdās says:

The girls of Braj say again and again:
Rādhā, you are blessed; he who lifted the mountain is your slave.
Blessed is the son of Nand, blessed art thou and blessed is your love.
Blessed are you both, expert in the arts of love.
You are the real companion of Krishna;
The two of you have two bodies, but one soul; we are turned away
  from him.
You are one heart, one mind, one consciousness;
You are bound by the selfsame love.
If you are out of his sight for even a moment—he becomes impatient.
On his flute the mighty one repeats your name again and again.
You have recognised the jewel, Śyām;
You are clever and wise.
They say that the Lord is the slave of your love.
Who can compare with you? says Sūrdās.[18]

Thus we see that Rādhā holds an important place in the poems of Sūrdās. She is the beloved favorite of Krishna who has known him since childhood. The milkmaids praise her close relationship with Krishna and her worthiness of his love. (She is less important and less distinguishable from the other *gopīs* as *virahiṇī*.) Rādhā has always been the beloved of Krishna (in all their previous existences); they are really the same—the difference between them is only verbal, and Krishna created Rādhā for *līlā,* she is the wife (*svakīyā*) of Krishna, this status being stressed by Vallabha and the theologians of his school.

Bhakti in the Works of Sūrdās

Sūrdās belonged to the sect of Vallabha, and Vallabhācārya's philosophy of Śuddhādvaita finds expression in his poems. Krishna was the personal deity whom he worshiped. However, he also wrote poems about Rāma and gave respectful attention to Śiva in his work. This attitude of reconciliation is a characteristic feature of the devotional poetry of India. The Āḻvārs of South India composed poems about Krishna as well as Rāma. Nammāḻvār treats Krishna, Śiva, and Brahmā as one entity. He says in one of his poems

Am I to speak of my lord of mystery (Krishna), who for the joy of deliverance created all the worlds, who wears this sweet blossoming *tulasī* for the worlds to praise, as the one with color like a shining jewel, or as he who wears matted hair and the cool crescent moon [Śiva], ever to be praised as the unique one, or as the four-faced god [Brahmā].[19]

Kulaśekhara, who has composed poems chiefly on Rāma, also composed poems on Krishna. We find this tendency in the later Hindi poems, too. Vidyāpati in the fifteenth century composed poems on Krishna and on Śiva. For this reason some scholars debate the question of whether Vidyāpati was a Śaivite or a Vaiṣṇavite poet. They do not realize that poems about Śiva in the works of Vidyāpati can only be indications of the syncretistic spirit of the poet. Later, Sūrdās and Tulsīdās followed the same path. Tulsīdās, in the sixteenth century, composed a complete Kṛṣṇagītāvalī. We have already said that Sūrdās composed a complete Rāmāyaṇa, but there is no doubt that Tulsīdās was a devotee of Rāma and Sūrdās was a devotee of Krishna. In the following pages we will discuss the forms of *bhaḳti* reflected in the poems of Sūrdās. Like all the *bhaḳta* poets, Sūrdās, too, emphasized the view that this life is transitory and fleeting. All worldly things are only for a day. If there is anything valuable in this world, it is *bhaḳti*. In the Vallabha sect, devotion to the child Krishna was widespread. In most of the temples of the Vallabha sect the child Krishna was worshiped. However, Vallabha did not reject *mādhurya bhaḳti*. It is said that in his later life, because of the influence of Caitanya, he shifted his major emphasis to *mādhurya bhaḳti*. In his *Subodhinī,* his commentary on portions of the *Bhāgavata Purāṇa,* he explained the significance of the *rāsapañcādhyāyī* (the five chapters of the circular dance), of flute songs, and of the bee songs (*bhramargīt*). Later we shall speak of how Sūrdās described the *rāsapañcādhyāyī* and the flute of Krishna. We shall also examine the significance of the bee songs in the framework of his *bhaḳti*.

Here it will be useful to discuss the philosophical background of Sūrdās. In his poems we see, as we have already mentioned, the influence of Vallabha's philosophy; for Vallabha, Krishna is supreme as *brahman* is in the Upaniṣads. He is *sat-cit-ānanda* (being-consciousness-bliss). Non-living objects have only *sat* (being); consciousness and bliss are absent in them. The animate creation has being and consciousness, but no bliss. Krishna, the supreme being has all three qualities: being, consciousness, and bliss. In his *Tattvanibandha,* Vallabha says, "I salute that Krishna who created the world in his *līlā* and who dwells in the world in various forms. He is both *saguṇa* and *nirguṇa*. The individual souls come out of him as sparks from fire." *Bhakti* is the only way to salvation and *bhakti* for Vallabha is love (*prema*) and service (*sevā*). *Bhakti* can be attained only through the mercy of the supreme being. A *bhakta* can attain this mercy through complete surrender to the supreme and by purity of heart. Vallabha does not advocate renunciation or *saṃnyāsa*. *Māyā* is the power of *brahman* and is not different from *brahman*. God manifests himself as many through *māyā*. The manifestation is not an illusion. It is a real manifestation of the supreme being in his diverse forms and in some of his aspects. *Māyā* is not the original cause; it serves to make God manifest in the world.

In the poems of Sūrdās, Krishna is the object of his worship and is also the supreme being. He says:

> He, whose glory is sung by the Upaniṣads and whom the Upaniṣads speak of as *nirguṇa* has come as *saguṇa* and is playing at Nanda's door. He is the inexpressible *brahman* [who is] beyond the reach of mind and speech. His influence is limitless. He incarnates himself in the world for the good of *bhaktas*.[20]

In the poems of Sūrdās, his foster parents Nanda and Yaśodā, the cowherd boys, and the *gopīs* are all *bhaktas* who are devoted to Krishna in various ways. In *bhakti,* love of god is essential. This love can be expressed in many ways. Vallabhācārya has described four kinds of *bhakti:* (1) *vātsalya,* (2) *dāsya,* (3) *sākhya,* and (4) *mādhurya*.

The devotion of *vātsalya bhāva* is that in which parental love is expressed. Nanda and Yaśodā and Vasudeva and Devakī are the *bhaktas* who express parental love for Krishna. The devotion of *dāsya bhāva* is that in which a devotee feels himself a servant of his particular personal deity. In the devotion of *sākhya bhāva* the devotee feels himself a friend of his personal deity. The last, *mādhurya bhāva,* is that in which the *bhakta* worships the supreme being as a husband. A devotee in this form of *bhakti* is considered a beloved of god. Each of the *gopīs* feels herself to be the beloved of Krishna.

In the poems of Sūrdās, *vātsalya bhāva* and *mādhurya bhāva* are most prominent. Though the friends of Krishna have also been described as *bhaktas,* they do not attain the importance of Nanda and Yaśodā or the milkmaids. *Dāsya bhakti* has been expressed by Sūrdās in only a few poems of salutation. Tulsīdās was a follower of *dāsya bhakti.* In his *Rāmcaritmānas* Bharata, Lakṣmaṇa, and Hanumān all delight in serving Rāma. Rāma is their master and they are his servants (*sevaka*). Among the several kinds of devotion, *mādhurya bhakti* has been accepted by many scholars as the highest form of *bhakti.* An Indian wife in her various roles comprehends all the attitudes that are to be found in the various kinds of *bhakti.* She is a mother, a servant, a friend, and a beloved. Therefore *mādhurya bhakti* includes everything involved in *vātsalya, dāsya,* and *sākhya.* This is why the milkmaids occupy a very important place among the Krishnaite *bhaktas.* Vallabhācārya himself in his *Nirodhalakṣaṇa* says, "I wish my heart could feel the separation from Krishna that the *gopīs* felt."

Sūrdās says that the milkmaids are manifestations of Krishna himself.

> The *gopīs* and the *gwāls* and Krishna are not two;
> they are not in the least different from one another.
> Whenever Hari appears he doesn't forget them for a single moment.[21]

In the poems of Sūrdās, the other milkmaids are—like Rādhā—friends of Krishna from their earliest childhood. Their love for Krishna increases as time goes on. We see the full development of their love during the *rāsalīlā*. Sūrdās has given a very detailed description of this. On an autumn night Krishna plays his flute. The milkmaids are disturbed by this music. They leave their children and husbands and run to meet Krishna, their lord and the deity they worship. Krishna teaches them that a woman's duty is to love her husband and tells them to go back home. But the milkmaids cannot go, since they know in their hearts that their real lover is Krishna, and that he can be attained only through detachment from worldly things, including husbands and children. When Krishna sees their extreme devotion, he fulfills their desires. They wanted to have him as their husband, therefore he dances with them in the circular dance. The milkmaids enjoy their relation with Krishna. He manifests himself in as many forms as there are milkmaids. Each milkmaid feels that Krishna is with her alone. She becomes proud and begins to believe that Krishna is under her influence. Krishna who dwells in everyone's heart, sees this and disappears. The milkmaids discover their error and regret their pride. Krishna then appears before them again. Here Sūrdās follows the *Bhāgavata Purāṇa,* in which this episode has been introduced to explain that *bhaḳti* should be free from all pride. This episode also throws light on the divinity of Krishna, who appears as the lover of his *bhaḳtas* but at the same time shows himself to be beyond all attachment.

The milkmaids' love for Krishna becomes more intense when he leaves them in Braj and goes off to Mathurā. Sūrdās excels in the description of *viraha* (separation); the tenth chapter of the *Sūrsāgar* is full of poems of separation. *Viraha* has been depicted in greater detail in the *Sūrsāgar* for various reasons. Separation, of course, is a standard theme of court and folk literature in India. Also, it is in separation that love is tested; if the love is real, the pangs of separation will be strong. *Bhaḳti* is nothing but the feelings of sorrow in separation from God and the effort toward union with him.

In one poem a *gopī* says that the creeper of separation has spread throughout her body and that it is now difficult to remove it:

The creeper of separation was planted in my eyes.
They water it, friend, and its roots have gone deep.
It grows in its way; it casts thick shadows now.
How can I leave it? It has spread all through me.
Who knows what it wants? It is always new.
The *gopīs* complain that Śyām is gone,
And this has cankered the bud of love.[22]

In their separation from Krishna, the milkmaids are extremely dejected, so much so that they have not been able to sleep. They remain awake all night. Natural beauty no longer gives them pleasure. In the following poem their miserable condition is described. The groves and the Yamunā River which used to please them when Krishna was there, no longer please them in his absence. They say that without Krishna the groves have become their enemies.

Without Hari these groves have become enemies.
When he was here these creepers felt cool to our bodies, but now they have become a mass of flames.
The Yamunā flows in vain, the birds sing in vain, and in vain the bees hover around the lotus.
The air, the betel leaves, the camphor, and the moonbeams that used to refresh us now burn like the sun.
O Uddhav, go and tell Mādhav that Kāmdev has beaten us and crippled us.
Sūrdās says: O Prabhu, these eyes that have watched the road for a glimpse of you have grown dim with watching.[23]

They cannot appreciate the sweet music of the birds. The peacocks and the partridges are all antipathetic to them now. In one poem, Sūrdās gives a very gloomy description of the milkmaids who see the projection of their own thoughts in the partridge that speaks in the dead of night.

We burn in the separation from Mohan, but why do *you* burn?
O sinner cuckoo, why do you call *"piya piya"* [beloved, beloved] at midnight?
It shows nothing heroic that you pound these lifeless, helpless women.
O wicked one, you make others suffer and do not know this, since you do not suffer.
The world is happy, but you are unhappy without water; nevertheless you are not aware of sorrow.
The milkmaids say, "Why do you ruin your next life by speaking in this Braj that is deprived of Śyām?" Sūr says.[24]

Krishna wants to test the strength of the love of the milkmaids for him. To do this he sends his friend Uddhava to them. Uddhava goes to teach them about *nirguṇa brahman* and the doctrines of *jñāna yoga*. He meets with strong criticism from them. The milkmaids, who are devotees of Krishna, will not hear anything against Krishna *bhakti*. In the following poem we can see how the milkmaids criticize Uddhava and refuse to accept *nirguṇa brahman* and *jñāna yoga*.

Uddhav, we are not worthy of *yoga*. How can a weak woman know the essence of knowledge? How can she meditate? O bee, such deceptive words we will not listen to. Who wants to suffer having the ears pierced and letting the hair grow wild and matted? You tell us to give up sandalwood [paste] and to smear ashes [on our bodies], we who have been badly burned by the fire of separation from him. The one for whom the *yogī* wanders around forgetting himself, he, that same one, is in our hearts. Sūrdās says [the milkmaids say] we do not want to be away from him for an instant. He is the body and we are his shadow.[25]

All such poems are *bhramargīts,* or bee songs. Uddhava is represented here as a black bumblebee. Uddhava goes to the milkmaids to preach meditation and *jñāna yoga,* which they have no use for, and they call him a bee, presumably for his buzzing, bumbling behavior. In the *Bhāgavata Purāṇa* they are prepared to accept the doctrine preached by Uddhava, but in the works of Sūrdās there is a conscious attempt to establish *bhaḳti* as supreme. In the *Sūrsāgar,* Uddhava fails miserably in his mission. The milkmaids make fun of him and drive him to distraction. Afterward, very much impressed by the quality of their devotion, he returns to Krishna and tells him of the sorrow of the *gopīs*. He pleads on their behalf and asks Krishna to go back to them and take their grief away.

The tradition of bee songs, which began with Sūrdās, continued into the twentieth century. Many poets wrote bee songs in imitation of Sūrdās. Nanddās is the next great poet after Sūrdās whose bee songs became famous. The last important poet of the tradition was Ratnākar, who flourished in the twentieth century and wrote an *Uddhav Śataḳ*.

Some concluding comments on the *bhaḳti* and on the poetry of Sūrdās emerge from a somewhat perfunctory comparison of Sūrdās with Mīrābāī, a Hindi Krishnaite poetess, not of the Aṣṭchāp, but a poetess—probably the only one—at least as popular as Sūr. If one compares in their works the relations of the poet-singer and devotee to the action of the poems and the implications of these, one finds sharp differences. In the common medieval Sanskritic and Persian tradition, the name of the poet[26] is indicated by its mention—in Hindi, in a peculiar syntactic fashion—in the final verse of the poem. Such verses are often translated "Sūr says: . . ." All, or almost all, of the poems in the *Sūrsāgar* mention Sūr's name in this way. In these poems, in all but one group of the *vinaya padas,* he describes in a dramatic way and in a colloquial idiom the acts and the feelings of the *virahinīs,* of the child Krishna, of Uddhava, and so on. In a very small number of the *padas* in the *Sūrsāgar,* his name in the final verse is mentioned in a context that lets him figure, peripherally, in the action he describes. The minimum "role" possible is the use of a phrase such as "Sūr's *ṭhākur*" [deity] for "Krishna" (*SS* 781). Less perfunctory but still very peripheral "roles" are found in such statements as "Sūrdās says that he [Sūr] is a wayward man, but will sing auspicious songs in the groom's party at the wedding" (*SS* 811), or "Sūrdās [says] that he knows what will happen and therefore is worried" (*SS* 681).

Sūr speaks out in the first person only in the *vinaya padas.* These can be divided into two classes: the hortatory poems, in which he advises and admonishes his hearers as to what sort of life to lead, and those in which he uses "I" and "my" more centrally, characteristically describing himself as a great sinner. In those of the first category, Sūr usually does not speak of himself, but directly exhorts the listener. For example:

> The day when the bird of your life flies away, all the leaves of the beautiful tree of your body will fall.
> Do not be proud of this body. Jackals, crows, and vultures will eat it
> [One of] three things [will happen]: [your] body [will be gotten at by] insects, or [it will become] filth, or, as dust, it will fly away.
> Where [then] will this water of life, beauty, and form-and-color be seen?
> The people you loved, seeing you, will hate you.
> Your household will say: "Take him outside quickly, or he will become a ghost and catch hold [of us] and eat [us].
> Your sons, whom you brought up so carefully, will pray to the gods and goddesses [for their own welfare].
> They will break your skull open with a bamboo stick and scatter the pieces.
> Fool, go today and associate with saintly persons; from them, you will get something.
> If you have a human body and are not a devotee of Hari, Yama's assaults will consume you.
> Sūr says, "Without devotion to Hari your life is in vain."[27]

Sometimes in the poems of exhortation, he uses the first person for introducing his *pada,* "Where else could my soul find happiness [but in Hari]?" (*SS* 168), and then goes on to make his general points—in this case, by asking a number of pointed rhetorical questions. But it is only in the second group of *padas* that he speaks out strongly in the first person. Thus "Lord, I have been standing and waiting for a long time" (*SS* 137), or:

Who can be more devious, vile, and lustful than I?
What is hidden from you, O compassionate Lord who pervades [the hearts] of all?
You have given me a human body, but I am such an ingrate that I have forgotten.
Full of rebellion, I run to lust like a village pig.[28]

To quote one poem in full:

Now I have danced too much, Gopāl,
Wearing the garment of lust and anger, on my neck a garland of sensuality.
The ankle bells of delusion peal out sweet words of malice; envy sounds in my body in all kinds of beats.
Sunk in error, my mind has become a drum that keeps bad time.
My waist is tied with the sash of Māyā, and I wear the *tilak* of greed on my forehead.
Fully warmed up, I have demonstrated crores of dance techniques, oblivious to land, sea, and time.
Sūrdās says, O Nandlāl, take away my ignorance.[29]

He speaks of himself, then, as a great sinner: "I am the crown of sinners" (*SS* 96), "a sinner for the last seven generations, [who has] committed all the sins" (*SS* 134) and asks to be saved and thus to live eternally. "The sinner can rise only when you help him gladly" (*SS* 134), and "I want to board the boat, but can't pay the boatman./ Take me across, great Lord, Lord of Braj" (*SS* 108). He often speaks of the redemption of so great a sinner as Sūr as a test of Hari as savior: "You have redeemed only ordinary sinners (so far), all these accomplishments are vain and worthless./ When you redeem Sūr, then your fame will be world-wide" (*SS* 96). Elsewhere: "Now I want to dance naked [i.e., shamelessly] and destroy your reputation" (*SS* 134), and "Accept your defeat, or live up to your reputation [and save Sūr]" (*SS* 137).

Sūr uses the imagery of dancing to indicate the perfection, the power, and the attraction of the great sinner who must be bested, i.e., saved, by Hari or who must defeat him and destroy his "reputation." Sūr magnifies himself—as sinner—to exalt his Lord as savior. Sūr must be saved because it is Hari's place as *patitapāvana* (purifier of sinners) and *dīnabandhu* (friend of the poor) to save him, and because Sūr wants to and asks to be saved.

How the redemption comes about in the sinner is not mentioned. What one aspect of the *mukti* is like is described in a few poems. It is, of course, not the complete absorption into the godhead of, say, Kabīr and the *sant* poets. In the following poem the scene described and the imagery are quite traditional:

> O *cakai* bird, go to that lake—where there is no longer love and separation,
> Where the night of illusion never comes—which is the sea of happiness;
> Where Sanak, Śiv, the swans and the fish and the sages live, and the stars and the sun shine,
> Where the lotuses are without a moment's fear of moonbeams, where the path hums with fragrance,
> The lake where fine pearls and the fruits of *mukti* are, where the nectar of good deeds is drunk.
> If you give up that lake, O stupid bird, what will you do here?
> There, with Lakṣmī, the lovely sport goes on perpetually, says Sūr.[30]

To characterize Sūr's *padas* summarily, it can be said that they are short devotional poems, written in an idiomatic vernacular and that they give lively genre pictures of medieval village life in North India. Sūr is particularly happy in portraying women and children, and the domestic scenes and ceremonial occasions that involve them prominently. These are presented in a devout but lively and dramatic fashion in the *Bālakṛṣṇa* poems. His hero and his deity is Krishna as infant, child, and youth. He gives us idyllic pastoral pictures celebrating the traditional *saṃskāras* and ways of rural life that center around the young god-hero. Krishna as an adult is largely out of the picture, although he remains vital to the motivation of the limited "action" of the *viraha* poems, the longing of the *gopīs* for Krishna, who has gone from Braj to Mathurā and left them behind. In the hundreds of *viraha* poems in the *Sāgār,* Sūr takes these more traditional themes of separation and treats them in a more traditional language than he uses in the *Bālakṛṣṇa padas,* in a number of them very movingly and effectively.

The *bhramargīt* poems display the one kind of challenge to and mockery of authority—here the false authority of Uddhava, who comes to preach *jñāna yoga.*

> Paṇḍe came to teach us *yoga,*
> Loaded with scripture books like a traveling merchant with his string of pack animals.
> We move toward our lotus-eyed husband; those who study *yoga* are whores.[31]

Sūrdās is no radical; he depicts and advocates a traditional Brahmanism and asserts the authority of the *śrutis* as interpreted by Vallabha and his followers. He does not approve of the arid *nirguṇa jñāna* whose advocates are represented in the poems of Uddhava. The details of Sūr's ideal devotional life have not been thoroughly explored. For instance, Sūr seems to make little of the *guru* and the need for *guru*ship, but the implications of this are not clear. It is worth noting that the people of Braj who mock and reject Uddhava and his doctrine are the women. "We are weak women, and not worthy of *yoga,*" they tell him sarcastically (*SS* 4542). This is, of course, consistent enough with their positions as *virahiṇīs* who long for Hari and will accept no dehydrated substitutes, but it should be noted that there are no men in Sūr's poems who reject so bitingly this or any other traditional value.

In his *vinaya padas,* he tells his hearers to give up sensual indulgence and to become devotees of Hari and to associate with the pious, and thereby to avoid the ravages of death and live forever near the deity. Sūr is no theologian here, nor does he offer much in the way of ethical teaching. In other *padas* of this group he presents himself in somewhat hyperbolic language as the greatest of sinners (not, however, as utterly miserable and thoroughly meek, as some contemporary devotional poets of the *dāsya bhāva* persuasion present themselves) who "in the darkness of [his] ignorance [has] lost sight of his great destination" (*SS* 47) and who now pleads and demands to be saved.

Mīrā is much more limited in her choice of subject; she writes almost always of her love for Hari, and usually speaks in the first person. She is hardly concerned with story-telling and the life of Krishna, with Rādhā and the *gopīs,* or with *līlā,* with Uddhava, or *vinaya,* or sin, or elaborate description, although a few poems on some of these subjects have been attributed to her. She takes Giridhar as her husband and affirms and celebrates her love for him in her songs. "Giridhar Gopāl is mine; I have no other."[32] Her devotion met with a great deal of opposition from the family of her husband and derogation from people in general. She mentions this in the *padas*. "I am sold into the hands of Giridhar, but people say that I am loose" (*MP* 14). She makes comparatively little use of the traditional *alaṃkāras,* although some of her *padas* are much like the *gopī bhāva* poems of *viraha* in Sūr and other Hindi Krishnaite poets. There is much less of the luxuriant physical imagery in the description of Krishna and of her love and her longing than there is in the poems of Sūr, to say nothing of the stronger and more explicit language of physical passion used by Caṇḍīdās. Mīrā does use the traditional erotic imagery—"I have adorned myself, I have made the bed of pleasure" (*MP* 15)—but only up to a point in the individual poems. Usually, in the culminating final verse, the physical conceit is not followed up in similarly physical terms. The union Mīrā speaks of is essentially a mystical one. She does not use the metaphor of the consummation of physical union to represent it. For example, in the final verse, immediately following that quoted above, she says: "My Lord is the clever Giridhar: I make myself a sacrifice to him again and again" (*MP* 15); this verse has more overtones of physical love than other final verses, such as "mix my light in your light" (*MP* 46), or the common conceit (not in a final line) "I am deep-dyed in Giridhar's color" (*MP* 23). Neither the language nor the spiritual goals here are those of Sūr.

The physical descriptions in some of the *padas* serve to present Krishna more directly (at the beginning of a *pada*), but they are traditional, and usually perfunctory, and are neither physically suggestive nor emotionally highly charged. When she says, "Friend, the arrow [of his glance] struck my eyes./ Its head pierced my heart and his sweet image entered my soul" (*MP* 14), she is speaking in traditional Krishnaite terms, and, apart from the first-person "my," sounds like Sūr and others. But she differs considerably from Sūr in saying what her devotion has cost her.

My friend, I bought Govind
You say secretly, I say openly—after beating the drum I bought him.

You say dearly, I say cheaply; after weighing him on the scale I bought him.
I sacrificed my body, my life and [all my] priceless things.
[Mīrā says:] Lord, give me your *darśan;* in a previous life you promised me [this].[33]

In summary, Mīrā speaks almost always in the first person, and speaks of her love for Hari. She says she has, at considerable cost, "established a relationship with the great house" (*MP* 24), and must continually struggle to maintain it, to keep the deity from abandoning her. She also speaks of the opposition and the vilification of the world. Her world is less simple, comfortable, and homely than is Sūr's, and she usually speaks at a higher pitch of intensity. Thus, she says, "I am maddened by love; no one knows my pain./ My bed is on the point of a stake; how can I sleep?" (*MP* 70).[34] The love she speaks of is less amenable to the traditional classification of *śṛṅgāra* as *saṃyoga* and *vipralambha* than is that of Sūr's *gopīs* and Rādhā, since her Krishna is less physical, less a person, and is considered, at least sometimes, to be indwelling. The ultimate union she craves is more spiritual and abstract. She is not infrequently eager to sacrifice herself: "I make myself a sacrifice to him [Krishna] again and again." Pleading for mystical union, she makes use of a personal, often anguished, woman's voice along with a directness of language uncommon in Hindi and an aptness of metaphor, and she can sound, at her infrequent best, like no other poet in Hindi. For instance: ". . . show me the way./ Let me become a pyre of sandalwood; light it with your hand/ And when [it] burns to a heap of ashes, apply [it] to your body./ Mīrā says, Lord Giridhar, mix my light in yours" (*MP* 46).

Mīrābāī's voice is closer than that of any other Hindi poet to the voice of the *sant* poets and, in language and feeling, closer to some of the European mystics comparable to the *sant* poets than are Sūrdās and his fellow Krishnaite poets.

VIII. THE FEAST OF LOVE

by McKim Marriott

I shall try here to interpret Krishna and his cult as I met them in a rural village of northern India while I was conducting my first field venture as a social anthropologist. The village was Kishan Garhi,[1] located across the Jumnā from Mathurā and Vrindaban, a day's walk from the youthful Krishna's fabled land of Vraja.

As it happened, I had entered Kishan Garhi for the first time in early March, not long before what most villagers said was going to be their greatest religious celebration of the year, the festival of Holī. Preparations were already under way. I learned that the festival was to begin with a bonfire celebrating the cremation of the demoness Holikā. Holikā, supposedly fireproofed by devotion to her demon father, King Harnākas, had been burned alive in the fiery destruction plotted by her to punish her brother Prahlāda for his stubborn devotion to the true god, Rāma.[2] I observed two priests and a large crowd of women reconstructing Holikā's pyre with ritual and song: the Brahman master of the village site with a domestic chaplain consecrated the ground of the demoness's reserved plot; the women added wafers and trinkets of dried cow-dung fuel,[3] stood tall straws in a circle around the pile, and finally circumambulated the whole, winding about it protective threads of homespun cotton. Gangs of young boys were collecting other combustibles—if possible in the form of donations, otherwise by stealth—quoting what they said were village rules, that everyone must contribute something and that anything once placed on the Holī pyre could not afterward be removed. I barely forestalled the contribution of one of my new cots; other householders in my lane complained of having lost brooms, parts of doors and carts, bundles of straw thatch, and an undetermined number of fuel cakes from their drying places in the sun.

The adobe houses of the village were being repaired or whitewashed for the great day. As I was mapping the streets and houses for a preliminary survey, ladies of the village everywhere pressed invitations upon me to attend the festival. The form of their invitations was usually the oscillation of a fistful of wet cow-dung plaster in my direction, and the words, "Saheb will play Holī with us?" I asked how it was to be played, but could get no coherent answer. "You must be here to see and to play!" the men insisted.

I felt somewhat apprehensive as the day approached. An educated landlord told me that Holī is the festival most favored by the castes of the fourth estate, the Śūdras. Europeans at the district town advised me to stay indoors, and certainly to keep out of all villages on the festival day. But my village friends said, "Don't worry. Probably no one will hurt you. In any case, no one is to get angry, no matter what happens. All quarrels come to an end. It is a *līlā*—a divine sport of Lord Krishna!" I had read the sacred *Bhāgavata Purāṇa's* story about Prahlāda and had heard many of its legends of Krishna's miraculous and amorous boyhood.[4] These books seemed harmless enough. Then, too, Radcliffe-Brown had written in an authoritative anthropological text that one must observe the action of rituals in order to understand the meaning of any myth.[5] I had been instructed by my reading of B. Malinowski, as well as by all my anthropological preceptors and elders that one best observes another culture by participating in it as directly as possible.[6] My duty clearly was to join in the festival as far as I might be permitted.

The celebration began auspiciously, I thought, in the middle of the night as the full moon rose. The great pile of blessed and pilfered fuel at once took flame, ignited by the village fool, for the master of the village site had failed to rouse with sufficient speed from his slumbers. "Victory to Mother Holikā!" the shout went up, wishing her the achievement of final spiritual liberation rather than any earthly conquest, it seemed. A hundred men of all twenty-four castes in the village, both Muslim and Hindu, now crowded about the fire, roasting ears of the new, still green barley crop in her embers. They marched around the fire in opposite directions and exchanged roasted grains with each other as they passed, embracing or greeting one another with "Rām Rām!"—blind in many cases to distinctions of caste. Household fires throughout the village had been extinguished, and as the assembled men returned to their homes, they carried coals from the collective fire to rekindle their domestic hearths. Many household courtyards stood open with decorated firepits awaiting the new year's blaze. Joyful celebrants ran from door to door handing bits of the new crop to waking residents of all quarters or tossing a few grains over walls when doors were closed. As I entered a shadowy lane, I was struck twice from behind by what I thought might be barley, but found in fact to be ashes and sand. Apart from this perhaps deviant note, the villagers seemed to me to have expressed through their unified celebration of Holikā's demise their total dependence on each other as a moral community. Impressed with the vigor of these communal rites and inwardly warmed, I returned to my house and to bed in the courtyard.

It was a disturbing night, however. As the moon rose high, I became aware of the sound of racing feet: gangs of young people were howling "Holī!" and pursuing each other down the lanes. At intervals I felt the thud of large mud bricks thrown over my courtyard wall. Hoping still to salvage a few hours of sleep, I retreated with cot to the security of my storeroom. I was awakened for the last time just before dawn by the crash of the old year's pots breaking against my outer door. Furious fusillades of sand poured from the sky. Pandemonium now reigned: a shouting mob of boys called on me by name from the street and demanded that I come out. I perceived through a crack, however, that anyone who emerged was being pelted with bucketfuls of mud and cow-dung water. Boys of all ages were heaving dust into the air, hurling old shoes at each other, laughing and cavorting "like Krishna's cowherd companions"—and of course, cowherds they were. They had captured one older victim and were making him ride a donkey, seated backward, head to stern. Household walls were being scaled, loose doors broken open, and the inhabitants routed out to join these ceremonial proceedings. Relatively safe in a new building with strong doors and high walls, I escaped an immediate lynching.

I was not sure just what I could find in anthropological theory to assist my understanding of these events. I felt at least that I was sharing E. Durkheim's sense (when he studied Australian tribal rites) of confronting some of the more elementary forms of the religious life. I reflected briefly on the classic functional dictum of Radcliffe-Brown, who had written that the "rites of savages persist because they are part of the mechanism by which an orderly society maintains itself in existence, serving as they do to establish certain fundamental social values." [7] I pondered the Dionysian values that seemed here to have been expressed, and wondered what equalitarian social order, if any, might maintain itself by such values.

But I had not long to reflect, for no sooner had the mob passed by my house than I was summoned by a messenger from a family at the other end of the village to give first aid to an injured woman. A thrown water pot had broken over her head as she opened her door that morning. Protected by an improvised helmet, I ventured forth. As I stepped into the lane, the wife of the barber in the house opposite, a lady who had hitherto been most quiet and deferential, also stepped forth, grinning under her veil, and doused me with a pail of urine from her buffalo. Hurrying through the streets, I glimpsed dances by parties of men and boys impersonating Krishna and company as musicians, fiddling and blowing in pantomime on wooden sticks, leaping about wearing garlands of dried cow-dung and necklaces of bullock bells. Again, as I returned from attending to the lacerated scalp, there was an intermittent hail of trash and dust on my shoulders, this time evidently thrown from the rooftops by women and children in hiding behind the eaves.

At noontime, a state of truce descended. Now was the time to bathe, the neighbors shouted, and to put on fine, fresh clothes. The dirt was finished. Now there would be solemn oblations to the god Fire. "Every cult," Durkheim had written, "presents a double aspect, one negative, the other positive."[8] Had we then been preparing ourselves all morning by torture and purgation for other rites of purer intent? "What is it all going to be about this afternoon?" I asked my neighbor, the barber. "Holī," he said with a beatific sigh, "is the Festival of Love!"

Trusting that there would soon begin performances more in the spirit of the *Gītagovinda* or of Krishna's *rāsa* dances in the *Bhāgavata Purāṇa*, I happily bathed and changed, for my eyes were smarting with the morning's dust and the day was growing hot. My constant benefactor, the village landlord, now sent his son to present me with a tall glass of a cool, thick green liquid. This was the festival drink, he said; he wanted me to have it at its best, as it came from his own parlour. I tasted it, and found it sweet and mild. "You must drink it all!" my host declared. I inquired about the ingredients—almonds, sugar, curds of milk, anise, and "only half a cup" of another item whose name I did not recognize. I finished off the whole delicious glass, and, in discussion with my cook, soon inferred that the unknown ingredient—*bhāng*—had been four ounces of juice from the hemp leaf known in the West as hashish or marijuana.

Because of this indiscretion, I am now unable to report with much accuracy exactly what other religious ceremonies were observed in the four villages through which I floated that afternoon, towed by my careening hosts. They told me that we were going on a journey of condolence to each house whose members had been bereaved during the past year. My many photographs corroborate the visual impressions that I had of this journey: the world was a brilliant smear. The stained and crumpled pages of my notebooks are blank, save for a few declining diagonals and undulating scrawls. Certain steaming scenes remain in memory, nevertheless. There was one great throng of villagers watching an uplifted male dancer with padded crotch writhe in solitary states of fevered passion and then onanism; then join in a remote *pas de deux* with a veiled female impersonator in a parody of pederasty, and finally in telepathic copulation—all this to a frenzied accompaniment of many drums. I know that I witnessed several hysterical battles, women rushing out of their houses in squads to attack me and other men with stout canes, while each man defended himself only by pivoting about his own staff, planted on the ground, or, like me, by running for cover. The rest was all hymn singing, every street resounding with choral song in an archaic Śākta style. The state of the clothes in which I ultimately fell asleep told me the next morning that I had been sprayed and soaked repeatedly with libations of liquid dye, red and yellow. My face in the morning was still a brilliant vermilion, and my hair was orange from repeated embraces and scourings with colored powders by the bereaved and probably by many others. I learned on inquiry what I thought I had heard before, that in Kishan Garhi a kitchen had been profaned with dog's dung by masked raiders, that two housewives had been detected in adultery with neighboring men. As an effect of the festivities in one nearby village, there had occurred an armed fight between factional groups. In a third, an adjacent village, where there had previously been protracted litigation between castes, the festival had not been observed at all.

"A festival of *love?*" I asked my neighbors again in the morning.

"Yes! All greet each other with affection and feeling. Lord

Krishna taught us the way of love, and so we celebrate Holī in this manner."

"What about my aching shins—and your bruises? Why were the women beating us men?"

"Just as the milkmaids loved Lord Krishna, so our wives show their love for us, and for you, too, Saheb!"

Unable at once to stretch my mind so far as to include both "love" and these performances in one conception, I returned to the methodological maxim of Radcliffe-Brown: the meaning of a ritual element is to be found by observing what it shares with all the contexts of its occurrence.[9] Clearly, I would need to know much more about village religion and about the place of each feature of Holī in its other social contexts throughout the year. Then perhaps I could begin to grasp the meanings of Krishna and his festival, and to determine the nature of the values they might serve to maintain.

There were, I learned by observing throughout the following twelve months in the village, three main kinds of ritual performances—festivals, individual sacraments, and optional devotions. Among sacraments, the family-controlled rites of marriage were a major preoccupation of all villagers. In marriage, young girls were uprooted from their privileged situations in the patrilineally extended families of their birth and childhood. They were wedded always out of the village, often many miles away, to child husbands in families that were complete strangers. A tight-lipped young groom would be brought by his uncles in military procession, and after three days of receiving tribute ceremoniously, he would be carried off with his screaming, wailing little bride to a home where she would occupy the lowest status of all. Hard work for the mother-in-law, strict obedience to the husband, and a veiled, silent face to all males senior to herself in the entire village—these were the lot of the young married woman. Members of the husband's family, having the upper hand over the captive wife, could demand and receive service, gifts, hospitality, and deference from their "low" affines on all future occasions of ceremony. Briefly, sometimes, there would be little outbreaks of "Holī playing" at weddings, especially between the invading groom's men and the women of the bride's village: in these games, the men would be dared to enter the women's courtyards in the bride's village and would then be beaten with rolling pins or soaked with colored water for their boldness. Otherwise, all ceremonies of marriage stressed the strict formal dominance of men over women, of groom's people over bride's. When married women returned to their original homes each rainy season for a relaxed month of reunion with their "village sisters" and "village brothers," the whole village sang sentimental songs of the *gopīs'* never-fulfilled longing for their idyllic childhood companionship with Krishna and with each other. Sexual relations between adults of humankind were conventionally verbalized in metaphors of "war," "theft," and rape, while the marital connection between any particular husband and his wife could be mentioned without insult only by employing generalized circumlocutions such as "house" and "children," and so on. The idiom of Holī thus differed from that of ordinary life both in giving explicit dramatization to specific sexual relationships that otherwise would not be expressed at all and in reversing the differences of power conventionally prevailing between husbands and wives.

Aside from the Holī festival, each of the other thirteen major festivals of the year seemed to me to express and support the proper structures of patriarchy and gerontocracy in the family, of elaborately stratified relations among the castes, and of dominance by landowners in the village generally. At Divālī, ancestral spirits were to be fed and the goddess of wealth worshiped by the head of the family, acting on behalf of all members. The rites of Gobardhan Divālī, another Krishna-related festival, stressed the unity of the family's agnates through their common interest in the family herds of cattle. On the fourth day of the lunar fortnight which ends at Divālī [10]—indeed, on certain fixed dates in every month—the wives fasted for the sake of their husbands. On other dates they fasted for the sake of their children. The brother-sister relation of helpfulness, a vital one for the out-married women, had two further festivals and many fasts giving it ritual support; and the Holī bonfire itself dramatized the divine punishment of the wicked sister Holikā for her unthinkable betrayal of her brother Prahlāda. At each other festival of the year and also at wedding feasts, the separation of the lower from the higher castes and their strict order of ranking were reiterated both through the services of pollution-removal provided by them, and through the lowering gifts and payments of food made to them in return. Since the economy of the village was steeply stratified, with one third of the families controlling nearly all the land, every kind of ritual observance, sacramental or festival, tended through ritual patronage and obeisance to give expression to the same order of economic dominance and subordination. Optional, individual ritual observances could also be understood as expressing the secular organization of power, I thought. Rival leaders would compete for the allegiance of others through ceremonies. A wealthy farmer, official, or successful litigant was expected to sponsor special ceremonies and give feasts for lesser folk "to remove the sins" he had no doubt committed in gaining his high position; he who ignored this expectation might overhear stories of the jocular harassment of misers at Holī, or of their robbery on other, darker nights. Once each year, a day for simultaneous worship of all the local deities required a minimal sort of communal action by women, and smaller singing parties of women were many, but comradeship among men across the lines of kinship and caste was generally regarded with suspicion. In sum, the routine ritual and social forms of the village seemed almost perfect parallels of each other: both maintained a tightly ranked and compartmentalized order. In this order, there was little room for behavior of the kinds attributed to Krishna's roisterous personality.

"Why do you say that it was Lord Krishna who taught you how to celebrate the festival of Holī?" I inquired of the many villagers who asserted that this was so. Answers, when they could be had at all, stressed that it was he who first played Holī with the cowherd boys and with Rādhā and the other *gopīs*. But my searches in the *Bhāgavata's* tenth book, and even in that book's recent and locally most popular adaptation, the *Ocean of Love,*[11] could discover no mention of Holī or any of the local festival's traditional activities, from the bonfire to the game of colors. "Just see how they play Holī in Mathurā district, in Lord Krishna's own village of Nandgaon, and in Rādhā's village of Barsana!" said the landlord. There, I was assured by the barber, who had also seen them, that the women train all year long, drinking milk and eating ghee like wrestlers, and there they beat the men *en masse,* before a huge audience of visitors, to the music of two hundred drums.

"I do not really believe that Lord Krishna grew up in just that village of Nandgaon," the landlord confided in me, "for Nanda, Krishna's foster father, must have lived on this side of the Jumnā River, near

Gokula, as is written in the Purāṇa. But there in Nandgaon and Barsana they keep the old customs best."

The landlord's doubts were well placed, but not extensive enough, for, as I learned from a gazetteer of the district, the connection of Krishna, Rādhā, and the cowgirls with the rising of the women at Holī in those villages of Mathurā could not have originated before the early seventeenth-century efforts of certain immigrant Bengali Gosvāmin priests. The Gosvāmīs themselves—Rūpa, Sanātana, and their associates—were missionaries of the Krishnaite devotional movement led by Caitanya[12] in sixteenth-century Bengal, and that movement in turn had depended on the elaboration of the new notion of Rādhā as Krishna's favorite by the Telugu philosopher Nimbārka, possibly in the thirteenth century, and by other, somewhat earlier sectarians of Bengal and southern India.[13] The village names "Nandgaon" (village of Nanda) and "Barsana" (to make rain—an allusion to the "dark-as-a-cloud" epithet of Krishna) were probably seventeenth-century inventions, like the formal choreography of the battles of the sexes in those villages, that were contrived to attract pilgrims to the summer circuit of Krishna's rediscovered and refurbished holy land of Vraja.[14] Of course, privileged attacks by women upon men must have existed in village custom long before the promotional work of the Gosvāmīs—of this I was convinced by published studies of villages elsewhere, even in the farthest corners of the Hindī-speaking area, where such attacks were part of Holī, but not understood as conveying the message of Lord Krishna.[15] But once the great flow of devotees to Mathurā had begun from Bengal, Gujarat, and the South, the direction of cultural influence must have been reversed: what had been incorporated of peasant practice and local geography into the *Brahmavaivarta Purāṇa* and other new sectarian texts must have begun then to reshape peasant conceptions of peasant practice. At least the Krishnaite theology of the "love battles" in Kishan Garhi, and possibly some refinements of their rustic hydrology and stickwork, seemed to have been remodeled according to the famous and widely imitated public performances that had been visible in villages of the neighboring district for the past three centuries or so. The Mathurā pilgrimage and its literature appeared also to have worked similar effects upon two other festivals of Krishna in Kishan Garhi, in addition to Holī.[16]

To postulate the relative recency of the association of Rādhā and Krishna with the battles of canes and colors in Kishan Garhi was not to assert that the entire Holī festival could have had no connection with legends of Krishna before the seventeenth century. Reports on the mythology of Holī from many other localities described the bonfire, not as the burning of Holikā, but as the cremation of another demoness, Pūtanā.[17] Pūtanā was a demoness sent by King Kaṃsa of Mathurā to kill the infant Krishna by giving him to suck of her poisonous mother's milk. The Pūtanā story could no doubt claim a respectable antiquity, occurring as it did in the *Viṣṇu Purāṇa* and the *Harivaṃśa;* it was known in Kishan Garhi, although not applied currently to the rationalization of the Holī fire, and represented an acquaintance with a Krishna senior in type to the more erotic Krishna of the *Bhāgavata Purāṇa* and the later works. Even if I peeled away all explicit references to Krishna, both older and more recent, I would still have confronted other layers of Vaiṣṇavism in the Holī references to Rāma, whose cult centered in the middle Gangetic plain and in the South. And then there was the further Vaiṣṇava figure Prahlāda, another of ancient origin. Finally, I had to consider the proximity of Kishan Garhi to Mathurā, which was more than merely generically Vaiṣṇavite in its ancient religious orientations: Mathurā was thought to have been the original source of the legends of the child Krishna and his brother Balarāma, as suggested by Greek evidence from the fourth century B.C. as well as by the Purāṇic traditions.[18] Assuming that urban cults may always have been influential in villages and that such cults often carried forward what was already present in rural religious practice,[19] I thought it probable that the ancestors of the people of Kishan Garhi might well have celebrated the pranks of some divine ancestor of the Purāṇic Krishna even before their less complete adherence to the cults of Rāma and other gods later known as avatars of Viṣṇu. If these historical evidences and interpretations were generally sound, if Krishna had indeed waxed and waned before, then what both I and the villagers had taken to be their timeless living within a primordial local myth of Krishna appeared instead to represent rather the latest in a lengthy series of revivals and reinterpretations mingling local, regional, and even some quite remote movements of religious fashion.

Beneath the level of mythological enactment or rationalization, with its many shifts of contents through time, however, I felt that one might find certain more essential, underlying connections between the moral constitution of villages like Kishan Garhi and the general social form of the Holī festival—so the functional assumption of Radcliffe-Brown had led me to hope. Superficially, in various regions and eras, the festival might concern witches or demonesses (Holikā or Holākā, Pūtanā, Ḍhoṇḍhā), Viṣṇu triumphant (as Rāma, Narasiṃha, or Krishna), Śiva as an ascetic in conflict with gods of lust (Kāma, Madana, or the nonscriptural Nathurām), or others.[20] Festival practices might also vary greatly. Were there enduring, widespread features, I wondered? From a distributional and documentary study by N. K. Bose, I learned that spring festivals featuring bonfires, a degree of sexual license, and generally saturnalian carousing had probably existed in villages of many parts of India for at least the better part of the past two thousand years.[21] Spring festivals of this one general character evidently had remained consistently associated with many of India's complex, caste-bound communities. Even if only some of such festivals had had the puckish, ambiguous Krishna as their presiding deity, and these only in recent centuries, many seemed since the beginning of our knowledge to have enshrined divinities who sanctioned, however briefly, some of the same riotous sorts of social behavior.

Now a full year had passed in my investigations, and the Festival of Love was again approaching. Again I was apprehensive for my physical person, but was forewarned with social structural knowledge that might yield better understanding of the events to come. This time, without the draft of marijuana, I began to see the pandemonium of Holī falling into an extraordinarily regular social ordering. But this was an order precisely inverse to the social and ritual principles of routine life. Each riotous act at Holī implied some opposite, positive rule or fact of everyday social organization in the village.

Who were those smiling men whose shins were being most mercilessly beaten by the women? They were the wealthier Brahman and Jāṭ farmers of the village, and the beaters were those ardent local Rādhās, the "wives of the village," figuring by both the real and the fictional intercaste system of kinship. The wife of an "elder brother" was properly a man's joking mate, while the wife of a "younger brother" was properly removed from him by rules of extreme respect, but both were merged here with a man's mother-surrogates, the wives of his "father's younger brothers," in one revolutionary cabal of "wives" that cut across all lesser lines and links. The boldest beaters in this veiled battalion were often in fact the wives of the farmers' low-caste field laborers, artisans, or menials—the concubines and kitchen help of the victims. "Go and bake bread!" teased one farmer, egging his assailant on. "Do you want some seed from me?" shouted another flattered victim, smarting under the blows, but standing his ground. Six Brahman men in their fifties, pillars of village society, limped past in panting flight from the quarterstaff wielded by a massive young Bhañgin, sweeper of their latrines. From this carnage suffered by their village brothers, all daughters of the village stood apart, yet held themselves in readiness to attack any potential husband who might wander in from another, marriageable village to pay a holiday call.

Who was that "King of the Holī" riding backward on the donkey? It was an older boy of high caste, a famous bully, put there by his organized victims (but seeming to relish the prominence of his disgrace).

Who was in that chorus singing so lustily in the potters' lane? Not just the resident caste fellows, but six washermen, a tailor, and three Brahmans, joined each year for this day only in an idealistic musical company patterned on the friendships of the gods.

Who were those transfigured "cowherds" heaping mud and dust on all the leading citizens? They were the water carrier, two young Brahman priests, and a barber's son, avid experts in the daily routines of purification.

Whose household temple was festooned with goat's bones by unknown merrymakers? It was the temple of that Brahman widow who had constantly harassed neighbors and kinsmen with actions at law.

In front of whose house was a burlesque dirge being sung by a professional asectic of the village? It was the house of a very much alive moneylender, notorious for his punctual collections and his insufficient charities.

Who was it who had his head fondly anointed, not only with handfuls of the sublime red powders, but also with a gallon of diesel oil? It was the village landlord, and the anointer was his cousin and archrival, the police headman of Kishan Garhi.

Who was it who was made to dance in the streets, fluting like Lord Krishna, with a garland of old shoes around his neck? It was I, the visiting anthropologist, who had asked far too many questions, and had always to receive respectful answers.

Here indeed were the many village kinds of love confounded—respectful regard for parents and patrons; the idealized affection for brothers, sisters, and comrades; the longing of man for union with the divine; and the rugged lust of sexual mates—all broken suddenly out of their usual, narrow channels by a simultaneous increase of intensity. Boundless, unilateral love of every kind flooded over the usual compartmentalization and indifference among separated castes and families. Insubordinate libido inundated all established hierarchies of age, sex, caste, wealth, and power.

The social meaning of Krishna's doctrine in its rural North Indian recension is not unlike one conservative social implication of Jesus' Sermon on the Mount. The Sermon admonishes severely, but at the same time postpones the destruction of the secular social order until a distant future. Krishna does not postpone the reckoning of the mighty until an ultimate Judgment Day, but schedules it regularly as a masque at the full moon of every March. And the Holī of Krishna is no mere doctrine of love: rather it is the script for a drama that must be acted out by each devotee passionately, joyfully.

The dramatic balancing of Holī—the world destruction and world renewal, the world pollution followed by world purification—occurs not only on the abstract level of structural principles, but also in the person of each participant. Under the tutelage of Krishna, each person plays and for the moment may experience the role of his opposite: the servile wife acts the domineering husband, and vice versa; the ravisher acts the ravished; the menial acts the master; the enemy acts the friend; the strictured youths act the rulers of the republic. The observing anthropologist, inquiring and reflecting on the forces that move men in their orbits, finds himself pressed to act the witless bumpkin. Each actor playfully takes the role of others in relation to his own usual self. Each may thereby learn to play his own routine roles afresh, surely with renewed understanding, possibly with greater grace, perhaps with a reciprocating love.

NOTES

CHAPTER I

1. F. E. Pargiter, *Ancient Indian Historical Tradition* (London: Oxford University Press, 1922), p. 55.
2. M. Winternitz, *A History of Indian Literature,* S. Ketkar and H. Kohn, trans. (Calcutta: University of Calcutta, 1927), I, p. 528.
3. *Ibid.*, p. 556..
4. R. C. Hazra, *Studies in the Puranic Records on Hindu Rites and Customs* (Dacca: University of Dacca, 1940), p. 55.
5. Pargiter, *op. cit.*, p. 57. F. E. Pargiter, *The Purāṇa Text of the Dynasties of the Kali Age* (London: Oxford University Press, 1913), pp. xvi–xvii, 86.
6. R. Mukerjee, *The Lord of the Autumn Moons* (Bombay: Asia Publishing House, 1957), pp. 65–66.
7. J. N. Farquhar, *An Outline of the Religious Literature of India* (London: Oxford University Press, 1920), pp. 231–233.
8. C. V. Vaidya, "The Date of the Bhāgavata Purāṇa," *Journal of the Bombay Branch of the Royal Asiatic Society*. New Series, I (1925), 144–156.
9. K. A. Nīlakaṇṭa Śāstrī, *A History of South India* (2nd ed.; London: Oxford University Press, 1958), p. 329.
10. Winternitz, *op. cit.*, p. 556.
11. Farquhar, *op. cit.*, pp. 232–233. (References are to *Bhāgavata Purāṇa,* XI.5.38–40 and *Bhāgavata Māhātmya* I.27.)
12. *Ibid.*, p. 233.
13. Vaidya, *op. cit.*, pp. 156–158. (References are to *Bhāgavata Purāṇa,* X.79.10 ff. and XI.5.38–40.
14. Nīlakaṇṭa Śāstrī, *op. cit.*, p. 329.
15. Mukerjee, *op. cit.*, pp. 63–74.
16. For a discussion of Buddhist influence on the *Bhāgavata,* see Mukerjee, *op. cit.*, pp. vii, 31–32, and 37–38.
17. Nīlakaṇṭa Śāstrī, *op. cit.*, pp. 415–416.
18. *Bhāgavata Purāṇa,* III.29.14–19. All translations from the *Bhāgavata Purāṇa* are by the author.
19. XI.2.45, 48–52.
20. I.5.17–19.
21. III.27.4–5; IV.29.79–80.
22. VII.5.23–24.
23. XI.14.23–24.
24. XI.27.48–53; XI.11.34–40.

25. XI.27.15–18; X.81.3–4.
26. VI.1.41.
27. X.4.41.
28. I.5.8–11.
29. XI.11.20.
30. IV.31.11–12 and IV.29.44–47.
31. XI.12.1–2 and XI.14.20–22.
32. X.47.58.
33. X.23.9–11.
34. III.14.27 and IV.31.21.
35. XI.5.5–7.
36. XI.21.32–34.
37. XI.23.17.
38. X.60.14.
39. X.88.8–9.
40. X.10.13–18.
41. See, for example, *Mahābhārata* 3.177.20–21, 26–28 and 30–32 (crit. ed.); 3.206.12 (crit. ed.); 5.43.29 (crit. ed.); 12.181.10–15 (crit. ed.); 12.182.4–8 (crit. ed.); and 13.143.6 and 46–51 (Calcutta ed.).
42. The most important sections are VII.11.13–30 and XI.17.16–21.
43. See III.29.32–33 and X.86.53.
44. X.7.13.
45. VII.11.24.
46. III.6.33.
47. VII.9.9–10.
48. VII.11.8–12.
49. XI.19.36–40.
50. VII.11.35.
51. VII.11.17.
52. I.17.30.
53. V.8.10.
54. VIII.16.56.
55. I.4.24–25.
56. XII.12.65.
57. IV.23.32.
58. III.16.6.
59. III.33.6.
60. VI.16.44; III.33.7; and X.70.43.
61. X.23.42–43.
62. I.18.18.
63. VII.9.12.
64. I.5.23, 28–32, and VII.15.72–74.
65. XI.12.4–7.
66. II.4.18.
67. X.41.40 and 43, and X.42.13.
68. X.88.1.
69. XI.22.59.

CHAPTER II

1. On the textual layers of this text, see my study, *The Maitrāyaṇīya Upaniṣad: A Critical Essay* (The Hague, 1962).
2. Edited by H. Grube (Berlin, 1875).
3. *Mahābhārata* I.3.60 ff. (critical edition). One could also quote such deliberately vedicizing stanzas in classical Sanskrit, e.g., Bhavabhūti, *Mālatīmādhava,* stanza 5 (*kalyāṇānām tvam asi . . .*), but the concern there is to echo rather than to identify.
4. Yāska's *Nirukta.* See Lakshman Sarup, *The Nighaṇṭu and the Nirukta* (2nd ed.; Benares, 1962).
5. "Der Archaismus in der Sprache des Bhāgavata-Purāṇa," *Zeitschrift für Indologie und Iranistik,* VIII (1931), 33–79.
6. *Ibid.,* 36–37. Although permitted by Pāṇini (VII.1.35) and not absent from classical literature, these imperatives regularly bring along Vedic associations, especially in the *Bhāgavata Purāṇa.* I would not exclude them from the archaistic tendency generally displayed.
7. *Ibid.,* pp. 36–37.
8. Truman Michelson, "Additions to Bloomfield's Vedic Concordance, *Journal of the American Oriental Society,* XXIX (1909), 284.
9. *Bhāgavata Purāṇa,* IX.xiv.34 ff. (from *Ṛgveda* X.95) and IX.xvi.29 ff. (from *Aitareya Brāhmaṇa,* VII.17–18), respectively.
10. F. J. Meier, *op. cit.,* p. 39.
11. Thomas Hopkins, "The Social Teaching of the *Bhāgavata Purāna,*" this volume, pp. 3–22.
12. On the function of *Akṣara* here, see my paper, "Akṣara," *Journal of the American Oriental Society,* LXXIX (1959), 176–187.
13. *Bṛhadāraṇyaka Upaniṣad* 3.8.10.
14. The *Bhāgavata Purāṇa* here reads *"trikāṇḍaviṣayāḥ,"* which corresponds to *"traiguṇya-viṣayā vedāḥ"* in the *Bhagavad Gītā* (II.45). Note that the *Bhāgavata* tacitly corrects the *Bhagavad Gītā* here by adding *"brahmātmaviṣayāḥ"!*
15. Certainly to be compared with the *Taittirīya Upaniṣad* II.3 for the *prāṇamaya* and *manomaya ātmans,* the latter having *yajus, ṛc, sāman,* and *atharvāṅgirasaḥ* as its members; in other words, the *śabdabrahman,* "the Sound Brahman, viz. the Veda" as distinguished from the "higher" Brahman.
16. Cf. *Bhāgavata Purāṇa* XI.5.9–10; discussed by Hopkins, this volume, p. 12.
17. See *Alberuni's India,* edited (in Arabic original) by E. Sachau (London, 1887); al-Bīrūnī lists the *Bhagbat Purān* (i.e., *Bhāgavatā-purāṇa*) and adds *alias Vāsudeva* (sc. *Purāṇa*), a title that no longer survives. It is noteworthy that al-Bīrūnī quotes the list in which the *Bhāgavata Purāṇa* figures as the alternative of a list in which it does not; this may suggest that the latter list was more authoritative at the time of his writing. The second list including the *Bhāgavata Purāṇa* he quotes on the authority of the *Viṣṇu Purāṇa* (Sachau ed., p. 63, line 10). In fact, the list tallies exactly and in sequence with that in the *Viṣṇu Purāṇa* (III.vi.21).
18. F. Otto Schrader, *The Kashmir Recension of the Bhagavadgītā* (Stuttgart, 1930), p. 7 and note. He remarks: "This passage, then, if authentic throughout, would be the earliest reference so far discovered to the *Bhāgavata*

Purāṇa." Doubt as to its authenticity is admissible: quotations from standard works are of course vulnerable to use by later scribes. One would feel more assured if the *Bhāgavata* quotation had been central to Abhinavagupta's discourse, or if several quotations had been scattered throughout the text—instead of only four and a half *ślokas* appended to another quotation in one locus.

19. See my Rāmānuja's *Vedārthasaṃgraha* (Poona, 1956), pp. 33 ff.
20. My annotated translation, based on Rāma Miśra Śāstrī's edition [reprinted from the *Pandit* (Benares, 1934–36)] has now been awaiting publication in India for four years.
21. *Āgamapramāṇya,* ed. Miśra Śāstrī, pp. 6–10.
22. Viz., those of *smṛti* and *śruti;* the basic assumption is that customs observed by the Vaidikas are thereby proved to be normative.
23. *Śiṣṭa,* the final arbiter of rectitude and correctness.
24. *Parivrājaka.*
25. *Sātvata,* apparently derived from *satvant-* (according to Pāṇini, *gaṇa* on IV.1.86, a people from the South), has occurred as the name of a people since the *Aitareya Brāhmaṇa* VIII.14 and the *Śatapatha Brāhmaṇa* XIII.v.3–21. It has become a name for Krishna and, by further derivation (?), for a Krishnaite. *Pāñcarātra* is known in the epic as *Sātvatamatam* (e.g., *Mahābhārata,* XII.cccxxii.19, crit. ed.). Perhaps because this Krishnaism was associated with classes other than Brahmans (*Mahābhārata* III.clxxxix.9–10 states that Nārāyaṇa was worshiped by *kṣatriyas* and *vaiśyas*), the name may subsequently have become the name of a low caste living off Krishna worship.
26. *Manusmṛti* X.23.
27. I.e., by occupation.
28. I have been unable to identify the quotation in the extant *Auśanasasmṛti* [in *Smṛtīnām Samuccayaḥ* (Ānandāśrama Sanskrit series, 48, Poona, 1905), p. 46 ff.] On the problem of Uśanas, see P. V. Kane, *History of Dharmaśāstra* (Poona, 1930), Vol. I, pp. 110 ff. *Manu* (X.23) likewise lists the *Ācāryas* with the *Sātvatas.*
29. Not in the present vulgate. The closest statement is *Manu* IX.228, but the context is different: *pracchannaṃ vā prakāśaṃ vā tān niṣeveta yo naraḥ/ tasya daṇḍavikalpaḥ syād yatheṣṭaṃ nṛpates tathā.*
30. Name of a Pāñcarātra text.
31. A special fast; see *Manu* XI.106 ff.
32. *Devalaka,* a pejorative term, used in *Manu* III.152, where it is said that he (along with a physician, a meat seller, and a market trader) is to be avoided. Kullūka *ad loc.* has Yāmuna's quotation from Devala. *Manu* III.180 has it that a gift to a *devalaka* (for icon worship?) is lost.
33. *Upabrāhmaṇa.*
34. *Brāhmaṇacāṇḍāla;* quoted from *Mahābhārata* XII.77.8 (crit. ed.).
35. *The Philosophy of Viśiṣṭādvaita* (Adyar, 1946), p. 511.
36. Eventually, however, a fission did occur in *Viśiṣṭādvaita,* in the Teṅkalai who favored Tamil and the Vaḍakalai who favored Sanskrit. Traditionally, the chief exponent of Tamil was Piḷḷai Lokācārya. Is it possible that the sack

of Madurai by Alā'-ud-Dīn's General Malik Naib Kafur, in 1310, and subsequently the sack of Śrīraṅgam consolidated the schism?

37. Not one of the recognized *śākhās.* Although it is probable that some early form of theistic devotion existed in late Vedic times (cf. the *Vaikhānasas,* themselves linked with Viṣṇuism), traditional accounts do not list the Ekāyana school as Vedic. The assumption of the early existence of such a school seems to be based on several mentions of it in the *Chāndogya Upaniṣad* and the *Mahābhārata.*
38. Note the orthopraxy. There is not a word about their dogma.
39. For details, see J. Brough, trans. *The Early Brahmanical System of Gotra and Pravara* (London: Cambridge University Press, 1953).
40. It is interesting to note not only that in the *Bhāgavata Purāṇa* (XI.v.27–31) obviously Pāñcarātra practices are referred to, but also that such practices occurred in the Dvāpara Age, which immediately preceded the present Kali Age. Whereas people in the Dvāpara Age worshiped the spirit as "great king" (*mahārājopalakṣaṇam*) according to Vedas and Tantras and praised the Lord of the world by paying homage to Vāsudeva, Saṃkarṣaṇa, Pradyumna, and Aniruddha (the Pāñcarātra *vyūhas*), the wise men of the Kali Age worship Krishna with offerings mainly consisting of *samkīrtanas*—as though Pāñcarātra as a decisive system of *bhakti* was, for the common people, already a thing of the past.
41. He flourished under Bukka I and Harihara; died in 1387.
42. I use Smārta in the general sense of a Brahman who traditionally practices the rites and observes the customs whose main sources are such *Dharmaśāstras* as *Manusmṛti* and *Yājñavalkyasmṛti,* and who is not "sectarian," in the sense that he has no defining theistic or Tantric affiliation.
43. So far only available in MS; an edition by Mr. Subhadra Jha, accompanied by a translation by the present writer, is due to appear in the the Harvard Oriental Series.
44. Technically known as *jñānakarmasamuccaya;* it is definitely prior to Śaṃkara, who refers to another exponent, Bhartṛprapañca. See M. Hiriyanna, "Fragments of Bhartṛprapañca," in *Proceedings and Transactions of the Third Oriental Conference* (Madras, 1924).
45. Kumārila (probably sixth century A.D.) was the exponent of what since has become the principal school of Mīmāṃsā.
46. Notably in *Religion and Society among the Coorgs of South India* (Oxford, 1952), but continued in "A Note on Sanskritization and Westernization," *The Far Eastern Quarterly,* XV, No. 4 (1956), 481–496.
47. The increasing use of the qualification "Sanskritic" by Western anthropologists, who are inclined to equate it with "Sanskrit," arouses the legitimate impatience of the Sanskritist, who knows that much Sanskrit literature would not qualify as "Sanskritic" in this sense.
48. The "exemplary person" in the Smārta opposition to Yāmuna; literally, "the educated man of culture, the literatus."
49. "Text and Context in the Study of Contemporary Hinduism," *Adyar Library Bulletin* (Madras), XXV (1961), 274 ff.
50. See my Rāmānuja's *Vedārthasaṃgraha* (Poona, 1956), pp. 31 ff.

CHAPTER III

1. Though the supreme deity of the Bengal sect was Krishna, not Viṣṇu, Bengal Vaiṣṇavas so call themselves in their own texts; I shall therefore do so throughout this chapter.
2. The most thorough and incisive work on the Bengal movement is S. K. De, *History of the Vaisnava Faith and Movement in Bengal* (Calcutta: General Printers and Publishers, 1942. 2nd ed.; Calcutta, K. L. Mukhopadhyaya, 1961). The work will hereafter be cited as *VFM*.
3. The earliest major work of the Bengal school is the *Gītagovinda* of Jayadeva, who was court poet to Lakṣmaṇa Sena in the latter part of the twelfth century. But, from a mention of Rādhā and Krishna in a Sanskrit verse by the eleventh-century Bengali poet Ḍimboka, it seems evident that a sect of Rādhā and Krishna had developed by that time. See Daniel H. H. Ingalls, "A Sanskrit Poetry of Village and Field: Yogeśvara and his Fellow Poets," *Journal of the American Oriental Society,* LXXIV (1954), 119–131; the verse in question is quoted on p. 125.
4. Bāladeva was himself a follower of Madhva; see his *Prameyaratnāvalī* (Calcutta, 1927). There is a suggestion of earlier Mādhva affiliation in a late sixteenth-century Vaiṣṇava work, but the text is open to question. See *VFM,* p. 11.
5. There is, however, some doubt about the specific order into which he went. De (*VFM,* p. 12) feels that it was the Daśanāmī order of Śaṃkara *saṃnyāsins,* "even though the ultimate form which he gave to Vaiṣṇava *bhakti* has nothing to do with Śaṃkara's extreme Advaitavāda." Caitanya was born a Brahman. In this regard, note the prominence in the *bhajana* movement in Madras of Smārta (i.e., advaitin) Brahmans. See Milton Singer, "The Rādhā-Krishna *Bhajanas* of Madras City," in this volume (pp. 113–121), and T. K. Venkateswaran, "Rādhā-Krishna *Bhajana* of South India" (pp. 144–148).
6. Nimbārka was a Telugu Brahman; he lived about the eleventh century A.D. I have noted above that the indications from Dimboka are that a Rādhā-Krishna sect had developed in Bengal by that time. There is at least a possibility that one of the sculptures found on a Pāla period (Dharma-pāla, late eighth century) building in the excavations at Paharpur represents a joint figure of Rādhā and Krishna. See *Memoirs of the Archaeological Survey of India,* Nos. 52–56. The fully developed legend of Rādhā and Krishna appears in both the *Nārada-pañcarātra* and the *Brahma-vaivarta Purāṇa,* but the dates of both these texts are open to question. Neither is accepted as canonical by the Bengal Vaiṣṇavas. In general, the problem of how the Rādhā-concept developed is a very vexing one, and there is hardly space here to deal with all the possibilities.
7. "The Social Teaching of the Bhāgavata Purāṇa," in this volume, pp. 3–22.
8. See Jīva Gosvāmin's *Tattva-Saṃdarbha;* cf. *VFM,* p. 169.
9. This is not to say that emotionalism in devotional worship was new with Caitanya. As Thomas J. Hopkins points out in a letter to me, "Emotionalism similar to that of Caitanya is stressed in the *Bhāgavata,* and Śrīdharasvāmin

knows of a later stage of development of Vaiṣṇava practice which probably also has this element."

10. The best source is De, *VFM.* Another English work that treats the biographical data is Melville Kennedy, *The Caitanya Movement* (Calcutta, 1925). There is a brief sketch of Caitanya's life in my "The Place of Gauracandrikā in Bengali Vaiṣṇava Lyrics," *Journal of the American Oriental Society,* LXXVIII (1958), 153–169.
11. Caitanya made pilgrimages to the south of India also, and most of his Bengali biographies mention them. There is a probably spurious work, the *Kaṛacā* of Govinda-dāsa (Calcutta: Calcutta University, 1926), which purports to be the diary of a companion of Caitanya on such a trip; whether or not there is any factual information in it is still a matter of controversy. In any case, little is known as to what effect, if any, these trips had upon the areas visited.
12. Kṛṣṇadāsa, *Caitanya-caritāmṛta,* Rādhāgovinda Nāth, ed. (Calcutta, 1949–1950), hereafter cited in the notes as *CC. CC Ādi* XIII:40 and *CC Madhya* X:113 have: "Vidyāpati, Caṇḍīdāsa, and the Śrīgītagovinda—these three gave Prabhu [i.e., Caitanya] great joy." *CC Madhya* I:111 has: "The *Brahma-saṃhitā* and the *Karṇāmṛta*—he obtained these two manuscripts and brought them with him to the north."
13. See, for example, the lyric of Vāsudeva Ghoṣ in my, "The Place of Gauracandrikā," *op. cit.* In the *CC Madhya* (XVIII:104–105) Caitanya denies that he is either.
14. See, for example, *CC Ādi*:49–50. There are interesting parallels to this concept in the Hermetic philosophy, which held that the primal man, the *homo adamicus,* carried about with him Eve, hidden in his body. The concept of a hermaphroditic deity is found also in Plato (*Symposium* 190b) and in Philo, where Abraham is conceived as uniting with Sarah (Sophia) in such a way that she was masculine and he feminine. (See Erwin Goodenough, *An Introduction to Philo Judaeus,* New Haven: Yale University Press, 1940, pp. 187 ff.) Nor is the concept unique in India. The *Bṛhadāraṇyaka-upaniṣad* I:4 expounds a creation theory in which the primal being created by bringing forth the female from within himself and copulating with her. For a general discussion of the matter, see C. G. Jung, *Psychology and Religion* (Bollingen Series, 20, New York: Pantheon Books, 1958), pp. 29 ff. and *passim.*
15. These verses are collectively called the *Śikṣāṣṭaka.* They are found in various places, including the last chapter of the *CC* and in Rūpa Gosvāmin's anthology *Padyāvalī.*
16. Sanātana's commentary on the third *śloka* of his own *Bṛhadbhāgavatāmṛta,* cited by Bimanbihari Majumdar, *Śrīcaitanyacāriter upādān* (Calcutta: Calcutta University, 1939), p. 124.
17. B. B. Majumdar (*op. cit.,* p. 123) feels that there is some evidence that their father was a convert. Citing an article in *Bhāratbarṣa* 1341 B.S. (A.D. 1935), pp. 177–78, he writes: "Some conclude that Rūpa and Sanātana or their father Kumāradeva had become Muslim. Paṇḍit Basantakumār Caṭṭopādhyāya writes that shortly before the birth of Rūpa and Sanātana, a Muslim by the name of Pīrali Khān came to Yasohara district, preaching the Muslim

pīr-dharma. Possibly it was at this time . . . that the father of Rūpa and Sanātana adopted Islam."

18. In several places in the *CC,* Sanātana is made to say such as the following: "I am of low caste; I have kept low companions, and have done low work" (*Madhya* I:179); "I have served Muslims; I have associated with the murderers of Brahmans and cows" (*Madhya* I:186).
19. See *VFM,* pp. 111–112.
20. Narahari Cakravarti, *Bhakti-ratnākara,* Gauṛiya Maṭh, ed. (Calcutta, 1940), I:120 ff.
21. *CC Ādi* VII:44.
22. *CC Antya* XIII:19.
23. *Ibid.,* VI, *passim.*
24. *Ibid.,* VII:22; Gopala Bhaṭṭa, *Haribhakti-vilāsa* I:2.
25. There were also others at Vṛndāvan, some of them even instructed by Caitanya to go there. For example, Lokanātha, whose biography is given in *Bhakti-ratnākara* I:299 ff., "abandoned everything and came to Navadvīpa, to the side of Prabhu. Prabhu was gracious to him, and instructed him to go to Vṛndāvana." Lokanātha is not as famous as many other residents of Vṛndāvana, since he had no part in producing the doctrinal literature. He was, however, *guru* of the great Vaiṣṇava Śrīnivāsa, who was prominent in the spread of the movement.
26. *CC Ādi* V:139, *Madhya* XII:186, *Bhakti-ratnākara* VIII:171 ff. The Avadhūtas (Pure Ones) are ascetics; Nityānanda, when he became a member of their order, gave up his caste.
27. Akiñcana-dāsa [*Vivarta-vilāsa* (Calcutta, 1948), p. 22], contends that Jīva Gosvāmin did not want Kṛṣṇadāsa to write the *CC* in Bengali, on the grounds that the truth of the Caitanya *līlā* was too sacred to spread among the masses in the vernacular. The *Vivarta-vilāsa,* however, is a biased Sahajiyā text, and its word cannot be taken too seriously on such matters.
28. The following discussion is based primarily on Jīva Gosvāmin's *Ṣaṭsaṃdarbha* (Murshidabad, 1935). This edition, however, contains only the *Bhakti-saṃdarbha* and the *Kṛṣṇa-saṃdarbha,* with the commentary of Bāladeva. I have therefore also referred to the summary of the complete work in De, *VFM,* pp. 193–320. Also, most of the substance of Jīva's Sanskrit work has been given in Kṛṣṇadāsa's Bengali *CC.* The outline which follows is a painfully simplified summary of a very subtle and careful theological system.
29. The giving of pleasure, of course, works both ways. By giving pleasure to Krishna, the *bhakta* experiences pleasure. But this return must not be at the root of the *bhakta's* desire to please Krishna.
30. *CC Madhya* XIX:135: "Brahman is the qualityless manifestation [*nirviśeṣaprakāśa*] of the Bhagavat, that which gives grandeur to his body."
31. These theories are far too complex to develop here. The basic texts on the matter are Rūpa Gosvāmin's *Bhakti-rasāmṛta sindhu* and *Ujjvala-nīlamaṇī.*
32. The term *"līlā"* is extremely difficult to translate. It is frequently rendered as "sport," and indeed it does suggest sportiveness, in the sense that divine activity is beyond human comprehension and unmotivated by consideration of mankind. In the Vaiṣṇava sense, it refers specifically to the revelation of Krishna's eternal self and his eternal surroundings in the earthly Vṛndāvan.

33. There are many lyrics written by Caitanya's companions and followers that give us such a picture. A lyric by Jñānadāsa runs: "The limbs of Gaurā ["the golden one"—Caitanya] are supported by the limbs of his companions. He cannot walk—from time to time he slips to the ground, fainting, his body so weak that he cannot hold it up. Fallen to the earth, he gazes up at the faces of his companions, sobbing, 'O Lord of my life, where are you? . . .' In the fever of his former *viraha* [i.e., the separation of Rādhā from Krishna as related in the *Bhāgavata*] he has no peace." The Vaiṣṇava devotee or poet often sees himself as a woman, a *gopī,* so complete is his transformation in *bhāva.*
34. Some do not consider *śānta* a *bhāva* at all, since they believe that true emotion can be directed only toward an object that is known, and therefore can be loved or hated, and that the supreme deity cannot be put in such a category.
35. Cf. Hopkins, this volume, pp. 7–11.
36. *Kīrtana* can be of three varieties: dancing and group singing of religious lyrics which celebrate the story of Krishna, repetitive singing of the names of the deity, and street processionals with singing and dancing. The name of the deity is all-powerful; see Venkateswaran, "Rādhā-Krishna *Bhajanas* of South India," this volume, pp. 139–172.
37. There are two types of *gurus: śravaṇa-guru,* from whom one hears the truths (who may also be the *śikṣā-guru,* or the *guru* who instructs) and the *mantra-guru* or *dīkṣā-guru,* who initiates the aspirant to *bhakti* and gives him the formula upon which he is to meditate. Jīva Gosvāmin says that "one's *guru* is to be looked upon as the Bhagavat himself [*sva-gurau bhagavad-dṛṣṭiḥ kartavyaḥ*]."
38. Cf. Singer, "The Rādhā-Krishna *Bhajanas* of Madras City," this volume, pp. 90–138. The ritual gesture, if repeated, eventually brings about the appropriate attitude of mind.
39. The religious value of such separation will be treated below. It might be appropriate at this point, however, to note the view that separation is essential to pure and profound love. Denis de Rougemont, in his *Love in the Western World* (hereafter cited as *LWW*) (New York, 1957, p. 148), speaking of the Tristan and Iseult legend, writes that "in the Romance the repeated partings of the lovers answer to an altogether internal necessity of their passion. . . . The more Tristan loves, the more he wants to be parted from the beloved."
40. *CC Ādi* IV:149.
41. *CC Ādi* XVII:23.
42. *CC Madhya* XXII:45 ff.
43. Cf. Hopkins, "The Social Teaching of the *Bhāgavata Purāṇa,* this volume, pp. 16–18.
44. Rāmacandra Gosvāmi, *Pāṣaṇḍa-dalana,* in the anthology *Vaiṣṇava-granthāvalī* (Calcutta, 1936), the opening lines. The author goes on to cite the *Padma-purāṇa* as his authority.
45. A *pada* attributed to Nityānanda-dāsa, in *Sahajiyā-sāhitya,* M. M. Basu, ed. (Calcutta, 1932), No. 12.
46. *CC Madhya* VIII:100, *Ādi* VIII:18, etc.
47. *CC Madhya* VIII:18 ff.: "Prabhu asked—Are you Rāmānanda Rāya? And

Rāmānanda said: I am he, your servant and a lowly Śūdra. Then Caitanya caught him in a firm embrace. . . . Seeing this, the Brahmans were astonished. Those Vedic Brahmans said to one another: How can he weep and embrace a Śūdra?"

48. See Singer, *op. cit.*, this volume, pp. 123–128. It seems that, apart from the religious context, Caitanya abided by the rules. For example, although he stayed with a Śūdra in Benares, it seems that he took his food in the house of a Brahman (*CC Ādi* VII:44).
49. Narahari-dāsa, *Narottama-vilāsa* (Murshidabad, 1918), p. 9: "Puruṣottama was the elder brother of Kṛṣṇānanda Datta; his son Narottama is famous throughout the world." Datta is a non-Brahman and usually a Kāyastha surname. In another place in the same text (pp. 146–147), Narottama is called a Śūdra.
50. *Ibid., Narottama-vilāsa,* p. 157.
51. The antagonism of the *Bhāgavata* is toward Brahmans who feel superior because of birth. Brahmans who are devotees, however, are the best of *bhaktas* because of their natural superiority to other classes of men.
52. Vṛndāvana-dāsa, *Caitanya-bhāgavata,* Gauṛiya Maṭh, ed. (Calcutta, 1934), *Antya* VI:8 ff.
53. *Bhakti-ratnākara* VIII:174.
54. Dinesh Chandra Sen [*History of Bengali Language and Literature* (2nd ed. Calcutta, 1954), p. 483] records the story, and is followed in it by Melville Kennedy (*op cit.*, p. 70) with some variation. The earliest textual evidence for the story which I have been able to find is in the late Sahajiyā work *Ānanda-bhairava* of Prema-dāsa, which is given in M. M. Basu's *Sahajiyā-sāhitya* (Calcutta, 1932). This text, however, attributes the action to Nityānanda's son (p. 148): "Virabhadra Gosvāmi . . . gave initiation to twelve hundred *neṛas* [*lit.*, "shaven-headed ones"], and thirteen hundred *neṛis.*"
55. *Caitanya-bhāgavata, Antya* V:222 ff.
56. For example, he is reluctant to sit at table with Nityānanda; see *CC Madhya* XII:185–186.
57. Nityānanda-dāsa, *Prema-vilāsa* (Murshidabad, 1912), p. 2.
58. *CC Ādi* XII:65–67.
59. *CC Ādi* XVII: 32 ff.
60. See *VFM*, p. 275.
61. *Caitanya-bhāgavata, Ādi* V:96 ff., XVI:347 ff. Apart from Rūpa and Sanātana themselves, Caitanya's most famous convert was Haridāsa, the story of whose heroism in the face of torture is told in *CC Antya* III. The orthodox Brahmans also accused Caitanya of immorality (*CC Ādi* VII:203–211).
62. The story is told in *CC Madhya* VI:209 ff.
63. *Bhāgavata* X:33:34–35; from Hopkins, "The Vaiṣṇava Bhakti Movement in the *Bhāgavata Purāṇa*" (unpublished doctoral dissertation; Yale University, 1961), p. 117. The position of the Purāṇa on this matter was pointed out in a personal communication from Hopkins.
64. Hopkins' translation, "Vaiṣṇava Bhakti Movement in the *Bhāgavata Purāṇa,*" p. 114.

65. De Rougemont, *LWW,* suggesting that the Cathars were the inheritors of Manichaean dualism, makes the following relevant remark (p. 136) :". . . to love with pure passion, even without physical contact—the sword laid between a couple's bodies and the theme of partings—is the supreme virtue, and the true way to divinization."
66. Maurice Valency, *In Praise of Love* (New York: Macmillan, 1961), p. 16
67. *Sermones de diversis,* VIII:9. Bernard also writes (*Cantica canticorum* vii, commenting on *Song of Songs* 1:2, "Let him kiss me with the kisses of his mouth"): "Who is it who speaks these words? It is the Bride. It is the soul thirsting for God. . . . She who asks this is held by the bond of love to him from whom she asks it. Of all the sentiments of nature, this of love is most excellent, especially when it is rendered back to him who is the source of it—that is, God. Nor are there found any expressions equally sweet to signify the mutual affection between the Word of God and the soul, as those of Bridegroom and Bride . . . They have one inheritance, one table, one dwelling-place, they are in fact one flesh."
68. *Systematic Theology* (Chicago: University of Chicago Press, 1960), Vol. I, p. 124.
69. John Frederick Nims, *The Poems of St. John of the Cross* (New York: Grove Press, 1959), p. 121.
70. See de Rougemont, *LWW, passim.*
71. Valency, *op. cit.,* p. 1.
72. Alfred Jeanroy, *Anthologie des troubadours* (Paris, n.d.), p. 22.
73. John Frederick Rowbotham, *The Troubadours and Courts of Love* (London, 1895), quoting from André, *Livre de l'art d'aimer,* fol. 56.
74. The story can be found in many texts, including the *Karṇānanda* of Yadunandana-dāsa and the *Vivarta-vilāsa* of Akiñcana-dāsa.
75. Khagendranāth Mitra *et al.,* eds., *Vaiṣṇava-padāvalī* (Calcutta, 1952), p. 91. The poem appears in other places with the signature line "Śekhara," who was probably in fact the author.
76. Harekṛṣṇa Mukhopādhyāya, ed., *Vaiṣṇava-padāvalī* (Calcutta: Sahitya Samsad, 1961), p. 205.

CHAPTER IV

1. Translated from the original Bengali, in S. C. Roy, *The Mundas and their Country* (Calcutta, 1921), p. 176.
2. *Op. cit.,* pp. 176–179.
3. See E. T. Dalton, *Descriptive Ethnology of Bengal* (Calcutta, 1872), p. 174; and H. H. Risley, *The People of India* (2nd ed.; Calcutta, 1915), p. 75.
4. The *gurus* are householders who are Vaiṣṇava by caste; the *sādhus* are casteless wandering mendicants professing the Vaiṣṇava religious doctrine.
5. An outline of the territorial and power hierarchy in Barabhum has been presented in my "State Formation and Rajput Myth in Tribal Central India," *Man in India,* XLII, No. 1 (1962), 38–57
6. Some details on the internal structure of the various orders of Vaiṣṇavas have been given in H. H. Risley, *The Tribes and Castes of Bengal* (Calcutta,

1891), II, pp. 339–348. This general information needs verification in terms of narrower regions.

7. *Op. cit.* (1915), p. 118.
8. See my paper, "Some Aspects of Changes in Bhūmij Religion in South Manbhum," *Man in India,* XXXIII, No. 2 (1953), 154–164.
9. *Ibid.,* pp. 154–157.
10. An account of the activities of the *sādhus* was presented in two of my papers: "Some Aspects of Changes in Bhūmij Religion in South Manbhum," *loc. cit.,* pp. 148–164, and "Bhūmij-Kṣatriya Social Movement in South Manbhum," *Bulletin of the Department of Anthropology,* VIII, No. 2 (1959), 9–32.
11. See my article, "Some Aspects of Changes in Bhūmij Religion in South Manbhum," *loc cit.,* p. 164.
12. "A Note on the Concept of Sexual Union for Spiritual Quest Among the Vaiṣṇava Preachers in the Bhūmij Belt of Purulia and Siṅgbhum," *Eastern Anthropologist,* XIV, No. 2 (1961), 194–196.
13. *Ibid.,* pp. 194–195. Several minor changes (in spelling, punctuation, etc.) have been made in this quotation for the sake of consistency within the chapter.
14. Robert Redfield uses the concept of "hinge groups" in his *Peasant Society and Culture* (Chicago: University of Chicago Press, 1956), pp. 43–46. In connection with the concept of "cultural brokers," see Eric R. Wolf, "Aspects of Group Relations in a Complex Society: Mexico," *American Anthropologist,* LVIII (1956), 1075–1076.

CHAPTER V

1. Milton Singer, "The Great Tradition in a Metropolitan Center: Madras," in Milton Singer, ed., *Traditional India: Structure and Change* (Philadelphia: American Folklore Society, 1958, 1959).
2. The present paper is based on observations and interviews in and around Madras City during 1954–1955 and 1960–1961 as well as on continuing correspondence and conversation with friends from Madras. To Dr. V. Raghavan, who first took me to some Rādhā-Krishna *bhajanas,* to T. S. Krishnaswami and his son, T. K. Venkateswaran, who have taught me so much about the *bhajanas,* and to the many devotees who welcomed a foreigner into their midst, I am deeply indebted. I am also obliged to Edward C. Dimock, McKim Marriott, J. A. B. van Buitenen, T. P. Meenakshisundaran, R. Rangaramanujan, A. K. Ramanujan, and Helen Singer for their helpful comments on an earlier draft of the paper. My two trips to India were made possible by a grant from the Ford Foundation to the University of Chicago for the Program on Comparative Studies of Cultures and Civilizations which Robert Redfield organized and directed until 1958
3. These stanzas are translated and discussed in the chapter by T. K. Venkateswaran, "Rādhā-Krishna *Bhajanas* of South India: A Phenomenological, Theological, and Philosophical Study," this volume, pp. 139–172. Translations of other stanzas and songs that follow, unless otherwise identified, are his.

4. A very popular *bhajana* book whose program is widely followed is that edited by Gopālakrishna Bhāgavatār.
5. *Supreme Court Journal,* XVI (1954), 335–361.
6. This biographical material has been made available to me through the kindness of S. V. Aiyer's son.
7. Biographical material made available through the kindness of T. S. Vasudevan.
8. This biographical information came to me through the kindness of T. S. Krishnaswami.
9. This life-history material is based on personal interviews and on correspondence.
10. The earlier historical role of Smārtas in Krishna-worship is discussed by T. K. Venkateswaran, this volume, pp. 144–148.
11. N. Venkata Ramanayya, *Studies in the History of the Third Dynasty of Vijayanagara* (Madras: University of Madras, 1935); K. R. Subramanian, *The Maratha Rajas of Tanjore* (Madras, 1928); and V. Vriddhagirisan, *The Nayaks of Tanjore* (Annamalainagar: Annamalai University, 1942).
12. T. K. Venkateswaran, this volume, pp. 141–144, 161–165.
13. The philosophy and theology of Krishna devotion is discussed in chapters in this volume by Thomas J. Hopkins (pp. 3–22), Edward C. Dimock, Jr. (pp. 41–63), and T. K. Venkateswaran (pp. 139–172). See also W. G. Archer, *The Loves of Krishna* (New York: Grove Press, n.d.), and Rādhākamal Mukerjee, *The Lord of the Autumn Moons* (Bombay: The Asia Publishing House, 1957).
14. *Cf.* Dimock, this volume, p. 51.
15. Swāmī Śāradānanda, *Sri Rama Krishna, The Great Master* (2nd rev. ed.; Madras: Śrī Rāmakrishna Maṭh, n.d.).

CHAPTER VI

1. For these aspects and other details, see chapter two by J. A. B. van Buitenen in this volume.
2. See Milton Singer, "The Great Tradition in a Metropolitan Center: Madras," in Milton Singer, ed., *Traditional India: Structure and Change.* Publication of the American Folklore Society, Bibliographical and Special Series, Vol. X (Philadelphia, 1959), pp. 141–182, or in the *Journal of American Folklore,* LXXI (1958), 347–388.
3. V. Raghavan. "Śrī Nārāyaṇa Tīrtha," *Rūpa-Lekhā,* XXVI, No. 2, pp. 1–7.
4. The several compositions from which the rich tapestry of the *bhajana* is drawn are listed in the bibliography at the end of this volume.
5. This and several other stanzas from the Purāṇas are quoted in the commentary on the *Viṣṇu-sahasra-nāma-stotra,* attributed to Śaṃkara. In the beginning of his commentary, Śaṃkara discusses the reasons for the pre-eminence of this way of singing and praising God in order to reach him.
6. The word used here is *"adhīte,"* the same verb as that used for studying and chanting the Vedas.
7. This reminds one of the words of Jesus: "For when two or three are gathered in my name there am I in the midst of them." Also, the rabbinical

statements mention that God's Shekinah descends and abides with even two or three persons when they gather for the study of the *Torah*.

8. *Viṣṇu Purāṇa* VI.2.17. This stanza is cited by Śaṃkara in his commentary.
9. *Bhāgavata Purāṇa* XII.3.51.
10. For their available works and for articles on the lives of some of them, see the bibliography at the end of this chapter.
11. For details of some of these interactions, see A. S. Altekar, *Sources of Hindu Dharma in its Socio-Religious Aspects.* Sain Das Foundation Lectures, 1952 (Sholapur: Institute of Public Administration, 1952).
12. From V. Veṅkaṭācalam, "The Śālagrāma: A Study." A paper read at the All India Oriental Conference, 1955.
13. Śiva, Viṣṇu, Devī (God as She), Āditya (sun), and Gaṇapati. They are invoked, respectively, in a *liṅga*-like black stone, in *śālagrāmas* (black fossils of shells, flat or with spiral markings), in a type of stone with golden streaks, in circular crystals, and in conical red stones. The *liṅga* stones, known as *bāṇa liṅga,* are secured from the bed of the Narmadā River; *śālagrāmas,* from the Gaṇḍakī River. The golden stones, the crystals, and the red conical stones are available from Vallam, the Svarṇamukhī River, and the Śoṇabhadra River, respectively.
14. Madhusūdana Sarasvatī, *Advaita Siddhi,* Sambaśiva Iyer, ed. (Kumbakōṇam, 1893), p. 234. Unfortunately, this Sanskrit work has not been fully translated into English or any other European language.
15. Quoted by Kāmakoṭi Śaṃkarācārya in *The Call of the Jagadguru: Discourses of His Holiness Śrī Jagadguru,* P. Śaṃkaranārāyaṇan, trans. (Madras: Ganesh and Co., 1958), p. 240.
16. Oft-quoted verse. Author unknown.
17. Kāmakoṛi Śaṃkarācārya, *op. cit.,* p. 240.
18. *Ibid.,* p. 243.
19. This involvement that follows "a temporary withdrawal" is discussed in great detail, along with the meaning of *saṃnyāsa,* in works such as the *Siddhāntaleśa-saṃgraha* of Appaya Dīkṣita, and has a history of its own. Unfortunately, this subject has not yet received adequate treatment.
20. From Louis Dumont and D. Pocock, eds., *Contributions to Indian Sociology,* No. 1, 1957, p. 17.
21. Sadāśiva Brahmendra, *Works and Compositions* (Madras: Kāmakoṭikośasthanam, 1951), p. 60. A few minor changes in spelling, punctuation, etc., have been made for the sake of consistency. For an article on his life, see V. Raghavan, "Sadāśiva Brahman," in T. M. P. Mahedevan, ed., *A Seminar on Saints* (Madras, 1960), pp. 117–124.
22. Sadāśiva Brahmendra, *op. cit.,* p. 35.
23. *Bhāgavata Purāṇa,* I.3.28.
24. T. R. V. Murti, "The Two Definitions of Brahman in the Advaita," in *Krishna Chandra Bhattacharya Memorial Volume* (Amalner, 1958), p. 149.
25. *Bhāgavata Purāṇa,* X.44.15.
26. For a description, see Milton Singer, in this volume, pp. 90–138.
27. *Bhāgavata Purāṇa,* X.29.4.
28. *Ibid.,* X.29.8.
29. These ideas, which are implicit in the *Bhāgavata Purāṇa* and are brought

into bold relief in several places by Śrīdhara Svāmī, the commentator, also form the theme of some of the Smārta expositions, both oral and written, in dealing with the theme of the love of the *gopīs* for Krishna. See, e.g., Varakavi, A. Subramaṇya Bharati, *Svayamprakāśavijayam: Life and Teachings of an Advait-Sanyasin* (Madras: Svayamprakasa Svami, 1935), p. 530.

30. See Rādhākamal Mukerjee, *The Lord of the Autumn Moons* (Bombay: Asia Publishing House, 1957), p. 145.
31. *Bhāgavata Purāṇa,* X.31.3
32. *Ibid.,* X.31.4.
33. *Bhagavadgītā,* II.47.
34. *Ibid.,* XVIII.46.
35. See the following articles by Milton Singer: "Cultural Values in India's Economic Development," in *Annals of the American Academy of Political and Social Science, CCCV* (May, 1956), 81–91; "India's Cultural Values and Economic Development: A Discussion" (with John Goheen, M. N. Srinivas, and D. G. Karve), in *Economic Development and Cultural Change,* VII (October, 1958), 1–12; and his review of *The Religion of India: The Sociology of Hinduism and Buddhism* by Max Weber in *American Anthropologist,* LXIII (February, 1961), 143–151.
36. *Bhagavadgītā* XVII.65, 66.
37. Vedāntadeśika, *Śrīmad Rahasyatrayasāra,* M. R. Rājagopāla Ayyangar, trans. (Kumbakōṇam, 1956), p. xxxvi; see also chapters in the work itself.
38. Max Weber, *The Hindu Social System,* Hans Garth and Don Martindale, trans. *University of Minnesota Sociology Club Bulletin,* Vol. 1, No. 1 (1950), 63 ff.
39. Rāmānuja, *Śrībhāṣya* I.1.1.
40. Śaṃkara, *Brahmasūtrabhāṣya* I.1.1.
41. For more details on such interactions, see Milton Singer, this volume, pp. 90–138.
42. *Kaṭha Upaniṣad* I.2.23.
43. From V. Rāghavan and C. Rāmānujācāri, *The Spiritual Heritage of Tyāgarāja* (Mylapore, Madras: Ramakrishna Mission Students Home, 1957), p. 251.
44. *Ibid.,* p. 576.
45. *Ibid.,* p. 398.
46. In this connection, see the following articles: McKim Marriott, "Little Communities in an Indigenous Civilization," in McKim Marriott, ed., *Village India: Studies in the Little Community* (Chicago: University of Chicago Press, 1955), pp. 171–222; V. Rāghavan, "Variety and Integration in the Pattern of Indian Culture," *Far Eastern Quarterly,* XV (August, 1956), 497–505; Milton Singer, "Text and Context in the Study of Contemporary Hinduism," *Adyar Library Bulletin* (Madras), XXV, Parts I–IV (1961), 274 ff.; Milton Singer, "The Great Tradition in a Metropolitan Center: Madras," in *Traditional India: Structure and Change* (Philadelphia, 1959), pp. 141–182; M. N. Srinivas, "A Note on Sanskritization and Westernization," *Far Eastern Quarterly,* XV (August, 1956), 481–496; and M. N. Srinivas, *Religion and Society Among the Coorgs of South India* (Oxford: Oxford University Press, 1952).

47. Personal communication.
48. Marriott, *Village India: Studies in the Little Community,* pp. 171–222.
49. N. Raghunāthan, "Bodhendra and Sadguru Svāmī," in T. M. P. Mahadevan, ed., *A Seminar on Saints,* p. 137.
50. *Ibid.*, p. 131.
51. Sadgurusvāmī, *Bhakti-saṃdeha-dhvānta-bhāskara,* A. B. S. Ramasvami, ed. (rev. ed.; New Delhi: Delhi Bhajana Samaj, 1958), p. 37.
52. *Ibid.*, p. 32.
53. *Ibid.*, p. 11.
54. *Ibid.*, p. 15.
55. *Bhāgavata Purāṇa,* VII.9.44.
56. The author is in the midst of an elaborate study of certain aspects of *jīvan-mukti* and *jīvan-muktas.*
57. Śaṃkara *Brahmasūtrabhāṣya,* III.3.32; see also his commentary on the second chapter of the *Bhagavadgītā.*
58. Bhartṛhari, *Vākyapadīya;* Vacaspati Miśra, *Tattvabindu;* and Maṇḍana, *Sphoṭasiddhi.*
59. *Bhāgavata Purāṇa,* I.5.11.
60. Quoted by V. Rāghavan in his introduction to Śrīdhara Veṅkaṭeśa, *Ākhyaṣaṣṭi* (Madras: Kāmakoṭi Kośasthanam, 1944), p. 13.
61. Sadgurusvāmī, *op. cit.,* p. 17.
62. *Bhāgavata Purāṇa,* XI.29.16.
63. Sadgurusvāmī, *op. cit.,* pp. 51, 52.
64. *Bhāgavata Purāṇa,* XI.14.15, 16, 17.

CHAPTER VII

1. Prabhudayāl Mītal and Dwārikāprasād Parīkh, *Sūr-Nirṇay* (Mathurā: Agrawāl Press, 1951), p. 52.
2. Mītal and Parīkh, *op. cit.,* pp. 99, 103.
3. *Sūrdās* (Allahabad: Allahabad University, 1957).
4. Prabhudayāl Mītal, ed., *Sūrdās Kī Vārtā* (Mathurā: Agrawāl Press, n.d.), p. 17.
5. *Sūrsāgar,* chap. 1, *pada* 225.
6. *Ibid.,* chap. 10, *padas* 13–47.
7. C. Vaudeville, "Evolution of Love-Symbolism in Bhāgavatism," *Journal of the American Oriental Society,* LXXXII (1962), 31–40.
8. Narmadeśwar Caturvedī, ed., *Gāthāsaptaśati.* (Banaras: Chaukhamba Vidyā Bhavan, 1960), chap. 1, verse 89.
9. The lines from Svayambhū are quoted in Hemacandra's *Prakrit Grammar,* P. L. Vaidya, ed., Bombay Sanskrit and Prakrit Series, LX, 1958, p. 616. We owe this reference to Professor R. S. Tomar (personal communication).
10. B. Upādhyāy, "Hindī Meṃ Vaiṣṇava Padāvalī Kā Pratham Racayitā," *Nāgarī Pracāriṇī Patrikā* (Banaras), LXVI (1961), 2–4.
11. *Pada* 68 in S. M. Pandey and Norman Zide, *The Poems of Sūrdās.* Anthology (unpublished), South Asia Language and Area Center, University of Chicago, 1962.
12. Govardhannāth Śukla, *Paramānandsāgar* (Aligarh, 1958), p. 105.

13. Brajratna Dās, *Nanddās Granthāvalī* (Banaras, 1957), p. 207.
14. It would be of considerable interest to examine the history of the treatment of the marriage of Rādhā and Krishna in Hindi literature but this has yet to be done.
15. Mīrā sees Krishna as *her* husband and has no use for or need of Rādhā in her poems.
16. *Sūrsāgar,* (hereafter *SS*), *pada* 4709.
17. See C. Vaudeville, *loc cit.*
18. Pandey and Zide, *The Poems of Sūrdās, pada* 62.
19. J. S. M. Hooper, *Hymns of the Āḻvārs* (Calcutta, 1929), p. 58.
20. *Sūrsāgar, pada* 4.
21. *Ibid., pada* 2223.
22. *Ibid., pada* 3864
23. *Ibid., pada* 4686.
24. *Ibid., pada* 3956.
25. *Ibid., pada* 4542.
26. The several problems of authorship in devotional and court literature of India—the problems involved in the attribution of poems to particular authors and of the identification of these authors with other, more famous, poets—are ignored here. The wide popularity of the *padas* of Sūr and Mīrābāī led to a great deal of popular refashioning of these *padas* which, in almost all cases, were never written down by their authors. For our purposes we accept the edition of Mīrā of Paraśurām Caturvedī. We are not unaware of the difficulties of interpretation, but the conclusions here are presumably independent of textual difficulties in the poems alluded to.
27. *Sūrsāgar, pada* 86.
28. *Ibid., pada* 148.
29. *Ibid., pada* 153.
30. *Ibid., pada* 337.
31. *Ibid., pada* 4222.
32. Paraśurām Caturvedī, *Mīrāṃ bāī ḳī Padāvalī, pada* 18.
33. *Ibid., pada* 22.
34. These two lines are not accepted by Caturvedī in his edition but are to be found in numerous other editions.

CHAPTER VIII

1. "Kishan Garhi," a pseudonymous village in Aligarh district, Uttar Pradesh, was studied by me from March 1951 to April 1952, with the assistance of an Area Research Training Fellowship grant from the Social Science Research Council. For his comments on this paper, I am indebted to David E. Orlinsky.
2. In this local version of the Prahlāda story, King Harnākas will readily be recognized as Hiraṇya Kaśipu of the Purāṇas, e.g., *Viṣṇu Purāṇa* 1.17 (p. 108 in the translation by Horace Hayman Wilson [Calcutta: Punthi Pustak, 1961]). Holā or Holākā, in the oldest texts a name for the bonfire or festival and unconnected with the story of Prahlāda or other scriptural gods (see the sources cited by Pandurang Vaman Kane, *History of Dharmaśāstra* [Poona,

1958], Vol. V, pp. 237–239), appears only in recent popular stories as a female, and as a relative of Prahlāda. For Holī stories of the Hindi region generally, see William Crooke, *The Popular Religion and Folk-Lore of Northern India* (London: Archibald Constable & Co., 1896), Vol. II, p. 313; for similar tales from Delhi State, see Oscar Lewis, with the assistance of Victor Barnouw, *Village Life in Northern India* (Urbana: University of Illinois, 1958), p. 232; and from the Alwar district of Rajasthan, see Hilda Wernher, *The Land and the Well* (New York: John Day Co., 1946), pp. 199–200.

3. Some of the cow-dung objects for the Holī fire are prepared after the Gobardhan Divālī festival in autumn, with the materials of Gobardhan Bābā's (= Krishna's ?) body. See McKim Marriott, "Little Communities in an Indigenous Civilization," in McKim Marriott, ed., *Village India* (Chicago: University of Chicago Press, 1955), pp. 199–200. Other objects are prepared on the second or fifth days of the bright fortnight of the month of Phāgun, whose last day is the day of the Holī fire.
4. Books VII and X, as in *The Śrīmad-Bhagbātam of Krishna-Dwaipāyana-Vyāsa,* J. M. Sanyal, trans. (Calcutta, n.d.), Vols. IV and V.
5. Alfred Reginald Radcliffe-Brown, "Religion and Society," in *Structure and Function in Primitive Society* (London: Cohen & West, 1952), pp. 155, 177.
6. Bronislaw Malinowski, *Argonauts of the Western Pacific* (London, 1932), pp. 6–8.
7. "Taboo," in Radcliffe-Brown, *Structure and Function,* p. 152.
8. Émile Durkheim, *The Elementary Forms of the Religious Life,* Joseph Ward Swain, trans. (Glencoe, Ill.: Free Press, 1947), p. 299.
9. *The Andaman Islanders* (Glencoe, Ill.: Free Press, 1948), p. 235.
10. Details of some of these festivals are given in McKim Marriott, *op. cit.,* pp. 192–206. The social organization of Kishan Garhi is described more fully in McKim Marriott, "Social Structure and Change in a U.P. Village," in M. N. Srinivas, ed., *India's Villages* (London, 1960), pp. 106–121.
11. Lallu Lal, *Premasāgara,* Frederic Pincott, trans. (London, 1897).
12. Frederic Salmon Growse, *Mathurā: A District Memoir* (2nd ed., 1880), pp. 72, 93, 183–184.
13. *Ibid.,* pp. 178–221; John Nicol Farquhar, *An Outline of the Religious Literature of India* (London: Oxford University Press, 1920), pp. 238–240.
14. Growse, *Mathurā: A District Memoir,* pp. 71–94.
15. Women beat men at or near the time of Holī among the Gonds of Mandla district, according to Verrier Elwin, *Leaves from the Jungle* (London: J. Murray, 1936), p. 135; in Nimar, according to Stephen Fuchs, *The Children of Hari* (New York: Praeger, 1950), pp. 300–301; and elsewhere in Madhya Pradesh, according to Robert Vane Russell and Hira Lal, *The Tribes and Castes of the Central Provinces of India* (London, 1916), Vol. II, p. 126, and Vol. III, p. 117. The usage is reported also from Alwar in Rajasthan by Hilda Wernher, *op. cit.,* p. 208, and from Delhi by O. Lewis and V. Barnouw, *op. cit.,* p. 232.
16. At Krishna's birthday anniversary, biographies of his life by poets of Mathurā are read. At the Gobardhan Divālī, the circumambulation of the hill by the

pilgrims is duplicated in model; see McKim Marriott, "Little Communities," in *op. cit.*, pp. 199–200.

17. See W. Crooke, *op. cit.*, Vol. II, pp. 313–314; and Ṛgvedi (pseud.), *Āryāncā Saṇāncā Prācīna va Arvācīna Itihāsa* (in Marathi) (Bombay, n.d.), p. 399.
18. F. S. Growse, *Mathurā: a District Memoir,* p. 103.
19. R. Redfield and M. Singer, "The Cultural Role of Cities," *Economic Development and Cultural Change,* III (1954), pp. 53–74.
20. W. Crooke, *op. cit.*, Vol. II, pp. 313–314, 319–320; P. V. Kane, *op. cit.*, Vol. V, pp. 237–240; Ṛgvedi, *op. cit.*, pp. 399–400, 405.
21. Nirmal Kumar Bose, "The Spring Festival of India," in *Cultural Anthropology and Other Essays* (Calcutta, 1953), pp. 73–102.

BIBLIOGRAPHIES

CHAPTER I

Mahābhārata

The Mahābhārata. Critically edited by Vishnu S. Sukthanker (1925–1943) and S. K. Belvalkar (in progress). Poona: Bhandarkar Oriental Research Institute, 1933——.

The Mahābhārata. Edited by the learned pandits of the Education Committee. 5 vols. Calcutta: Education Society Press, 1834–1839.

A Prose English Translation of the Mahābhārata. Edited by Manmatha Nath Dutt. 18 vols. Calcutta: H. C. Dass, 1895–1905.

Śrīmanmahābhāratam. Edited by T. R. Krishnacharya and T. R. Vyasacharya. 6 vols. Bombay: B. R. Ghanekar, 1906–1910.

Bhāgavata Purāṇa

A Prose English Translation of Śrīmadbhāgavatam. Edited by Manmatha Nath Dutt. 3 vols. Calcutta: H. C. Dass, 1895–1896.

The Śrīmad-Bhāgabatam. Translated by J. M. Sanyal. 5 vols. Calcutta: The Oriental Publishing Co. (Vol. I) and Datta Bose & Co. (Vols. II–V), 1929–1939.

Śrīmadbhāgavatam. Text with nine commentaries. 5 vols. Brindaban, 1904–1907.

Books and Articles

De, S. K. *Early History of the Vaishnava Faith and Movement in Bengal.* Calcutta: General Printers and Publishers, Ltd., 1942. 2nd ed., 1961.

Farquhar, J. N. *An Outline of the Religious Literature of India.* London: Oxford University Press, 1920.

Hazra, R. C. *Studies in the Puranic Records on Hindu Rites and Customs.* Dacca: University of Dacca, 1940.

Kane, P. V. *History of Dharma Śāstra.* 5 vols. Poona: Bhandarkar Oriental Research Institute, 1930–1958.

Krishnamurti Śarma, B. N. "The Date of the *Bhāgavata Purāṇa,*" *Annals of the Bhandarkar Oriental Research Institute,* XIV (1932–1933), 182–218.

Mukerjee, R. *The Lord of the Autumn Moons.* Bombay: Asia Publishing House, 1957.

Nīlakaṇṭa Śāstrī, K. A. *A History of South India from Prehistoric Times to the Fall of Vijayanagar.* 2nd ed. Madras and New York: Oxford University Press, 1958.

Pargiter, F. E. *Ancient Indian Historical Tradition.* London: Oxford University Press, 1922.
——— *The Purāṇa Text of the Dynasties of the Kali Age.* London: Oxford University Press, 1913.
Sharma, R. S. *Śūdras in Ancient India.* Delhi: Motilal Banarsidass, 1958.
Vaidya, C. V. "The Date of the *Bhāgavata Purāṇa,*" *Journal of the Bombay Branch of the Royal Asiatic Society,* New Series, I (1925), 144–158
Wilson, H. H. "Analysis of the Purāṇas," in *Essays Analytical, Critical and Philological,* in *Works by the Late Horace Hayman Wilson,* Vol. III. Edited by Reinhold Rost. London: Trübner & Co., 1864–1865, pp. 1–155.
——— *The Viṣṇu Purāṇa.* Calcutta: Punthi Pustak, 1961.
Winternitz, Moriz. *A History of Indian Literature.* Translated by S. Ketkar and H. Kohn. 2 vols. Calcutta: University of Calcutta, 1927–1933.

CHAPTER VI

I. *Primary textual sources and materials: Rādhākṛṣṇa Bhajana of South India*

Bhāgavata Purāṇa, with the commentary of Śrīdharasvāmī (Sanskrit).
Kṛṣṇa Caitanya, *Śikṣāṣṭaka,* eight important verses of instruction on *bhakti* (Sanskrit).
Bhagavad Gītā (Sanskrit).
Bilvamaṅgala (Līlāśuka), *Kṛṣṇakarṇāmṛta* (Sanskrit).
*Lakṣmīdhara, *Bhagavannāma Kaumudī* (Sanskrit).
†Bodhendra, *Nāmāmṛta-Rasāyana, Nāmāmṛta-Rasodaya, Nāmāmṛta-Sūryodaya, Bhagavannāmāmṛtārṇava* and certain other works (Sanskrit).
*Śrīdhara Veṅkaṭeśa (Ayyaval), *Ākhyāṣaṣṭi* (Sanskrit), translated into English and Tamil, edited with an introduction by V. Rāghavan, Kāmakoṭi Kośasthanam, Madras, 1944. Also *Bhagavannāma-bhūṣaṇa* and several other works (Sanskrit).
*Veṅkaṭarāmadeśika (Marudanallūr Sadgurusvāmī), *Bhakti-saṃdeha-dhvānta-bhāskara* (Sanskrit), in the form of a dialogue attributed to him and his disciple; edited, with a translation in Tamil, by Adambar Bharadvāja Rāmasvāmī, New Delhi: The Delhi Bhajana Samaj, 1937, 2nd ed., 1958. Also other songs in Telugu and Sanskrit on Lakṣmīdhara, Bodhendra, and Śrīdhara Veṅkaṭeśa.
†Nārāyaṇa Tīrtha, *Kṛṣṇalīlā Taraṅginī* (Sanskrit).
†Sadāśiva Brahmendra Sarasvatī, Songs and other works (Sanskrit). Madras: Kamakotikosasthanam, 1951.
†Upaniṣad Brahmendra, *Bhaktisvarūpaviveka, Upeyanāmaviveka,* and several other works, *nāmāvalis,* and songs (Sanskrit).
Jayadeva, *Gītagovinda* (Sanskrit).

*Indicates that the author belongs to the Smārta tradition.
†Indicates that the author became a *saṃnyāsin* from the Smārta tradition. These are *advaita-saṃnyāsins* who had accepted Śaṃkara's position in Vedānta. Only in instances of certainty have these marks been added. In the list are also to be found Vaiṣṇavas and Mādhvas (like Caitanya and Purandaradās respectively).

Rāmadās of Bhadrācalam, Devotional compositions (Telugu).
†Vijayagopālasvāmī, Songs, *divyanāmas* (Sanskrit and Telugu).
Bhadrādrivāsa (perhaps identical with Rāmadās), Songs (Telugu and Sanskrit).
†Tyāgarāja, Compositions (mainly Telugu).
Purandaradās, *Padas,* songs (Kannada).
Mīrābāī (woman-devotee-composer), *Dhuns,* songs and poems in a type of Hindi.
Kabīr, Songs. (Hindi).
Ekanāth, *Abhaṅgs,* songs (Marathi).
Nāmdev, *Abhaṅgs,* songs (Marathi).
Tukaram, *Abhaṅgs,* songs (Marathi).
Aruṇagirināthār, *Tiruppugal* (Tamil).
Dēvāram and *Tiruvācakam* (Tamil).
Gopālakṛṣṇa Bhāratī, Songs (Tamil).
Śaṃkara, *Brahmasūtra bhāṣya* on the *Brahmasūtras* (Sanskrit); *Viṣṇusahasra-nāma bhāṣya,* commentary on the *Thousand and Eight Names of Viṣṇu* (Sanskrit). *Gītā-bhāṣya,* commentary on the *Bhagavad Gītā* (Sanskrit).

II. Compilations: Songs in different languages, from the above composers for use in the bhajana (in Tamil script)

Bhāgavatār, Gopālakṛṣṇa, *Śrīmad Bhajanāmṛtam.* Pudukottah: Sanjivi, 1950, 1954.
Bhajanāvali. Madras: Rāmakṛṣṇa Maṭh, 1939, 1945, 1952.
Ayyaṅgar, M. Rāmakṛṣṇa, *Bhajanotsava Mañjari.* Udumalpet: Śrī Rāmakṛṣṇa Bhajana Sabhā, 1948, 1950, 1953, 1954, 1956, 1959.

III. Secondary Works: A Select Bibliography

Altekar, A. S., *Sources of Hindu Dharma in Its Socio-religious Aspects.* Sain Das Foundation Lectures, 1952. Sholapur: Institute of Public Administration, 1952.
Bharati, A. Subrahmaṇya, Varakavi, *Svayaṃprakāśa vijayam: Life and Teachings of an Advaita-sanyasin.* Madras: Svayaṃprakāśa Svāmī, 1935. (Tamil.)
Dhanapatisūri, *Gūḍhārthadīpikā.* Commentary on *Rāsapañcādhyāyī,* the five central chapters in the tenth book of the *Bhāgavata Purāṇa,* dealing with the mysticism and theology of Rāsakrīḍā. Benares Sanskrit Series, 1908 (Sanskrit).
Marriott, McKim, ed., *Village India: Studies in the Little Community.* Comparative studies of cultures and civilizations, No. 6. American Anthropological Association Memoir, 83. Chicago: University of Chicago Press, 1955.
Mukerjee, Rādhākamal, *The Lord of the Autumn Moons.* Bombay: Asia Publishing House, 1957.
Murti, T. R. V., "The two definitions of Brahman in the Advaita," in *Krishna Chandra Bhattacharya Memorial Volume.* Amalner, 1958.
Rāghavan, V., and C. Rāmānujāchari, *The Spiritual Heritage* of *Tyāgarāja* (text and translation of Tyāgarāja's songs, with an introductory thesis by V. Rāghavan). Mylapore, Madras: Ramakrishna Mission Students Home, 1957.
Rāghavan, V., "Śrī Nārāyaṇa Tīrtha" in *Rūpa-Lekhā,* XXVI.
——— "Upaniṣadbrahma Yogin" in *The Journal of Madras Music Academy* XXVII, and XXVIII.

——— "Methods of Popular Religious Instruction in South India," in Milton Singer, ed., *Traditional India: Structure and Change.* Philadelphia: American Folklore Society, 1959. Pp. 130–140.

——— "Sadāśiva Brahman," in T. M. P. Mahādevan, ed., *A Seminar on Saints.* Madras: Ganesh and Co., 1960. Pp. 117–124.

——— "Variety and Integration in the Pattern of Indian Culture," *Far Eastern Quarterly,* XV (August, 1956), 497–505.

Raghunāthan, N., "Bodhendra and Sadguru Svāmī," in T. M. P. Mahādevan, ed., *A Seminar on Saints.* Madras: Ganesh and Co., 1960. Pp. 133–140.

Rāmānuja, *Śrī Bhāṣya,* on the *Brahmasūtras* (Sanskrit).

Redfield, Robert, *Peasant Society and Culture: An Anthropological Approach to Civilization.* Chicago: University of Chicago Press, 1956.

——— "The Social Organization of Tradition," *Far Eastern Quarterly,* XV (November, 1955), 13–21.

Śaṃkarācārya, Kāñcī Kāmakoṭipīṭha, *The Call of the Jagadguru: Discourses of His Holiness Śrī Jagadguru . . .* compiled and translated into English by P. Śaṃkaranārāyaṇan. Madras: Ganesh and Co., 1958.

Sarasvatī, Madhusūdana, *Advaita Siddhi,* Sambaśiva Iyer, ed. Kumbakōṇam, 1893 (Sanskrit).

Singer, Milton, ed., *Traditional India: Structure and Change.* Publication of the American Folklore Society, Bibliographical and Special Series, Vol. X. Philadelphia: The American Folklore Society, 1959.

Singer, Milton, "The Great Tradition in a Metropolitan Center: Madras," in Milton Singer, ed., *Traditional India: Structure and Change,* pp. 141–82.

——— "Cultural Values in India's Economic Development," in *The Annals of the American Academy of Political and Social Science,* CCCV (May 1956), 81–91.

——— Review article on Max Weber, *The Religion of India: The Sociology of Hinduism and Buddhism, American Anthropologist,* LXIII (February, 1961), 143–151.

——— "Text and Context in the Study of Contemporary Hinduism," *The Adyar Library Bulletin* (Madras), XXV (1961), 274 ff.

——— and Robert Redfield, "The Cultural Role of Cities," *Economic Development and Cultural Change,* III (October, 1954), 53–73.

——— John Goheen, M. N. Srinivas, and D. G. Karve, "India's Cultural Values and Economic Development: A Discussion," *Economic Development and Cultural Change,* VII (October, 1958), 1–12.

Srinivas, M. N., *Religion and Society Among the Coorgs of South India.* Oxford: Oxford University Press, 1952.

——— "A Note on Sanskritization and Westernization," *Far Eastern Quarterly,* XV (August, 1956), 481–496.

——— "The Nature of the Problem of Indian Unity," *The Economic Weekly* (Bombay), X (April 26, 1958), 571–577.

Vedāntadeśika, *Śrīmad Rahasyatrayasāra,* M. R. Rajagopala Ayyaṅgar, trans. Kumbakōṇam, 1956.

Weber, Max, *The Hindu Social System,* Hans Garth and Don Martindale, trans. *University of Minnesota Sociology Club Bulletin.* I, No. 1 (1950), 63 ff.

——— *The Religion of India: The Sociology of Hinduism and Buddhism,* translated and edited by Hans Garth and Don Martindale. Glencoe, Ill.: The Free Press, 1958.

CHAPTER VII

Bājpeyī, Nanddulāre, *Sūrsāgar*. Banaras: Nāgarī Prācāriṇī Sabhā, 1955.
Caturvedī, Paraśurām, *Mīrāṃbāi Kī Padāvali.* 11th ed. Allahabad: Hindī Sāhitya Sammelan, Śaka 1886.
Dvivedī, Hajārīprasād, *Sūr Sāhitya.* Bombay: Hindī Granth Ratnākar, Ltd., 1956.
Gupta, Dīndayāl, *Aṣṭchāp Aur Vallabh Sampradāy.* 2 vols. Allahabad: Hindī Sāhitya Sammelan, 1947.
Miśra, Janārdan, *The Religious Poetry of Sūrdās.* Patna: United Press, Limited, 1935.
Mītal, Prabhudayāl, and Dwārikāprasād Parīkh, *Sūr-Nirṇay.* Mathura: Agrawāl Press, 1951.
Pāṇḍey, Śyāmmanohar, *Bhramargīt Aur Rāspañcādhyāyī.* Allahabad: Ganeś Prakāśan, 1956.
Pāṇḍey, Śyāmmanohar, and Norman Zide, *The Poems of Sūrdās.* Anthology (unpublished), The University of Chicago, South Asia Language and Area Center, 1962.
Pāṇḍey, Śyāmmanohar, and Norman Zide, *The Poems of Mīrāṃbāī.* The University of Chicago, South Asia Language and Area Center, 1964.
Śarmā, Harbaṃslāl, *Sūr Aur Unḳā Sāhitya.* Aligarh: Bhārat Prakāshan Mandir, 1958.
Śarmā, Munśīrām, *Bhāratīya Sādhanā Aur Sūr Sāhitya.* Kanpur: Ācārya Śukla Sādhanā Sadan, 1960.
——— *Sūr-Saurabh.* Kanpur: Ācārya Śukla Sādhanā Sadan, 1956.
Varmā, Vrajeśwar, *Sūrdās.* Allahabad: Allahabad University, 1957.

CONTRIBUTORS

EDWARD C. DIMOCK is currently Associate Professor in the Department of Linguistics and of Oriental Languages and Civilizations at the University of Chicago, specializing in Bengali language and literature, and Director of the South Asia Language and Area Center. His interests, however, also lie in the direction of the history of religions, and his Ph.D. dissertation, submitted to the Department of Sanskrit and Indic Studies at Harvard, was *A Study of the Vaiṣṇava-sahajiyā Movement in Bengal.* His publications include *The Thief of Love* (Bengali tales from court and village), *An Introduction to Bengali* (with Somdev Bhattacharji and Suhas Chatterjee), *The Mahārāshṭa Purāṇa: An Eighteenth-Century Bengali Historical* Text with P. C. Gupta), and various articles on Vaiṣṇavism, on the snake goddess in Bengal, and on the Bengali language. His current research is on the *Vaiṣṇava-sahajiyā* movement and on the central text of Bengali Vaiṣṇavism, the *Caitanya-caritāmṛta.*

THOMAS J. HOPKINS is Assistant Professor of Religion at Franklin and Marshall College. He attended the College of William and Mary (B.S. in physics, 1953); Massachusetts Institute of Technology (B.S. in mechanical engineering, 1953); and Yale Divinity School (B.D., 1958), where he concentrated on Christianity and Culture and Foreign Missions; and Graduate School of Yale University (M.A., 1959, and Ph.D. in religion, 1962). His graduate work was in comparative religion under Norvin Hein; related studies were Sanskrit (mainly with Paul Thieme), sociology of religion, and Indian history. His special interest is in Indian religion, Hinduism, and Vaiṣṇavism, in the order of increased concentration. His dissertation was *The Vaiṣṇava Bhaḳti Movement in the Bhāgavata Purāṇa,* directed by Norvin Hein.

DANIEL H. H. INGALLS is Wales Professor of Sanskrit, Harvard University, and Editor of the Harvard Oriental Series. He studied at Harvard: A.B., 1936; M.A., 1938; Junior Fellow of the Society of Fellows (1939–1942 and 1946–1949). He also studied at the Sanskrit Research Institute at the University of Calcutta. He was appointed Assistant Professor of Indic Studies at Harvard in 1949; Associate Professor of Sanskrit and Indian

Studies, Harvard, 1954; Wales Professor of Sanskrit, Harvard, 1958. His chief publications are *Materials for the Study of Navya-Nyāya Logic* (Harvard Oriental Series, 40, 1951) and *An Anthology of Sanskrit Court Poetry: Vidyākara's Subhāṣitaratnakośa* (Harvard Oriental Series, 44, 1964). His interest in Sanskrit started with philosophy and proceeded to Sanskrit literature in general.

McKIM MARRIOTT is Professor of Social Sciences in the College and Professor of Anthropology, University of Chicago. He was educated at Harvard and trained in anthropology at the University of Chicago (Ph.D., 1955). His dissertation, *Caste Ranking and Community Structure in Five Regions of India and Pakistan,* was published at Poona in 1960. He edited *Village India* (1955) and collaborated with Albert Mayer and Richard L. Park on *Pilot Project, India: The Story of Rural Development at Etawah, Uttar Pradesh* (1958). He has written elsewhere on Hindu social organization, on technological and medical innovations in the village context, and on the theory of peasant culture; and has conducted intensive field research both in rural Uttar Pradesh and in a sacred city of Maharashtra.

S. M. PANDEY was Research Associate and Lecturer in the South Asian Languages Program of the University of Chicago until 1965. He was born in district Ballia near Benares in 1936. He took his M.A. from Allāhabād University in 1956 and his Ph.D. in 1960 from the same university on the subject, "A Comparative Study of Sūfī and Non-Sūfī Literature in Hindi." His first book, *Bharmar Gīt Aur Rās Pañchādhyāyī,* was published in 1956. His *Madhyayugīn Premakhyāna* (1960) is a revised version of his doctoral dissertation. His research papers have been published in various Hindi research journals, such as *Sammelan Patrika, Hindustani, and Hindi Anushilan.*

MILTON SINGER is Paul Klapper Professor of the Social Sciences in the College and Professor of Anthropology at the University of Chicago. He received his Ph.D. at the University of Chicago in 1940. He has been Executive Secretary of the University's Committee on Southern Asian Studies since 1954 and was Co-Director of its South Asia Language and Area Center from 1959 to 1963. He was Associate Director of the Redfield project on Comparative Civilizations from 1951 to 1958 and Director from 1958 to 1961. From 1947 to 1953 he was Chairman of the College's Social Sciences Staff, and Chairman of its Indian Civilization Program from 1956 to 1959. He is a fellow of the American Anthropological Association and was Vice President of the American Institute of Indian Studies (1962–1964). He has made three study trips to India since 1954. His publications on India (as editor and contributor) include *Introducing India in Liberal Education: Proceedings of a Conference* (Chicago, 1957), *Traditional India:*

Structure and Change (Publications of the American Folklore Society, Bibliographical Series, X; 1958–1959), and a number of journal articles.

SURAJIT SINHA, a Fellow of the Center for Advanced Study in the Behavioral Sciences (1963–1964), is currently on the staff of the Indian Institute of Management, Calcutta. He had his training in Anthropology first in Calcutta and then at Northwestern University, where he received his Ph.D. in 1956. He was Superintending Anthropologist, Anthropological Survey of India (1958–1961); Secretary, Central Advisory Board of Anthropology, Government of India (1959–1961); and President, Anthropology and Archaeology Section, Indian Science Congress Association (1961–1962). He has taught anthropology at the University of Calcutta (1953), University of Chicago (1955–1956, 1961–1962), and Duke University (1962–1963). His main field work has been on the Bhūmij tribe of Bengal-Bihar, and his special interests include tribal transformation in Central India and the structure of Indian civilization.

J. A. B. VAN BUITENEN is Professor of Sanskrit and Indic Studies at the University of Chicago and was Director of its South Asia Language and Area Center (1963–65). He was born in The Hague and received all his formal education in The Netherlands. He received his degree of Doctor of Letters and Philosophy from the University of Utrecht in 1953. Since then he was sub-editor of the Sanskrit Dictionary, Deccan College, Poona (1953–56), Rockefeller Foundation Fellow at Harvard University and the University of Chicago (1956–59), Reader in Indian Philosophy at the University of Utrecht (1959–61), and has been connected with the University of Chicago since 1961. Among his publications are *Rāmānuja on the Bhagavadgītā, Rāmānuja's Vedārthasaṃgraha, Tales of Ancient India,* and the *Maitrāyaṇīya Upaniṣad.*

T. K. VENKATESWARAN is Professor of Far Eastern (Asian) studies in Colorado Woman's College at Denver. He was born in 1928 in the city of Madras. He received his B.A. Honours and M.A. degrees with numerous academic distinctions at the University of Madras in Sanskrit language and literature, and also received from that University the Diploma in Anthropology. He studied *Nyāya* logic and epistemology and *Advaita Vedānta* for six years, in addition, with a celebrated South Indian *guru.*

Mr. Venkateswaran has taught since 1948 in the Sanskrit departments of the Madras State Government Colleges, and from 1956 to 1959 was Assistant Professor of Sanskrit in Presidency College of Madras University, teaching postgraduate courses.

On leave from Presidency College in 1959, with a Fulbright Grant and a Harvard University Resident Fellowship, Mr. Venkateswaran was a resident research scholar from 1959 to 1962 in Harvard's Center for the Study of World Religions.

He was visiting Lecturer in Indic Studies at the University of Chicago for the summer quarter of 1961. A study, "Revelation and Learning: Some Hindu and other Eastern Approaches," will be published shortly by the Danforth Foundation in a volume of essays on revelation and learning by various authors.

NORMAN H. ZIDE is Associate Professor of Linguistics at the University of Chicago. He received his Ph.D. in Linguistics and South Asian Studies from the University of Pennsylvania in 1960. He is the author of several linguistics papers; editor of *Comparative Studies in Austroasiatic Linguistics* (in press); co-editor (with S. M. Pandey) of *Poems of Sūrdās,* a selection of poems with translations and introduction (South Asia Language and Area Center, University of Chicago).

INDEX

ABBREVIATIONS: *BhG* — *Bhagavad Gītā*
BhP — *Bhāgavata Purāṇa*
MBh — *Mahābhārata*
P. — *Purāṇa*
Ram. — *Rāmāyaṇa*
Up. — *Upaniṣad*

Abdul Qādir Badāyūnī, 174
abhaṅgs, Marathi songs, 96
Abhedānanda, Svāmī, 115
Abhinavagupta, 26
abhinaya, in *divya-nāma-bhajana* dancing, 164
Absolute, 137; marriage of Rādhā and Krishna symbolizes union with, 97, 130; *see also* Ātman; Brahman
Abul Fazl, 174
ācaraṇa, rite, 51
ācāras, customs, stressed in *smṛtis,* 161
ācārya, religious teacher, 28
Ācāryas, Vaiṣṇava teachers, 30; product of Southern *bhakti* movement, 5; Sadgurusvāmī, 165; Vedāntadeśika, 157–158
acculturation, Vaiṣṇava impact on Bhūmij, 87–89
acintya-bhedābheda; see *bhedābheda*
Acyuta; *see* Krishna
Acyuta Śataka, 133
adhikārī, 67, 70, 71
aḍiyār-kūṭṭam: and *smṛti* and Purāṇic tradition, 162; of Tamil Śaivism, 156
Advaita, 46, 48; elements of, in *BhP,* 4, 5; influence in *bhajana,* 172; and Madhusūdana Sarasvatī, 148 ff.; and *pañcāyatana pūjā,* 147; and reversion to *bhakti,* 150–151; and Śaṃkara, 4, 5, 42, 145, 146–147, 148; and scriptural texts of *bhajanas,* 125–126; and Smārta Brahmans, 117–119, 144–151
Advaita-ācārya, 46; differences with Nityānanda, 53–54
Advaita Ācāryas, influence on Mahratta rājas of Tanjore, 120–121
Advaitasiddhi, 148, 149
Advaitin, 119; and personal deity, 118–119, 137
Āgamaprāmāṇya, 27–29, 31–32
Āgamas: canonical status, 161–162; and *jñāna,* 162; Pāñcarātra, 38, 162; *pūjā,* 162; *śakta,* 162; Sanskritization of, 38; subject matter of, 161–162; and temple building and temple worship, 162; *vaikhānasa,* 162; and Vaiṣṇavism, 161–162; and Veda, 162; and *yoga,* 162
Āgneyapurāṇa Saṃgraha, and Rādhā, 171
Agni, 203
agnihotra, 27
ahaitukī bhakti, 150–151, 166, 167 f.
Ahilyā, in *Sūrsāgar,* 177
'Ain-i-Akbarī, 174
Aiyer, Kōthamarāma, 110, 112
Aiyer, Rāmacandra, 110
Aiyer, S. V., 105, 110–111; innovations of, 111
Ajāmila, in *Sūrsāgar,* 177
ākāra, form, of Brahman, 148
Akbar, 173
Akṣara, 25
alaṃkāras, 198